CAMBRIDGE LIBRARY COLLECTION

Books of enduring scholarly value

History

The books reissued in this series include accounts of historical events and movements by eye-witnesses and contemporaries, as well as landmark studies that assembled significant source materials or developed new historiographical methods. The series includes work in social, political and military history on a wide range of periods and regions, giving modern scholars ready access to influential publications of the past.

An Historical Survey of the French Colony in the Island of St. Domingo

Bryan Edwards (1743–1800) was a wealthy West Indian planter, politician and historian. He vigorously opposed the abolition of the slave trade, since the sugar industry relied heavily on it. *An Historical Survey of the French Colony in the island of St. Domingo* was published in 1797. St Domingo (now Haiti) had been one of the most prosperous West Indian economies, producing more sugar and coffee than all the British West Indies combined. The harsh treatment of the slaves under the French *code noir* led to a widespread revolt in 1791, in part inspired by the French Revolution. An alliance between white planters and the British to take over the island was unsuccessful. Edwards feared that the revolt would spread to other islands, destroying their trade. The rebellion in St Domingo was of major significance, as it led to the colony becoming the first independent black-ruled republic in 1804.

T0382595

Cambridge University Press has long been a pioneer in the reissuing of out-of-print titles from its own backlist, producing digital reprints of books that are still sought after by scholars and students but could not be reprinted economically using traditional technology. The Cambridge Library Collection extends this activity to a wider range of books which are still of importance to researchers and professionals, either for the source material they contain, or as landmarks in the history of their academic discipline.

Drawing from the world-renowned collections in the Cambridge University Library, and guided by the advice of experts in each subject area, Cambridge University Press is using state-of-the-art scanning machines in its own Printing House to capture the content of each book selected for inclusion. The files are processed to give a consistently clear, crisp image, and the books finished to the high quality standard for which the Press is recognised around the world. The latest print-on-demand technology ensures that the books will remain available indefinitely, and that orders for single or multiple copies can quickly be supplied.

The Cambridge Library Collection will bring back to life books of enduring scholarly value (including out-of-copyright works originally issued by other publishers) across a wide range of disciplines in the humanities and social sciences and in science and technology.

An Historical Survey of the French Colony in the Island of St. Domingo

BRYAN EDWARDS

CAMBRIDGE
UNIVERSITY PRESS

CAMBRIDGE UNIVERSITY PRESS

Cambridge, New York, Melbourne, Madrid, Cape Town, Singapore,
São Paolo, Delhi, Dubai, Tokyo, Mexico City

Published in the United States of America by Cambridge University Press, New York

www.cambridge.org
Information on this title: www.cambridge.org/9781108023221

© in this compilation Cambridge University Press 2010

This edition first published 1797
This digitally printed version 2010

ISBN 978-1-108-02322-1 Paperback

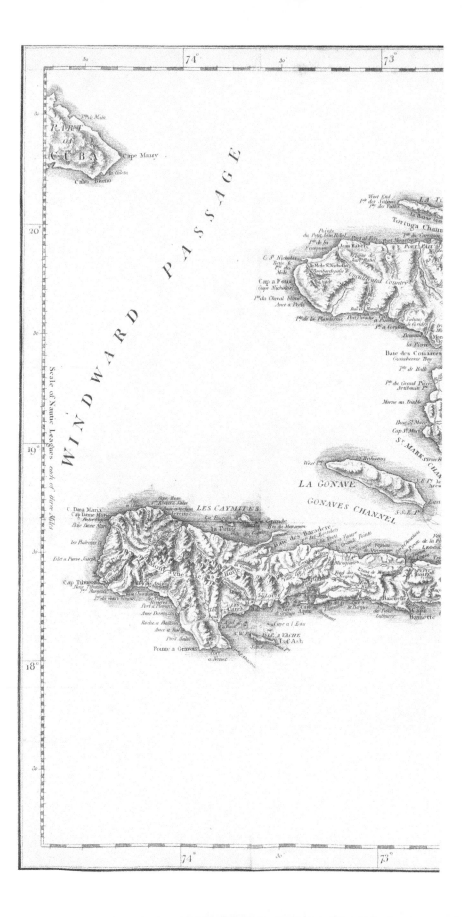

MAP OF ST. DOMINGO

British Miles

Published March 4th 1797, by John Stockdale, Piccadilly.

MAP OF St. DOMINGO

British Miles

Published March 4th 1797, by John Stockdale, Piccadilly.

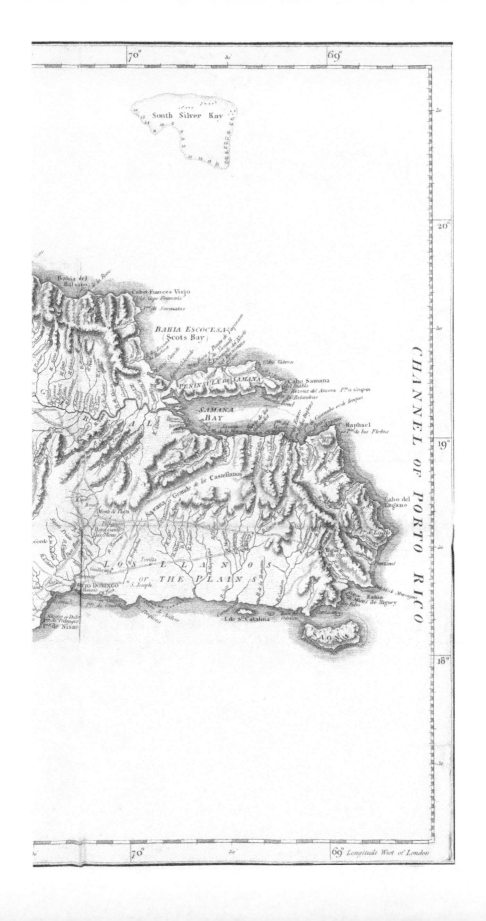

South Silver Kay

20°

Bahia del
Balsano

Cabo Frances Viejo
Old Cape François
Pta de Savanatas

BAHIA ESCOCESA
(Scots Bay)

Cabo Cabron

PENINSULA DE SAMANA

Cabo Samana
El Diablo
Rezona del Ancon   Pta a Grapin
de Balandras

SAMANA
BAY

19°

Raphael
Bahía de las Flechas

Savana Grande de la Castellanos

Cabo del
Engano

Monte de Plata

Higuey
Alto Guel

L O S   L L A N O S

or   T H E   P L A I N S

S.to DOMINGO
S. Joseph

Bahía
Hato el de Higuey

I. de S.ta Catalina

18°

AN

HISTORICAL SURVEY

OF THE

FRENCH COLONY

IN THE

ISLAND OF ST. DOMINGO:

COMPREHENDING

A SHORT ACCOUNT OF ITS ANCIENT GOVERNMENT,
POLITICAL STATE, POPULATION,
PRODUCTIONS, AND EXPORTS;

A NARRATIVE OF THE CALAMITIES WHICH HAVE DESOLATED
THE COUNTRY EVER SINCE THE YEAR 1789,

*WITH SOME REFLECTIONS ON THEIR CAUSES AND
PROBABLE CONSEQUENCES;*

AND

A DETAIL OF THE MILITARY TRANSACTIONS
OF THE BRITISH ARMY IN THAT ISLAND TO THE END OF 1794.

———————

BY *BRYAN EDWARDS*, Esq. M.P. F.R.S. &c.

AUTHOR OF THE HISTORY OF THE BRITISH COLONIES IN THE WEST INDIES.

———————

LONDON:

PRINTED FOR JOHN STOCKDALE, PICCADILLY.

1797.

CONTENTS.

A 2   CHAP.

CONTENTS.

CHAP. VI.

CHAP. VII.

CHAP. VIII.

C O N T E N T S.

CONTENTS.

PREFACE.

SOON after I had published the History of the British Colonies in the West Indies, I conceived the design of compiling a general account of the settlements made by all the nations of Europe in that part of the New Hemisphere, but more particularly the French, whose possessions were undoubtedly the most valuable and productive of the whole Archipelago. This idea suggested itself to my mind, on surveying the materials I had collected with regard to their principal colony in St. Domingo; not doubting, as the fortune of war had placed under the British dominion all or most of the other French islands, that I should easily procure such particulars of the condition, population, and culture of each, as would enable me to complete my design, with credit to myself, and satisfaction to the Publick. I am sorry to observe, that in this expectation I

b   have

PREFACE.

have hitherto found myfelf difappointed. The prefent publication therefore, is confined wholly to
St. Domingo; concerning which, having perfonally
vifited that unhappy country foon after the revolt
of the negroes in 1791, and formed connexions
there, which have fupplied me with regular com-
munications ever fince, I poffefs a mafs of evidence,
and important documents. My motives for going
thither, are of little confequence to the Publick; but
the circumftances which occafioned the voyage, the
reception I met with, and the fituation in which
I found the wretched Inhabitants, cannot fail of
being interefting to the reader; and I flatter myfelf
that a fhort account of thofe particulars, while it
confers fome degree of authenticity on my labours,
will not be thought an improper Introduction to
my book.

In the month of September 1791, when I was at
Spanifh Town in Jamaica, two French Gentlemen
were introduced to me, who were juft arrived from
St. Domingo, with information that the negro flaves
belonging to the French part of that ifland, to the
number, as was believed, of 100,000 and upwards,
                                                    had

had revolted, and were fpreading death and defolation over the whole of the northern province.
They reported that the governor-general, confiderng
the fituation of the colony as a common caufe among
the white inhabitants of all nations in the Weft Indies,
had difpatched commiffioners to the neighbouring
iflands, as well as to the States of North America,
to requeft immediate affiftance of troops, arms,
ammunition, and provifions; and that themfelves
were deputed on the fame errand to the Government
at Jamaica: I was accordingly defired to prefent
them to the Earl of Effingham, the commander in
chief. Although the difpatches with which thefe
gentlemen were furnifhed, were certainly a very fufficient introduction to his lordfhip, I did not he-
fitate to comply with their requeft; and it is fcarcely neceffary to obferve, that the liberal and enlarged
mind which animated every part of Lord Effingham's conduct, needed no folicitation, in a cafe of
beneficence and humanity. Superior to national
prejudice, he felt, as a man and a chriftian ought to
feel, for the calamities of *fellow men*; and he faw,
in its full extent, the danger to which every ifland
in the Weft Indies would be expofed from fuch an

b 2

example,

example, if the triumph of savage anarchy over all order and government should be complete. He therefore, without hesitation, assured the commissioners that they might depend on receiving from the government of Jamaica, every assistance and succour which it was in his power to give. Troops he could not offer, for he had them not; but he said he would furnish arms, ammunition, and provisions, and he promised to consult with the distinguished Officer commanding in the naval department, concerning the propriety of sending up one or more of his Majesty's ships; the commissioners having suggested that the appearance in their harbours of a few vessels of war might serve to intimidate the insurgents, and keep them at a distance, while the necessary defences and intrenchments were making, to preserve the city of Cape François from an attack.

ADMIRAL AFFLECK (as from his known worth, and general character might have been expected) very cheerfully co-operated on this occasion with Lord Effingham; and immediately issued orders to the captains of the Blonde and Daphne frigates to proceed,

ceed, in company with a sloop of war, forthwith to Cape François. The Centurion was soon afterwards ordered to Port au Prince. The Blonde being commanded by my amiable and lamented friend Captain William Affleck, who kindly undertook to convey the French commissioners back to St. Domingo, I was easily persuaded to accompany them thither; and some other gentlemen of Jamaica joined the party.

We arrived in the harbour of Cape François in the evening of the 26th of September, and the first object which arrested our attention as we approached, was a dreadful scene of devastation by fire. The noble plain adjoining the Cape was covered with ashes, and the surrounding hills, as far as the eye could reach, every where presented to us ruins still smoking, and houses and plantations at that moment in flames. It was a fight more terrible than the mind of any man, unaccustomed to such a scene, can easily conceive.—The inhabitants of the town being assembled on the beach, directed all their attention towards us, and we landed amidst a crowd of spectators who, with uplifted hands and streaming eyes, gave welcome to their deliverers (for such they considered us) and acclamations of *vivent les Anglois* resounded from every quarter.

THE

THE governor of St. Domingo, at that time, was the unfortunate General Blanchelande; a *marechal de camp* in the French service, who has since perished on the scaffold. He did us the honour to receive us on the quay. A committee of the colonial assembly, accompanied by the governor's only son, an amiable and accomplished youth *, had before attended us on board the Blonde, and we were immediately conducted to the place of their meeting. The scene was striking and solemn. The hall was splendidly illuminated, and all the members appeared in mourning. Chairs were placed for us within the bar, and the Governor having taken his seat on the right hand of the President, the latter addressed us in an eloquent and affecting oration, of which the following is as literal a translation as the idiom of the two languages will admit:

    " WE were not mistaken, Gentlemen, when we placed our confidence in your generosity; but we could hardly entertain the hope, that, besides sending us

* This young gentleman likewise perished by the guillotine under the tyranny of Roberspierre. He was massacred at Paris, on the 20th July 1794, in the twentieth year of his age.

I   succours,

fuccours, you would come in perfon to give us confolation. You have quitted, without reluctance, the peaceful enjoyment of happinefs at home, to come and participate in the misfortunes of ftrangers, and blend your tears with our's. Scenes of mifery (the contemplation of which, to thofe who are unaccuftomed to misfortune, is commonly difgufting) have not fuppreffed *your* feelings. You have been willing to afcertain the full extent of our diftreffes, and to pour into our wounds the falutary balm of your fenfibility and compaffion.

" THE picture which has been drawn of our calamities, you will find has fallen fhort of the reality. That verdure with which our fields were lately arrayed, is no longer vifible; difcoloured by the flames, and laid wafte by the devaftations of war, our coafts exhibit no profpect but that of defolation. The emblems which we wear on our perfons, are the tokens of our grief for the lofs of our brethren, who

were

were furprifed, and cruelly affaffinated, by the revolters.

" IT is by the glare of the conflagrations that every way furround us, that we now deliberate; we are compelled to fit armed and watchful through the night, to keep the enemy from our fanctuary. For a long time paft our bofoms have been depreffed by forrow; they experience this day, for the firft time, the fweet emotions of pleafure, in beholding you amongft us.

" GENEROUS iflanders! humanity has operated powerfully on your hearts;—you have yielded to the firft emotion of your generofity, in the hopes of fnatching us from death; for it is already too late to fave us from mifery. What a contraft between *your* conduct, and that of other nations! We will avail ourfelves of your benevolence; but the days you preferve to us, will not be fufficient to manifeft

our

our gratitude: our children ſhall keep it in remembrance.

" REGENERATED France, unapprized that ſuch calamities might befal us, has taken no meaſures to protect us againſt their effects: with what admiration will ſhe learn, that, without your aſſiſtance, we ſhould no longer exiſt as a dependency to any nation.

" THE Commiſſioners deputed by us to the iſland of Jamaica, have informed us of your exertions to ſerve us.—Receive the aſſurance of our attachment and ſenſibility.

" THE Governor-general of this iſland, whoſe ſentiments perfectly accord with our own, participates equally in the joy we feel at your preſence, and in our gratitude for the aſſiſtance you have brought us."

AT this juncture, the French coloniſts in St. Domingo, however they might have been divided in

c political

political fentiments on former occafions, feemed to be foftened, by the fenfe of common fuffering, into perfect unanimity. All defcriptions of perfons joined in one general outcry againft the National Affembly, to whofe proceedings were imputed all their difafters. This opinion was indeed fo widely diffeminated, and fo deeply rooted, as to create a very ftrong difpofition in all claffes of the whites, to renounce their allegiance to the mother country. The black cockade was univerfally fubftituted in place of the tri-coloured one, and very earneft wifhes were avowed in all companies, without fcruple or reftraint, that the Britifh adminiftration would fend an armament to conquer the ifland, or rather to receive its voluntary furrender from the inhabitants. What they wifhed might happen, they perfuaded themfelves to believe was actually in contemplation; and this idea foon became fo prevalent, as to place the author of this work in an awkward fituation. The fanguine difpofition obfervable in the French character, has been noticed by all who have vifited them; but in this cafe their credulity grew to a height that was extravagant and even ridiculous. By the kindnefs of the Earl of

Effingham,

Effingham, I was favoured with a letter of introduction to the Governor-general; and my reception,
both by M. Blanchelande and the colonial affembly,
was fuch as not only to excite the publick attention,
but alfo to induce a very general belief that no common .motive had brought me thither. The fug-
geftions of individuals to this purpofe, became per-
plexing and troublefome. Affurances on my part,
that I had no views beyond the gratification of cu-
riofity, had no other effect than to call forth com-
mendations on my prudence. It was fettled, that I
was an agent of the Englifh miniftry, fent purpofely
to found the inclinations of the Colonifts towards the
government of Great Britain, preparatory to an invafion of the country by a Britifh armament; and
their wifhes and inclinations co-operating with this
idea, gave rife to many ftrange applications which
were made to me; fome of them of fo ludicrous a
nature, as no powers of face could eafily withftand.

THIS circumftance is not recorded from the vain
ambition of fhewing my own importance. The
reader of the following pages will difcover its application; and, perhaps, it may induce him to make fome

allowance

allowance for that confident expectation of fure and fpeedy fuccefs, which afterwards led to attempts, by the Britifh arms, againft this ill-fated country, with means that muft otherwife have been thought at the time,—as in the fequel they have unhappily proved, —altogether inadequate to the object in view.

THE ravages of the rebellion, during the time that I remained at Cape François, extended in all directions. The whole of the plain of the Cape, with the exception of one plantation which adjoined the town, was in ruins; as were likewife the Parifh of Limonade, and moft of the fettlements in the mountains adjacent. The Parifh of Limbé was every where on fire; and before my departure, the rebels had obtained poffeffion of the bay and forts at l'Acul, as well as the diftricts of Fort Dauphin, Dondon, and La Grande Riviere.

DESTRUCTION every where marked their progrefs, and refiftance feemed to be confidered by the whites not only as unavailing in the prefent conjuncture, but as hopelefs in future. To fill up the meafure

of

of their calamities, their Spanish neighbours in the same island, with a spirit of bigotry and hatred which is, I believe, without an example in the world, refused to lend any assistance towards suppressing a revolt, in the issue of which common reason should have informed them, that their own preservation was implicated equally with that of the French. They were even accused not only of supplying the rebels with arms and provisions; but also of delivering up to them to be murdered, many unhappy French planters who had fled for refuge to the Spanish territories, and receiving money from the rebels as the price of their blood. Of these latter charges, however, no proof was, I believe, ever produced; and, for the honour of human nature, I am unwilling to believe that they are true.

To myself, the case appeared altogether desperate from the beginning; and many of the most respectable and best informed persons in Cape François (some of them in high stations) assured me, in confidence, that they concurred in this opinion. The merchants and importers of European manufactures, apprehending every hour the destruction of the town,

as

as much from incendiaries within, as from the rebels
without, offered their goods for ready money at half
the usual prices; and applications were made to Captain Affleck, by persons of all descriptions, for per-
mission to embark in the Blonde for Jamaica. The
interposition of the colonial government obliged him
to reject their solicitations; but means were contrived to send on board consignments of money to a
great amount; and I know that other conveyances
were found, by which effects to a considerable value
were exported both to Jamaica, and the states of
North America.

UNDER these circumstances, it very naturally occurred to me to direct my enquiries towards the state
of the colony previous to the revolt, and collect
authentick information on the spot, concerning the
primary cause, and subsequent progress, of the widely
extended ruin before me. Strongly impressed with
the gloomy idea, that the only memorial of this once
flourishing colony would soon be found in the records of history, I was desirous that my own country and fellow-colonists, in lamenting its catastrophe,
might at the same time profit by so terrible an
example.

example. My means of information were too valuable to be neglected, and I determined to avail
myfelf of them. The Governor-general furnifhed
me with copies of all the papers and details of
office that I folicited, with a politenefs that aug-
mented the favour. The fate of this unhappy
gentleman, two years afterwards, gave me infinite
concern. Like his royal mafter, he was unfortunately called to a ftation to which his abilities
were not competent; and in times when perhaps no
abilities would have availed him.

THE Prefident of the colonial affembly, at the
time of my arrival, was M. de Caducfh, who fome
time afterwards took up his refidence, and held an
important office, in Jamaica. He was a man of very
diftinguifhed talents, and withal ftrongly and fincerely attached to the Britifh government, of which,
if it were proper, I could furnifh unqueftionable
proof *. This gentleman drew up, at my requeft,
a fhort account of the origin and progrefs of the re-

* He afterwards accompanied General Williamfon back to St. Domingo, and
was killed (or, as I have heard, bafely murdered) in a duel at Port au Prince, by one
of his countrymen.

bellion;

bellion; and after my return to England, favoured me with his correspondence. Many important facts, which are given in this work, are given on his authority.

To M. Delaire, a merchant of confideration in the town of the Cape, who has fince removed, I believe, to the ftate of South Carolina, I was indebted for a fimilar narrative, drawn up by himfelf in the Englifh language, of which he is a very competent mafter. It is brief, but much to the purpofe; difplays an intimate knowledge of the concerns of the colony, and traces, with great acutenefs, its difafters to their fource.

But the friend from whofe fuperior knowledge I have derived my chief information in all refpects, is the gentleman alluded to in the marginal note to p. 112 of the following fheets; and I fincerely regret, that ill-fortune has fo purfued him as to render it improper in this work to exprefs to him, *by name*, the obligations I owe to his kindnefs. After a narrow efcape from the vengeance of thofe mercilefs men, Santhonax and Polverel, he was induced to return to St. Domingo, to look after his property ; and, I grieve to fay, that he is again fallen into the hands of his enemies. He found means, however, previous to his prefent confinement, to convey to me many valuable papers; and, among others, a copy of that moſt curious and important document, the dying depoſition or teſtament of Ogè, mentioned in the fourth chapter, and printed at large among the additional notes and illuſtrations at the end of my work. Of this paper (the communication of which, in proper time, would have prevented the dreadful ſcenes that followed) although I had frequently heard, I had long doubted the exiſtence. Its ſuppreſſion by the perſons to whom it was delivered by the wretched ſufferer, appeared to be an act of ſuch monſtrous and unexampled wickedneſs, that, until I ſaw the paper itſelf, I could not credit the charge. Whether M. Blanchelande was a party concerned in this atrocious proceeding, as my friend aſſerts, I know not. If he was guilty, he has juſtly paid the forfeit of his crime; and although, believing him innocent, I mourned over his untimely fate, I ſcruple not to avow my opinion, that if he had poſſeſſed a thouſand lives, the loſs of them all had not been a ſufficient

d   atonement,

atonement, in fo enormous a cafe, to violated juftice !

SUCH were the motives that induced me to undertake this Hiftorical Survey of the French part of St.
Domingo, and fuch are the authorities from whence
I have derived my information concerning thofe ca-
lamitous events which have brought it to ruin. Yet
I will frankly confefs, that, if I have any credit with
the publick as an author, I am not fure this work will
add to my reputation. Every writer muft rife or
fink, in fome degree, with the nature of his fubject ;
and on this occafion, the picture which I fhall exhibit, has nothing in it to delight the fancy, or to glad-
den the heart. The profpects before us are all dark
and difmal. Here is no room for tracing the beau-
ties of unfullied nature. Thofe groves of perennial
verdure; thofe magnificent and romantick land-
fcapes, which, in tropical regions, every where invite the eye, and oftentimes detain it, until wonder
is exalted to devotion, muft now give place to the
miferies of war, and the horrors of peftilence; to
fcenes of anarchy, defolation, and carnage. We
have to contemplate the human mind in its utmoft

deformity :

deformity: to behold favage man, let loofe from reftraint, exercifing cruelties, of which the bare recital
makes the heart recoil, and committing crimes which
are hitherto unheard of in hiftory; teeming

———— all monftrous, all prodigious things,
Abominable, unutterable, and worfe
Than fables yet have feign'd, or fear conceiv'd!
MILTON.

ALL therefore that I can hope and expect is, that
my narrative, if it cannot delight, may at leaft *inftruct*. On the fober and confiderate, on thofe
who are open to conviction, this affemblage of
horrors will have its effect. It will expofe the
lamentable ignorance of fome, and the monftrous
wickednefs of others, among the reformers of the
prefent day, who, urging onwards fchemes of perfection, and projects of amendment in the condition
of human life, fafter than nature allows, are lighting
up a confuming fire between the different claffes of
mankind, which nothing but human blood can ex-
tinguifh. To tell fuch men that great and beneficial
modifications in the eftablifhed orders of fociety, can
only be effected by a progreffive improvement in the

fituation

fituation of the lower ranks of the people, is to preach to the winds. In their hands reformation, with a fcythe more deftructive than that of time, mows down every thing, and plants nothing. Moderation and caution they confider as rank cowardice. Force and violence are the ready, and, in their opinion, the only proper application for the cure of early and habitual prejudice. Their practice, like that of other mountebanks, is bold and compendious; their motto is, *cure or kill.*

THESE reflections neceffarily arife from the circum-ftance which is incontrovertibly proved in the follow-ing pages, namely, that the rebellion of the negroes in St. Domingo, and the infurrection of the mulattoes, to whom Ogè was fent as ambaffador, had one and the fame origin. It was not the ftrong and irre-fiftible impulfe of human nature, groaning under oppreffion, that excited either of thofe claffes to plunge their daggers into the bofoms of unoffending women and helplefs infants. They were driven into thofe exceffes — reluctantly driven — by the vile machinations of men calling themfelves philofophers (the profelytes and imitators in France, of the Old

* Jewry

Jewry affociates in London) whofe pretences to philanthropy were as grofs a mockery of human reafon,
as their conduct was an outrage on all the feelings
of our nature, and the ties which hold fociety together !.

IT is indeed true, that negro-rebellions have heretofore arifen in this and other iflands of the Weft Indies, to which no fuch exciting caufes contributed :—
but it is equally certain, that thofe rebellions always
originated among the newly-imported negroes only;
many of whom had probably lived in a ftate of freedom in Africa, and had been fraudulently, or for-
cibly, fold into flavery by their chiefs. That cafes
of this kind do fometimes occur in the flave trade, I
dare not difpute, and I admit that revolt and infurrection are their natural confequences.

BUT, in St. Domingo, a very confiderable part of
the infurgents were—not Africans, but—Creoles, or
natives. Some of the leaders were favoured domef-
ticks among the white inhabitants, born and brought
up in their families. A few of them had even received thofe advantages, the perverfion of which,
under

under their philofophical preceptors, ferved only to render them pre-eminent in mifchief; for having been taught to read, they were led to imbibe, and enabled to promulgate, thofe principles and doctrines which led, and always will lead, to the fubverfion of all government and order.

LET me not be underftood, however, as affirming that nothing is to be attributed on this occafion to the flave-trade. I fcorn to have recourfe to concealment or falfhood. Unqueftionably, the vaft annual importations of enflaved Africans into St. Domingo, for many years previous to 1791, had created a black population in the French part of that ifland, which was, beyond all meafure, difproportionate to the white;—the relative numbers of the two claffes being as fixteen to one. Of this circumftance the leaders of the rebels could not be unobfervant, and they doubtlefs derived encouragement and confidence from it. Here too, I admit, is a warning and an admonition to ourfelves. The inference has not efcaped me:—it conftitutes my parting words with the reader, and I hope they are not urged in vain.

HAVING

HAVING thus pointed out the motives which induced me to write the following narrative; the sources from whence my materials are derived, and the purposes which I hope will be answered by the publication; nothing farther remains but to submit the work itself to the judgment of my readers, which I do with a respectful solicitude.

LONDON,
December, 1796.

ERRATA.

Page 3, line 4, for *its*, read *the*.

 4, note (a) for *ordonateur*, read *ordonnateur*.

 5, line 16, for 52, read *fifty-one*.

 10, line 8, from the bottom: dele the words *enflaved Negroes*, and place them in the margin. The paffage, as it now ftands, is wholly unintelligible.

 11, line 1, for *attending this*, read *attending it*.

 13, laft line but one: read *the chief aim*.

 20, line 2, for *in the metropolis*, read *of the metropolis*.

 24, line 4, for *in exclufion*, read *to the exclufion*.

 49, laft line; for *Machiavilian*, read *Machiavelian*.

 86, line 1, for *apprized*, read *believing*.

 109, line 2, for *eight*, read *fix*.

——line 9, after *governor*, infert *accompanied by a fleet of thirty tranfports*.

 132, line 10, for *fourteen*, read *fixteen*.

 135, line 5, from the bottom: after the word *freighted*, infert *for Europe*.

 152, line 1, inftead of *the whole of that extenfive bay*, read *the windward paffage, and the whole of that extenfive bay*.

A SHORT

HISTORY

OF THE

FRENCH Colony in ST. DOMINGO, &c.

CHAP. I.

Political State of ST. DOMINGO *previous to the Year* 1789.

THE inhabitants of the French part of St. Domingo, as of all the West Indian Islands, were composed of three great classes: 1st, pure whites. 2d, people of colour, and blacks of free condition. 3d, negroes in a state of slavery. The reader is apprised that the class which, by a strange abuse of language, is called *people of colour*, originates from an intermixture of the whites and the blacks. The genuine offspring of a pure white with a negro is called a mulatto; but there are various casts, produced by subsequent connections, some of which draw near to the whites, until all visible distinction between them is lost; whilst others fall retrograde to the blacks. All these were known in St. Domingo by the term *sang-melées*, or *gens de couleur*, (in com-

B

mon

mon parlance they are collectively called *mulattoes)* and it muſt be attributed, I preſume, to the greater diſcountenance which the married ſtate receives from the national manners, that in all the French iſlands theſe people abound in far greater proportion to the whites than in thoſe of Great Britain. In Jamaica, the whites out-number the people of colour as three to one. In St. Domingo, the whites were eſtimated at 30,000, the mulattoes at 24,000, of whom 4,700 were men capable of bearing arms, and accordingly, as a diſtinct people, actuated by an *eſprit de corps,* they were very formidable. Of the policy which it was thought neceſſary in St. Domingo to maintain towards this unfortunate race, I ſhall preſently treat; but it ſeems proper, in the firſt place, to give ſome account of the ſubordination in which, before the revolution of 1789, the parent country thought fit to hold the colony at large.

THE government was exerciſed by a Governor General, and an officer called Intendant, both of whom were nominated by the crown, on the recommendation of the miniſter of the marine, and generally conſidered as eſtabliſhed in their reſpective offices for three years. Their powers, in ſome caſes, were adminiſtered jointly; in others, they poſſeſſed ſeparate and diſtinct authority, which each of them exerciſed without the concurrence or participation of the other.

IN their joint adminiſtration their powers were unlimited, comprehending every part of colonial government, and extending even to detail, in the minuteſt branches of finance and police. They enacted the laws, nominated to all vacant offices,
                                                                    and

and diftributed the crown lands as they thought proper. They refpectively prefided at the fame time in each of the fupreme councils, or courts of juftice in the dernier refort; and as vacancies happened in thofe courts, by the death or removal of its members, they filled up the vacant places. Againft the abufe of powers, thus extravagant and unbounded, the people had no certain protection. Fortunately, it was rare that the governor and intendant agreed in opinion on the exercife of their joint authority, which therefore became neceffarily relaxed; and the inhabitants derived fome degree of fecurity from the difputes and diffenfions of the contending parties. In all fuch cafes, however, the greateft weight of authority fell to the fhare of the governor. He was, in truth, an abfolute prince, whofe will, generally fpeaking, conftituted law. He was authorized to imprifon any perfon in the colony, for caufes of which he alone was the judge; and having at the fame time the fupreme command of both the naval and military force, he had the means of exercifing this power whenever he thought proper. On the other hand, no arreft, by any other authority, was valid without the governor's approbation. Thus he had power to ftop the courfe of juftice, and to hold the courts of civil and criminal jurifdiction in a flavifh dependance on himfelf.

THE peculiar province of the intendant was that of regulating the publick revenues, or adminiftering the finances of the colony. The collectors and receivers of all duties and taxes were fubject to his infpection and controul. He paffed or rejected their accounts, and made them fuch allowances as he

alone

alone thought proper. The application of all the publick monies rested entirely with the intendant; — a province which created such temptation to himself as no virtue could resist, and furnished such means of corruption, as overcame all opposition from others *(a)*

FOR the better administration of justice, and the easier collection of the revenues, the colony was divided into three provinces; which were distinguished, from their relative situation, by the names of the Northern, the Western and Southern. In each of these provinces resided a deputy governor, or commander *en second,* and in each were established subordinate courts of justice, both civil and criminal; from whose determination appeals were allowed to the superior councils, of which there were two; one at *Cape François* for the Northern province, the other at *Port au Prince* for the Western and Southern. They were composed of the governor-general, the intendant, the deputy governors, the king's lieutenants *(b),* a president,

(a) The taxes and duties were laid and modified, as occasion required, by a court composed of the governor general, the intendant, the presidents of the provincial councils, the attorney general, the commissioner of the navy *(ordonateur)* and the several commandants of the militia. This court was dignified by the title of the *Colonial Assembly,* although the colonists had not a single delegate in it.

(b) These king's lieutenants were military officers residing in the several towns, commonly with the rank of colonel. There were also in each town *majors* and *aides-major.* All these officers were wholly independent of the civil power, and owned no superior but the governor-general, who could dismiss them at pleasure. It may be proper to observe too that the counsellors held their seats by a very uncertain tenure. One of the governors (the Prince de Rohan) sent the whole number state prisoners to France. They were seized on their seats of justice, and put on board a ship in irons, and in that condition conveyed to Paris, and shut up for a long time in the Bastile, without trial or hearing.

and

and twelve counsellors, four *assesseurs*, or assistant judges, together with the attorney general and register. In these councils, or courts of supreme jurisdiction, as in the parliaments of France, the king's edicts, and those of the governor and intendant, were registered. Seven members constituted a quorum for the hearing of appeal causes; but a hint from the governor-general was always sufficient to render much investigation unnecessary: and it is asserted (with what truth I pretend not to determine) that, besides their slavish dependance on the executive power, the members of these courts were notoriously and shamefully open to corruption and bribery. An appeal however lay to the king, in the last resort; and candour compels me to observe that, on such appeals, substantial justice was generally obtained *(c)*.

THE number of the king's troops on the colonial establishment was commonly from 2 to 3,000 men; and each of the 52 parishes into which the colony was divided raised one or more companies of white militia, a company of mulattoes, and a company of free blacks. The officers, both of the regular troops and the militia, were commissioned provisionally by the governor-general, subject to the king's approbation; but the militia received no pay of any kind.

FROM this recapitulation, it is evident that the peace and happiness of the people of St. Domingo depended very much on

(c) In the year 1787 these two superior councils were consolidated into one, which held its meetings at Port au Prince, this city being the seat of government *in time of peace*. In the event of a war, the governor-general removed to Cape François. The true, though not the ostensible, reason for this junction of the council boards, was an idea that a single board would be found more tractable in the registry of edicts and ordinances than two separate jurisdictions.

the

the perfonal qualities and native difpofition of the governor-general, who was always felected from the army. At the fame time it muft be honeftly admitted, that the liberality and mild-nefs, which of late years have dignified and foftened the military character among all the nations of Europe, had a powerful influence in the adminiftration of the government in the French colonies. It muft be allowed alfo, that the manifeft importance to which, as mankind become divefted of ancient prejudices, the commercial part of the community, even among the French, has imperceptibly rifen, infured to the wealthy and opulent planters a degree of refpect from perfons in power, which, in former times, attached only to noble birth and powerful con-nections; while the lower orders among the whites derived the fame advantage from that unconquerable diftinction which nature herfelf has legibly drawn between the white and black inhabitants; and from their vifible importance, in a country where, from the difproportion of the whites to the blacks, the common fafety of the former clafs depends altogether on their united exertions.

To contend, as fome philofophers have idly contended, that no natural fuperiority can juftly belong to any one race of peo-ple over another, to Europeans over Africans, merely from a difference of colour, is to wafte words to no purpofe, and to combat with air. Among the inhabitants of every ifland in the Weft Indies, it is the colour, with fome few exceptions, that diftinguifhes freedom from flavery: fo long therefore as free-dom fhall be enjoyed exclufively by one race of people, and flavery be the condition of another, contempt and degradation

x   will

will attach to the colour by which that condition is generally recognized, and follow it, in some degree, through all its varieties and affinities. We may trace a similar prejudice among the most liberal and enlightened nations of Europe. Although nothing surely ought to reflect greater lustre on any man than the circumstance of his having risen by industry and virtue above the disadvantages of mean birth and indigent parentage, there are, nevertheless, but few persons in the world who delight to be reminded of this species of merit. There is a consciousness of something disgraceful in the recollection; and it seems therefore reasonable to conclude, that if nature had made the same distinction in this case as in the other, and stamped, by an indelible mark, the condition and parentage on the forehead, the same, or nearly the same, effect would have resulted from it, as results from the difference of colour in the West Indies. I mean however only to account for in some degree, not to defend, the conduct of the whites of St. Domingo towards the coloured people; whose condition was in truth much worse than that of the same class in the British colonies, and not to be justified on any principle of example or reason.

In many respects their situation was even more degrading and wretched than that of the enslaved negroes in any part of the West Indies; all of whom have masters that are interested in their preservation, and many of whom find in those masters powerful friends and vigilant protectors. Although released from the dominion of individuals, yet the free men of colour in all the French islands were still considered as the property of the publick, and as publick property they were obnoxious to the

Free Mulattoes.

the caprice and tyranny of all thofe whom the accident of birth had placed above them. By the colonial governments they were treated as flaves in the ftricteft fenfe; compelled, on attaining the age of manhood, to ferve three years in a military eftablifhment called the *maréchauſſée (e)*, and on the expiration of that term they were fubject, great part of the year, to the burthen of the *corvées*;—a fpecies of labour allotted for the repair of the highways, of which the hardfhips were infupportable. They were compelled moreover to ferve in the militia of the province or quarter to which they belonged, without pay or allowance of any kind, and in the horfe or foot, at the pleafure of the commanding officer; and obliged alfo to fupply themfelves, at their own expence, with arms, ammunition, and accoutrements. Their days of mufter were frequent, and the rigour with which the King's lieutenants, majors, and aides-major, enforced their authority on thofe occafions over thefe people, had degenerated into the bafeft tyranny.

THEY were forbidden to hold any publick office, truft, or employment, however infignificant; they were not even allowed to exercife any of thofe profeffions, to which fome fort of liberal education is fuppofed to be neceffary. All the naval and military departments, all degrees in law, phyfick, and divinity, were appropriated exclufively by the whites. A mulatto could not

(*e*) It confifted of certain companies of infantry, which were chiefly employed *as rangers* in clearing the woods of *maron* or runaway flaves. This eftablifhment was afterwards very prudently diffolved, and the companies difbanded; it appearing that the mulattoes acquired, by communication with each other, a fenfe of common intereft and of common ftrength, which was beginning to render them formidable to their employers.

be

be a prieſt, nor a lawyer, nor a phyſician, nor a ſurgeon, nor an apothecary, nor a ſchoolmaſter. Neither did the diſtinction of colour terminate, as in the Britiſh Weſt Indies, with the third generation. There was no law, nor cuſtom, that allowed the privileges of a white perſon to any deſcendant from an African, however remote the origin. The taint in the blood was incurable, and ſpread to the lateſt poſterity. Hence no white man, who had the ſmalleſt pretenſions to character, would ever think of marriage with a negro or mulatto woman : ſuch a ſtep would immediately have terminated in his diſgrace and ruin.

UNDER the preſſure of theſe accumulated grievances, hope itſelf, too frequently the only ſolace of the wretched, was denied to theſe unfortunate people ; for the courts of criminal juriſdiction, adopting the popular prejudices againſt them, gave effect and permanency to the ſyſtem. A man of colour being proſecutor (a circumſtance in truth which ſeldom occurred) muſt have made out a ſtrong caſe indeed, if at any time he obtained the conviction of a white perſon. On the other hand, the whites never failed to procure prompt and ſpeedy juſtice againſt the mulattoes. To mark more ſtrongly the diſtinction between the two claſſes, the law declared that if a free man of colour preſumed to ſtrike a white perſon of whatever condition, his right hand ſhould be cut off; while a white man, for a ſimilar aſſault on a free mulatto, was diſmiſſed on the payment of an inſignificant fine.

IN extenuation of this horrible detail, it may be ſaid with truth that the manners of the white inhabitants ſoftened, in

ſome

some measure, the severity of their laws : thus, in the case last mentioned, the universal abhorrence which would have attended an enforcement of the penalty, made the law a dead letter. It was the same with the Roman law of the Twelve Tables, by which a father was allowed to inflict the punishment of death on his own child :—manners, not law, prevented the exertion of a power so unnatural and odious.

But the circumstance which contributed most to afford the coloured people of St. Domingo protection, was the privilege they possessed of acquiring and holding property to any amount. Several of them were the owners of considerable estates; and so prevalent was the influence of money throughout the colony, that many of the great officers in the administration of government scrupled not secretly to become their pensioners. Such of the coloured people therefore as had happily the means of gratifying the venality of their superiors, were secure enough in their persons; although the same circumstance made them more pointedly the objects of hatred and envy to the lower orders of the whites.

The next enslaved negroes, and lowest, class of people in the French islands were the negroes in a state of slavery; of whom, in the year 1789, St. Domingo contained no less than 480,000. It was in favour of this class that Louis XIV in the year 1685, published the celebrated edict, or code of regulations, which is well known to the world under the title of the *Code Noir*; and it must be allowed, that many of its provisions breathe a spirit of tenderness and philanthropy which reflects honour on the memory of its

6   author;

author;—but there is this misfortune attending this, and muſt attend all other ſyſtems of the ſame nature, that moſt of its regulations are inapplicable to the condition and ſituation of the
colonies in America. In countries where ſlavery is eſtabliſhed,
the leading principle on which government is ſupported, is *fear*;
or a ſenſe of that abſolute coercive neceſſity, which, leaving no
choice of action, ſuperſedes all queſtion of *right*. It is in vain
to deny that ſuch actually is, and neceſſarily muſt be, the caſe in
all countries where ſlavery is allowed. Every endeavour therefore to extend poſitive rights to men in this ſtate, as between one
claſs of people and the other, is an attempt to reconcile inherent
contradictions, and to blend principles together which admit not
of combination. The great and, I am afraid, the only certain
and permanent ſecurity of the enſlaved negroes, is the ſtrong circumſtance that the intereſt of the maſter is blended with, and in
truth, altogether depends on, the preſervation, and even on the
health, ſtrength, and activity, of the ſlave. This applies equally
to all the European colonies in America; and accordingly the
actual condition of the negroes in all thoſe colonies, to whatever
nation they belong, is I believe nearly the ſame. Of that condition I have given an account in another place *(f)*: I have therefore only to obſerve in this, that in all the French iſlands the general treatment of the ſlaves is neither much better nor much
worſe, as far as I could obſerve, than in thoſe of Great Britain.
If any difference there is, I think that they are better clothed
among the French, and allowed more animal food among the
Engliſh. The prevalent notion that the French planters treat

(f) Hiſt. Civil and Commercial of the Britiſh Colonies.

C 2

their

their negroes with greater humanity and tendernefs than the Britifh, I know to be groundlefs; yet no candid perfon, who has had an opportunity of feeing the negroes in the French iflands, and of contrafting their condition with that of the peafantry in many parts of Europe, will think them, by any means, the moft wretched of mankind.

On the whole, if human life, in its beft ftate, is a combination of happinefs and mifery, and we are to confider that condition of political fociety as relatively good, in which, notwithftanding many difadvantages, the lower claffes are eafily fupplied with the means of healthy fubfiftence; and a general air of cheerful contentednefs animates all ranks of people,—where we behold opulent towns, plentiful markets, extenfive commerce, and increafing cultivation—it muft be pronounced that the government of the French part of St. Domingo (to whatever latent caufes it might be owing) was not altogether fo practically bad, as fome of the circumftances that have been ftated might give room to imagine. With all the abufes arifing from the licentioufnefs of power, the corruption of manners, and the fyftem of flavery, the fcale evidently preponderated on the favourable fide; and, in fpite of political evils and private grievances, the figns of publick profperity were every where vifible.

Such were the condition and fituation of the French colony in St. Domingo in the year 1788—an eventful period; for the feeds of liberty which, ever fince the war between Great Britain and her tranfatlantick poffeffions, had taken root in the kingdom of France, now began to fpring up with a rank luxuriancy in all

parts

parts of her extensive dominions; and a thousand circumstances demonstrated that great and important changes and convulsions were impending. The necessity of a sober and well-digested arrangement for correcting inveterate abuses, both in the mother country and the colonies, was indeed apparent; but, unhappily, a spirit of subversion and innovation, founded on visionary systems inapplicable to real life, had taken possession of the publick mind. Its effects in St. Domingo are written in colours too lasting to be obliterated; for the pride of power, the rage of reformation, the contentions of party, and the conflict of opposing interests and passions, produced a tempest that swept every thing before it.

To trace those effects to their proper causes, to develop the atrocious purposes of pretended philanthropy, political fanaticism, and disappointed ambition; and to describe the vast and lamentable ruin which they occasioned, thereby to furnish a profitable lesson to other nations, is the aim of the following pages.

CHAP.

C H A P. II.

From the Revolution of 1789, to the Meeting of the First General Colonial Assembly.

ON the 27th of December 1788, the court of France came to the memorable determination to summon the States General of the kingdom; and resolved that the representation of the *tiers état* (or commons) should be equal to the sum of the representation of the other two orders.

THIS measure, as might have been foreseen, proved the basis of the great national revolution that followed; and it operated with immediate and decisive effect in all the French colonies. The governor of the French part of St. Domingo at that period was Monf. Duchilleau, a man who was supposed secretly to favour the popular pretensions. He was allowed therefore to continue unmolested in the seat of government; but the sceptre dropped from his hand; for when he attempted to prevent the parochial and provincial meetings, which were every where summoned, from assembling, his proclamations were treated with indignity and contempt: the meetings were held in spite of the governor, and resolutions passed declaratory of the right of the colonists to send deputies to the States General. Deputies were accordingly
elected

elected for that purpofe, to the number of eighteen (fix for each province) who forthwith, without any authority either from the French miniftry or the colonial government, embarked for France, as the legal reprefentatives of a great and integral part of the French empire.

THEY arrived at Verfailles the latter end of June, about a month after the States General had declared themfelves the national affembly. But neither the minifter nor the national affembly were difpofed to admit the full extent of their claims. The number of eighteen deputies from one colony was thought exceffive; and it was with fome difficulty that fix of them only were admitted to verify their powers, and feat themfelves among the national reprefentatives.

THERE prevailed at this time throughout the cities of France, a very ftrong and marked prejudice againft the inhabitants of the Sugar Iflands, on account of the flavery of their negroes. It was not indeed fuppofed, nor even pretended, that the condition of thefe people was worfe at this juncture than in any former period: the contrary was known to be the truth. But declamations in fupport of perfonal freedom, and invectives againft defpotifm of all kinds, had been the favourite topicks of many eminent French writers for a feries of years: and the publick indignation was now artfully raifed againft the planters of the Weft Indies, as one of the means of exciting commotions and infurrections in different parts of the French dominions. This fpirit of hoftility againft the inhabitants of the French colonies, was induftrioufly fomented and aggravated by the meafures of a fociety, who called themfelves

CHAP.   felves *Amis des Noirs* (Friends of the Blacks); and it muſt be ac-
II.   knowledged, that the ſplendid appearance, and thoughtleſs ex-
travagance, of many of the French planters reſident in the mother
country, contributed by no means to divert the malice of their
adverſaries, or to ſoften the prejudices of the publick towards
them.

The ſociety in France called *Amis des Noirs,* was I believe
originally formed on the model of a ſimilar aſſociation in London;
but the views and purpoſes of the two bodies had taken a different direction.   The ſociety in London *profeſſed* to have nothing more in view than to obtain an act of the legiſlature for
prohibiting the further introduction of African ſlaves into the
Britiſh colonies.   They diſclaimed all intention of interfering
with the government and condition of the negroes already in the
plantations; publickly declaring their opinion to be, that a general emancipation of thoſe people, in their preſent ſtate of ignorance and barbarity, inſtead of a bleſſing, would prove to them a
ſource of misfortune and miſery.   On the other hand, the ſociety of *Amis des Noirs,* having ſecretly in view to ſubvert the
ancient deſpotiſm of the French government, loudly clamoured
for a general and immediate abolition, not only of the ſlave
trade, but alſo of the ſlavery which it ſupported.   Proceeding
on abſtract reaſoning, rather than on the actual condition of human nature, they diſtinguiſhed not between civilized and unci-
vilized life, and confidered that it ill became them to claim
freedom for themſelves, and withhold it at the ſame time from
the negroes : it is to be lamented that a principle ſo plauſible in
appearance,

a¬pearance, fhould, in its application to this cafe, be vifionary and impracticable.

AT this juncture, a confiderable body of the mulattoes from St. Domingo and the other French iflands, were refident in the French capital. Some of thefe were young people fent thither for education: others were men of confiderable property, and many of them, without doubt, perfons of intelligence and amiable manners. With thefe people the fociety of *Amis des Noirs* formed an intimate connection; pointed out to them the wretchednefs of their condition; filled the nation with remonftrances and ap-peals on their behalf; and poured out fuch invectives againft the white planters, as bore away reafon and moderation in the torrent. Unhappily, there was too much to offer on the part of the mu-lattoes. Their perfonal appearance too, excited pity, and, co-operating with the temper of the times, and the credulity of the French nation, raifed fuch an indignant fpirit in all ranks of people againft the white colonifts, as threatened their total an-nihilation and ruin.

IN this difpofition of the people of France towards the inha-bitants of their colonies in the Weft Indies, the national affem-bly, on the 20th day of Auguft, voted the celebrated *aeclaration of rights*; and thus, by a revolution unparalleled in hiftory, was a mighty fabrick (apparently eftablifhed by every thing that was fecure and unaffailable) overturned in a moment. Happy had it been for the general interefts of the human race, if, when the French had gone thus far, they had proceeded no farther! Happy for themfelves, if they had then known—what painful ex-

1789

D   perience

perience has fince taught them—that the worft of all gov: :"
ments is preferable to the miferies of anarchy !

PERHAPS a diligent obferver might have difcovered, even in
the firft proceedings of this celebrated affembly, the latent feeds
of that violence, injuftice, and confufion which have fince produced fuch a harveft of crimes and calamities. Many of the
doctrines contained in the declaration of rights feem to have
been introduced for no other purpofe than to awaken a mif-
chievous fpirit of contention and cavil, and to deftroy all fubordination in the lower ranks of the people. Such, for inftance,
was the pofition, that " all men are born, and continue, free and
" equal as to their rights;" according to which, there ought to
be no diftinctions in fociety, nor (if the poffeffion of property
is *a right*) can any man have a right to poffefs or acquire
any thing to the exclufion of others; a pofition not only falfe,
but pernicious, and unfit for every condition of civilized life.
To promulgate fuch leffons in the colonies, as the declared fenfe
of the fupreme government, was to fubvert the whole fyftem of
their eftablifhments. Accordingly, a general ferment prevailed
among the French inhabitants of St. Domingo, from one end of
the colony to the other. All that had paffed in the mother
country concerning the colonifts,—the prejudices of the metropolis towards them,—the efforts of the fociety of *Amis des
Noirs* to emancipate the negroes,—and the conduct of the mulattoes,—had been reprefented to them through the medium
of party, and perhaps with a thoufand circumftances of exaggeration and infult, long before the declaration of rights was received in the colony; and this meafure crowned the whole.

They

They maintained that it was calculated to convert their peaceful and contented negroes into implacable enemies, and render the whole country a theatre of commotion and bloodſhed.

In the meanwhile, the French government, apprehenſive that diſorders of a very alarming nature might ariſe in the colonies from the proceedings in France, had iſſued orders to the gover- nor general of St. Domingo, to convoke the inhabitants, for the purpoſe of forming a legiſlative aſſembly for interior regulation. Theſe orders, however, being unaccountably delayed, the people had anticipated the meaſure. The inhabitants of the Northern diſtrict had already conſtituted a provincial aſſembly, which met at Cape Francois, and their example was followed in November in the Weſtern and Southern provinces; the Weſtern aſſembly met at Port au Prince, the Southern at *Aux Cayes.* Parochial com- mittees were, at the ſame time, every where eſtabliſhed, for the ſake of a more immediate communication between the people and their repreſentatives.

A RECITAL of the conduct and proceedings of theſe pro- vincial aſſemblies, would lead me too much into detail. They differed greatly on many important queſtions; but all of them concurred in opinion concerning the neceſſity of a full and ſpeedy colonial repreſentation; and they unanimouſly voted, that if inſtructions from the king for calling ſuch an aſſembly ſhould not be received within three months thenceforward, the colony ſhould take on itſelf to adopt and enforce the meaſure;—their immediate ſafety and preſervation being, they ſaid, an obligation paramount to all others.

D 2

DURING

CHAP.
II.

DURING this period of anxiety and alarm, the mulattoes were not inactive. Inftructed by their brethren in the metropolis in the nature and extent of their rights, and apprized of the favourable difpofition of the French nation towards them, they became, throughout the colony, actuated by a fpirit of turbulence and fedition; and difregarding all confiderations of prudence, with regard to time and feafons, determined to claim, without delay, the full benefit of all the privileges enjoyed by the whites. Accordingly large bodies of them appeared in arms in different parts of the country; but acting without fufficient concert, or due preparation, they were eafily overpowered. It is faid, that the temper of the provincial affemblies at this juncture,—how much foever inflamed againft the inftigators and abettors of thefe people in the mother country,—was not averfe to moderation and conceffion towards the mulattoes themfelves. Thus, when the party which had taken arms at *Jacmel* was defeated, and their chiefs imprifoned, the affembly of the Weft interpofed with effect in favour of the whole number; and at *Artibonite*, where the revolt was much more extenfive and alarming, a free and unconditional pardon was alfo chearfully granted on the fubmiffion of the infurgents.

AGAINST fuch of the whites as had taken any part in thefe difturbances, in favour of the people of colour, the rage of the populace knew no limits. Monf. *Dubois*, deputy *procureur general*, had not only declared himfelf an advocate for the mulattoes, but, with a degree of imprudence which indicated infanity, fought occafions to declaim publickly againft the flavery

of

of the negroes. The Northern affembly arrefted his perfon, and very probably intended to proceed to greater extremities; but the governor interpofed in his behalf, obtained his releafe, and fent him from the country.

Mons. *Ferrand de Beaudierre,* a magiftrate at *Petit Goave,* was not fo fortunate. This gentleman was unhappily ena-moured of a woman of colour, to whom, as fhe poffeffed a valuable plantation, he had offered marriage. Apprehenfive that by this ftep he might be difplaced from the magiftracy, and being a man of a warm imagination, with little judgment, he undertook to combat the prejudices of the whites againft the whole clafs.   He drew up, in the name and behalf of the mu-latto people, a memorial to the parochial committee, wherein, among other things, they were made to claim, in exprefs words, the full benefit of the national declaration of rights. Nothing could be more ill-timed or injudicious than this proceeding: it was evi-dent, that fuch a claim led to confequences of which the mu-lattoes themfelves (who certainly at this juncture had no wifh to enfranchife the flaves) were not apprized. This memorial therefore was confidered as a fummons to the negroes for a ge-neral revolt. The parochial committee feized the author, and committed him to prifon; but the mob took him from thence by force, and in fpite of the magiftrates and municipality, who exerted themfelves to ftop their fury, put him to death.

The king's order for convoking a general colonial affembly was received in St. Domingo early in the month of January 1790. It appointed the town of *Leogane,* in the Weftern pro-vince,

vince, for the place of meeting; and inftructions accompanied the order, concerning the mode of electing the members. Thefe inftructions, however, being confidered by the provincial affemblies as inapplicable to the circumftances of the colony, were difapproved; and another plan, better fuited, as they conceived, to the wealth, territory, and population of the inhabitants, was adopted. They refolved alfo to hold the affembly at the town of *St. Marc* inftead of *Leogane*, and the 25th of March was fixed for the time of its meeting. It was afterwards prorogued to the 16th of April.

In the meanwhile intelligence was received in France of the temper of St. Domingo towards the mother country. The inhabitants were very generally reprefented as manifefting a difpofition either to renounce their dependency, or to throw themfelves under the protection of a foreign power; and the planters of Martinico were faid to be equally difcontented and difaffected. The trading and manufacturing towns took the alarm; and petitions and remonftrances were prefented from various quarters, imploring the national affembly to adopt meafures for compofing the minds of the colonifts, and preferving to the French empire its moft valuable dependencies.

On the 8th of March 1790, the national affembly entered into the confideration of the fubject, with a ferioufnefs and folemnity fuited to its importance; and, after full difcuffion, a very large majority voted, " That it never was the intention of " the affembly to comprehend the interior government of the co- " lonies in the conftitution which they had framed for the mother " country,

" country, or to fubject them to laws which were incompatible
" with their local eftablifnments; they therefore authorife the in-
" habitants of each colony to fignify to the national affembly their
" fentiments and wifhes concerning that plan of interior legifla-
" tion and commercial arrangement, which would be moft con-
" ducive to their profperity." It was required, however, that the
plan to be offered fhould be conformable to the principles which
had connected the colonies with the metropolis, and be calculated for the prefervation of their reciprocal interefts.—To this
decree was annexed a declaration, " That the national affembly
" would not caufe any innovation to be made, directly or indi-
" rectly, in any fyftem of commerce in which the colonies were
" already concerned."

NOTHING could equal the clamour which this decree occafioned among the people of colour refident in the mother
country, and the philanthropick fociety of *Amis des Noirs*. The
declaration concerning commerce was interpreted into a tacit
fanction for the continuance of the flave trade; and it was even
contended, that the national affembly, by leaving the adjuftment
of the colonial conftitutions to the colonifts themfelves, had dif-
charged them from their allegiance. It was faid that they were
no longer fubject to the French empire, but members of an independent ftate.

NEVERTHELESS, if the circumftances of the times, and the
difpofition of the French colonifts at this juncture, be taken into
the account, candour muft acknowledge that it was a decree
not only juftifiable on the motives of prudence and policy, but
was

was founded also on the strong basis of moral necessity. The arguments that were urged against it seem to imply that the benefits of the French revolution were intended only for the people residing in the realm, in exclusion of their fellow subjects in the plantations. After that great event, to suppose that the inhabitants of those colonies (with the successful example too of the English Americans recent in their memories) would have submitted to be governed and directed in their local concerns by a legislature at the distance of 3,000 miles from them, is to manifest a very slender acquaintance with human nature. How little inclined the colonial assembly was to such submission, their proceedings, from the first day of their meeting, to their final dissolution, will demonstrate.—Of those proceedings I shall endeavour to furnish a brief account in the next Chapter.

C H A P. III.

*Proceedings of the General Colonial Assembly until its final Dissolu-
tion, and Embarkation of the Members for France, August 1790.*

THE General Assembly of St. Domingo met on the 16th
of April, at the town of *St. Marc.* It was composed of
213 members, of whom the city of *Cape François* elected
twenty-four, *Port au Prince* sixteen, and *Aux Cayes* eight. Most
of the other parishes returned two representatives each; and it
is allowed that, on the whole, the colony was fairly, fully, and
most respectably represented. The provincial assemblies, however, continued in the exercise of their functions as before, or appointed committees to act during their intermission.

THE session was opened by a discourse from the president,
wherein, after recounting various abuses in the constitution and
administration of the former colonial government, he pointed
out some of the many great objects that seemed to require immediate attention: among others, he recommended the case of
the mulattoes, and a melioration of the slave laws. The assembly concurred in sentiment with the orator; and one of their first
measures was to relieve the people of colour from the hardships
to which they were subject under the military jurisdiction. It

CHAP.
III.
1790.

E   was

was decreed, that in future no greater duty should be required of them in the militia than from the whites; and the harsh authority, in particular, which the king's lieutenants, majors, and aides-major, commanding in the towns, exercised over those people, was declared oppressive and illegal. These acts of indulgence were certainly meant as the earnest of greater favours, and an opening to conciliation and concession towards the whole class of the coloured people.

THE general assembly proceeded, in the next place, to rectify some gross abuses which had long prevailed in the courts of judicature, confining themselves however to such only as called for immediate redress, their attention being chiefly directed to the great and interesting object of preparing the plan for a new constitution, or system of colonial government; a business which employed their deliberations until the 28th of May.

1790.

M. PEYNIER was now governor general, from whom the partizans and adherents of the ancient despotism secretly derived encouragement and support. The whole body of tax-gatherers, and officers under the fiscal administration, were of this number. These therefore began to recover from the panick into which so great and sudden a revolution had thrown them, and to rally their united strength. Nothing could be more opposite to their wishes, than the success of the general assembly in the establishment of order and good government throughout the colony. Nor were these the only men who beheld the proceedings of this body with an evil eye. All the persons belonging to the courts of civil and criminal jurisdiction (and their numbers were

x   considerable)

confiderable) who were interefted in the maintenance of thofe
abufes which the affembly had corrected, were filled with indignation and envy. To thefe were added moft of the men who
held military commiffions under the king's authority. Habituated to the exercife of command, they indignantly beheld the
fubverfion of all that accuftomed obedience and fubordination
which they had been taught to confider as effential to the fupport
of government, and offered themfelves the willing inftruments
of the governor general in fubverting the new fyftem.

Such were the perfons that oppofed themfelves to the new
order of things in the colony, when the Chevalier Mauduit, colonel of the regiment of Port au Prince, arrived at St. Domingo.
He had not come directly from France, but circuitoufly by way
of Italy; and at Turin had taken leave of the Count d'Artois,
to whofe fortunes he was ftrongly attached. He was a man of
talents; brave, active, and enterprizing; zealous for his party,
and full of projects for a counter-revolution. By his dexterity
and addrefs, he foon acquired an afcendancy over the feeble and
narrow genius of Peynier, and governed the colony in his name.
His penetration eafily made him difcover that, in order effectually to difturb the new fettlement, it was abfolutely neceffary to
prevent a coalition of interefts between the colonial affembly,
and the free people of colour. He therefore proclaimed himfelf
the patron and protector of the mulattoes, and courted them on
all occafions, with fuch affiduity and fuccefs, as gained over the
whole body.

E 2

It

I T feems however extremely probable that the peace of the country would have been preferved, notwithftanding the machinations of Peynier and Mauduit, if the planters, true to their own caufe, had remained united among themfelves. But, unfortunately, the provincial affembly of the North was induced, through mifreprefentation or envy, to counteract, by all poffible means, the proceedings of the general affembly at St. Marc. Thus, difcord and diffention every where prevailed; and appearances feemed to indicate an approaching civil war, even before the plan for the new conftitution was publifhed. This was contained in the famous decree of the general colonial affembly of the 28th of May; a decree, which having been the fubject of much animadverfion, and made the oftenfible motive, on the part of the executive power, for commencing hoftilities, it is proper to ftate it at large.

May 1790.

I T confifted of ten fundamental pofitions, which are preceded by an introductory difcourfe or preamble (as ufual in the French decrees) wherein, among other confiderations, it is ftated, as an acknowledged principle in the French conftitution, that the right in the crown to confirm the acts of the legiflature, is a prerogative, inherent and *incommunicable*: of courfe that it cannot be delegated to a colonial governor, whofe authority is precarious and fubordinate. The articles are then fubjoined, in the order and words following:

" 1. The legiflative authority, in every thing which relates to the internal concerns of the colony *(regime interieur)*, is vefted
in

in the affembly of its reprefentatives, which fhall be called *the General Affembly of the French Part of St. Domingo.*

2. No act of the legiflative body, in what relates to the internal concerns of the colony, fhall be confidered *as a law definitive*, unlefs it be made by the reprefentatives of the French part of St. Domingo, freely and legally chofen, and confirmed by the king.

3. In cafes of urgent neceffity, a legiflative decree of the general affembly, in what relates to the internal concerns of the colony, fhall be confidered as a *law provifional.* In all fuch cafes, the decree fhall be notified forthwith to the governor general, who, within ten days after fuch notification, fhall caufe it to be publifhed and enforced, or tranfmit to the general affembly his obfervations thereon.

4. The neceffity of the cafe on which the execution of fuch provifional decree is to depend, fhall be a feparate queftion, and be carried in the affirmative by a majority of two-thirds of the general affembly; the names and numbers being taken down. *(Prifes par l'appel nominal.)*

5. If the governor general fhall fend down his obfervations on any fuch decree, the fame fhall be entered in the journals of the general affembly, who fhall then proceed to revife the decree, and confider the obfervations thereon in three feveral fittings. The votes for confirming or annulling the decree fhall be given in the words *Yes* or *No*, and a minute of the proceedings fhall be figned by the members prefent, in which fhall be enumerated the votes on each fide of the queftion; and if there appears a majority of two-thirds for confirming the decree, it fhall be immediately enforced by the governor general

6. As

6. As every law ought to be founded on the confent of thofe who are to be bound by it, the French part of St. Domingo fhall be allowed to propofe regulations concerning commercial arrangements, and the fyftem of mutual connection *(rapports commerciaux, et autres rapports communs)*, and the decrees which the national affembly fhall make in all fuch cafes *fhall not be enforced in the colony, until the general affembly fhall have confented thereto.*

7. In cafes of preffing neceffity, the importation of articles for the fupport of the inhabitants fhall not be confidered as any breach in the fyftem of commercial regulations between St. Domingo and France ; provided that the decrees to be made in fuch cafes by the general affembly fhall be fubmitted to the revifion of the governor general, under the fame conditions and modifications as are prefcribed in articles 3 and 5.

8. Provided alfo, that every legiflative act of the general affembly, executed provifionally, in cafes of urgent neceffity, fhall be tranfmitted forthwith for the royal fanction. And if the king fhall refufe his confent to any fuch act, its execution fhall be fufpended, as foon as the king's refufal fhall be legally notified to the general affembly.

9. A new general affembly fhall be chofen every two years and none of the members who have ferved in the former affembly fhall be eligible in the new one.

10. The general affembly decree that the preceding articles, as forming part of the conftitution of the French colony in St. Domingo, fhall be immediately tranfmitted to France for the acceptance of the national affembly, and the king. They fhall

likewife

likewife be tranfmitted to all the parifhes and diftricts of the colony, and be notified to the governor general."

THAT a decree of fuch comprehenfivenefs and magnitude
fhould have excited very general difquifition in the colony, and
have produced mifreprefentation and clamour, even among men
of very oppofite fentiments and tempers, is no way furprifing.
It muft be allowed, that fome of the articles are irreconcileable
to every juft principle of colonial fubordination. The refufing
to allow a negative voice to the reprefentative of the king, is
repugnant to all the notions which an Englifhman is taught to
entertain of a monarchical government, however limited: and
the declaration that no decree of the national affembly concerning the colony, in cafes of exterior regulation, fhould be ir
force until confirmed by the colonial affembly, was fuch an extravagant affumption of imperial authority, in a fubordinate part
of the French empire, as I believe is without a precedent.

ALL that can be urged in extenuation, feems to be that the circumftances of the cafe were novel, and the members of the colonial affembly unexperienced in the bufinefs of legiflation. That
they had any ferious intention of declaring the colony an independent ftate, in imitation of the Englifh American provinces, it is
impoffible to believe. Neverthelefs, the decree was no fooner
promulgated, than this notion was induftrioufly propagated by
their enemies from one end of the colony to the other; and when
this report failed to gain belief, it was pretended that the colony
was fold to the Englifh, and that the members of the general
                                                        affembly

affembly had received and divided among themfelves 40 millions of livres as the purchafe money.

If recent events had not demonftrated the extreme credulity and jealous temper of the French character, it would be difficult to believe that charges, thus wild and unfupported, could have made an impreffion on the minds of any confiderable number of the people. So great however was the effect produced by them, as to occafion fome of the Weftern parifhes to recal their deputies; while the inhabitants of Cape François took meafures ftill more decifive: they renounced obedience to the general affembly, and prefented a memorial to the governor, requefting him to diffolve it forthwith, declaring that they confidered the colony as loft, unlefs he proceeded with the utmoft vigour and promptitude in depriving that body of all manner of authority.

M. Peynier received this addrefs with fecret fatisfaction. It feemed indeed to be the policy of both parties to reject all thoughts of compromife by negociation; and there occurred at this juncture a circumftance which would probably have rendered all negociation abortive, had it been attempted. In the harbour of Port au Prince lay a fhip of the line, called the Leopard, commanded by M. Galifoniere. This officer, co-operating in the views of Peynier and Mauduit, made a fumptuous entertainment for the partizans of thofe gentlemen, and by this, or fome other parts of his conduct, gave offence to his failors. Whether thefe men had felt the influence of corruption (as afferted by one party) or were actuated folely by one of thofe

unaccountable

unaccountable freaks to which feamen are particularly fubject, the fact certainly is, that they withdrew their obedience from their proper officer, and declared themfelves to be in the inte-refts of the colonial affembly! Their conduct became at length fo turbulent and feditious, as to induce M. Galifoniere to quit the fhip, whereupon the crew gave the command to one of the lieutenants. The affembly, perceiving the advantages to be derived from this event, immediately tranfmitted a vote of thanks to the feamen for their patriotick conduct, and required them, in the name of the law and the king, to detain the fhip in the road, and await their further orders. The failors, gratified with this acknowledgement, promifed obedience, and affixed the vote of thanks on the main-maft of the fhip. Some par-tizans of the affembly, about the fame time, took poffeffion of a powder magazine at Leogane.

A CIVIL war feemed now to be inevitable. Two days after the vote of thanks had been tranfmitted from St. Marc's to the crew of the Leopard, M. Peynier iffued a proclamation to dif-folve the general affembly. He charged the members with en-tertaining projects of independency, and afferted that they had treacheroufly poffeffed themfelves of one of the king's fhips by corrupting the crew. He pronounced the members and all their adherents traitors to their country, and enemies to the na-tion and the king: declaring that it was his intention to employ all the force he could collect to defeat their projects, and bring them to condign punifhment; and he called on all officers, civil and military, for their co-operation and fupport.

CHAP. III.

27th July, 1790.

F

His

His firft proceedings were directed againſt the committee of the Weſtern provincial aſſembly.—This body held its meetings at Port au Prince, and in the exerciſe of its ſubordinate functions, during the intermiſſion of that aſſembly, had manifeſted ſuch zealous attachment to the general aſſembly at St. Marc, as ex-poſed its members to the reſentment of the governor and his party. It was determined therefore, at a council held the ſame day, to arreſt their perſons the following night, and M. Mau-duit undertook to conduct the enterprize. Having been in-formed that this committee held conſultations at midnight, he ſelected about one hundred of his ſoldiers, and formed a ſcheme to ſeize the members at their place of meeting. On arriving however at the houſe, he found it protected by four hundred of the national guards (g). A ſkirmiſh enſued; but the circum-ſtances attending it are ſo variouſly related, that no preciſe ac-count can be given of the particulars; nor is it aſcertained which party gave the firſt fire. Nothing further is certainly known, than that two men were killed on the part of the aſ-ſembly,—that ſeveral were wounded on both ſides, and that M. Mauduit returned without effecting any purpoſe but that of ſeizing, and bearing away in triumph, the national colours;—a circumſtance which afterwards (as will be ſeen in the ſequel) coſt him his life.

THE general aſſembly, on receiving intelligence of this attack, and of the formidable preparations that were making for di-

(g) The troops in St. Domingo, called *the National Guards*, were originally nothing more than the colonial militia. They were new organized in 1789, on the model of the national guards in the mother-country, and bore the ſame colours, and aſſumed the ſame name.

recting hoftilities againft themfelves, fummoned the people,
from all parts of the colony, to haften properly armed to protect their reprefentatives; and mcft of the inhabitants of the
neighbouring parifhes obeyed the fummons. The fhip Leopard
was brought from Port au Prince to St. Marc's for the fame purpofe. On the other hand, the Northern provincial affembly
joined the party of the governor, and fent to his affiftance a detachment from the regular troops in that quarter, which was
joined by a body of two hundred people of colour. A much
greater force was collected at the fame time in the Weftern province by M. Mauduit, and the preparations on both fides threatened an obftinate and bloody conflict; when, by one of thofe
wonderful eccentricities in the human mind which are feldom
difplayed except in times of publick commotion, a ftop was put
to the immediate fhedding of blood, by the fudden and unexpected determination of the general affembly to undertake a
voyage to France, and juftify their conduct to the king and
the national affembly in perfon. Their motives were thought
the more laudable, as all the Weftern and great part of the
Southern provinces gave a decided approbation of their conduct,
and armed in a very fhort time two thoufand men in their defence, which were in full march for Port au Prince. Their
refolution however was fixed, and accordingly, of about one
hundred members, to which the colonial affembly was reduced
by ficknefs and defertion, no lefs than eighty-five (of whom
fixty-four were fathers of families) actually embarked on board
the Leopard, and on the 8th of Auguft took their departure for
Europe:—a proceeding which created as much furprize in the
governor and his party, as admiration and applaufe among the

people

people at large.   Perfons of all ranks accompanied the members to the place of embarkation, pouring forth prayers for their fuccefs, and fhedding tears of fenfibility and affection for a conduct which was very generally confidered as a noble proof of felf-denial, and as fignal an inftance of heroick virtue and chriftian forbearance as any age has exhibited.   A momentary calm followed this event :—the parties in arms appeared mutually difpofed to fubmit their differences to the wifdom and juftice of the king and the national affembly, and M. Peynier refumed, though with a trembling hand, the reins of government.

Such was the iffue of the firft attempt to eftablifh a free conftitution in the French part of St. Domingo, on the fyftem of a limited monarchy ; and it affords occafion for fome important reflections.   That the general colonial affembly, in their decree of the 28th of May, exceeded the proper boundary of their conftitutional functions, has been frankly admitted.   This irregularity, however, might have been corrected without bloodfhed or violence ; but there is this misfortune attending every deviation from the rule of right, that, in the conflict of contending factions, the exceffes of one party are ever confidered as the fulleft juftification for the outrages of the other.   For fome parts of their conduct an apology may be offered.   The meafure of fecuring to their interefts the crew of the Leopard, and the feizure of the magazine at Leogane, may be vindicated on the plea of felf-defence.   It cannot be doubted that M. Peynier had long meditated how beft to reftore the ancient defpotick fyftem, and

that,

that, jointly with M. Mauduit and others, he had made preparations for that purpose. He had written to M. Luzerne, the minifter in France, that he never intended to fuffer the colonial affembly to meet; and let it be told in this place, in juftice to the French miniftry, that the anfwer which he received contained a tacit difapprobation of his meafures; for M. Luzerne recommended moderate and conciliatory councils. The governor proceeded notwithftanding in the fame career, and diftruftful perhaps of the fidelity of the French foldiers, he made application (as appeared afterwards) to the governor of the Havannah for a reinforcement of Spanifh troops from Cuba. It is evident therefore that he concurred entirely in the plans of Mauduit for effectuating a counter-revolution; and hence it is reafonable to conclude, that the difcord and diftruft which prevailed among the inhabitants, and above all, the fatal diffentions that alienated the provincial affembly of the North, from the general affembly at St. Marc's, were induftrioufly fomented and encouraged by M. Peynier and his adherents. Concerning the members of the colonial affembly, their prompt and decifive determination to repair to France, and furrender their perfons to the fupreme government, obviates all impeachment of their loyalty. Their attachment to the mother-country was indeed fecured by too many ties of intereft and felf-prefervation to be doubted.

Of their reception by the national affembly, and the proceedings adopted in confequence of their arrival in Europe, I fhall hereafter have occafion to fpeak. A paufe in this place

seems

feems requifite ;—for I have now to introduce to the reader the mournful hiftory of an unfortunate individual, over whofe fad fate (however we may condemn his rafh and ill-concerted en- terprize)

    " One human tear may drop, and be forgiven !"

CHAP. IV.

Rebellion and Defeat of Ogé, a free Man of Colour.

FROM the firſt meeting of the general aſſembly of St. Domingo, to its diſſolution and diſperſion, as related in the
preceding chapters, the coloured people reſident within the colony remained on the whole morc peaceable and orderly than
might have been expected. The temperate and lenient diſpoſition manifeſted by the aſſembly towards them, produced a beneficial and deciſive effect in the Weſtern and Southern provinces, and although 300 of them from theſe provinces, had been
perſuaded by M. Mauduit to join the force under his command,
they very ſoon became ſenſible of their error, and, inſtead of
marching towards St. Marc, as Mauduit propoſed, they demanded and obtained their diſmiſſion, and returned quietly to
their reſpective habitations. Such of the mulatto people however as reſided at that juncture in the mother-country, continued
in a far more hoſtile diſpoſition ; and they were encouraged in
their animoſity towards the white coloniſts by parties of very
different deſcriptions. The colonial decree of the 28th of
May, 1790, was no ſooner made known in France, than it excited
univerſal clamour. Many perſons who concurred in nothing
elſe, united their voices in reprobating the conduct of the inhabitants

bitants of St. Domingo. The adherents of the ancient government were joined on this occasion by the partizans of de-
mocracy and republicanism. To the latter, the constitution of
1789 was even more odious than the old tyranny; and these
men, with the deepest and darkest designs, possessed all that
union, firmness, and perseverance which were necessary to their
purposes; and which, as the world has beheld, have since rendered them irresistible. These two factions hoped to obtain
very different ends, by the same means; and there was another
party who exerted themselves with equal assiduity in promoting
publick confusion: these were the discordant class of specula-
tive reformers, whom it was impossible to reconcile to the new
government, because every man among them had probably
formed a favourite system in his own imagination which he was
eager to recommend to others. I do not consider the philanthropick society, called *Amis des Noirs*, as another distinct body,
because it appears to me that they were pretty equally divided
between the democratick party, and the class last mentioned.
Strengthened by such auxiliaries, it is not surprizing that the
efforts of this society should have operated powerfully on
the minds of those who were taught to consider their personal wrongs as the cause of the nation, and have driven some
of them into the wildest excesses of fanaticism and fury.

AMONG such of these unfortunate people resident in France
as were thus inflamed into madness, was a young man under
thirty years of age, named *James Ogé*: he was born in St. Domingo, of a mulatto woman who still possessed a coffee plantation in the Northern province, about thirty miles from Cape
François,

François, whereon she lived very creditably, and found means out of its profits to educate her son at Paris, and even to support him there in some degree of affluence, after he had obtained the age of manhood. His reputed father, a white planter of some account, had been dead several years.

Ogé had been introduced to the meetings of the *Amis des Noirs*, under the patronage of Gregoire, Briffot *(h)*, La Fayette, and Robespierre *(i)*, the leading members of that society; and was by them initiated into the popular doctrine of *equality*, and *the rights of man*. Here it was that he first learnt the miseries of his condition, the cruel wrongs and contumelies to which he and all his mulatto brethren were exposed in the West Indies, and the monstrous injustice and absurdity of that prejudice, " which, (said Gregoire) estimating a man's merit by the colour " of his skin, has placed at an immense distance from each other " the children of the same parent; a prejudice which stifles the " voice of nature, and breaks the bands of fraternity asunder."

THAT these are great evils must be frankly admitted, and it would have been fortunate if such men as Briffot and Gregoire, instead of bewailing their existence and magnifying their extent, had applied their talents in considering of the best practicable means of redressing them.

BUT these persons had other objects in view:—their aim, as I have shewn, was not to reform, but to destroy; to excite con-

(h) Guillotined 31 October, 1793.　　*(i)* Guillotined 28 July, 1794.

G

vulsions

vulfions in every part of the French empire; and the ill-fated Ogé became the tool, and was afterwards the victim, of their guilty ambition.

He had been led to believe, that the whole body of coloured people in the French iflands were prepared to rife up as one man againſt their oppreſſors; that nothing but a diſcreet leader was wanting, to fet them into action; and, fondly conceiving that he poſſeſſed in his own perſon all the qualities of an able general, he determined to proceed to St. Domingo by the firſt opportunity. To cheriſh the conceit of his own importance, and animate his exertions, the fociety procured him the rank of lieutenant-colonel in the army of one of the German electors.

As it was found difficult to export a fufficient quantity of arms and ammunition from France, without attracting the notice of the government, and awakening fufpicion among the planters re-fident in the mother country, the fociety refolved to procure thofe articles in North America, and it was recommended to Ogé to make a circuitous voyage for that purpofe. Accordingly, being furniſhed with money and letters of credit, he embarked for New England in the month of July 1790.

But, notwithſtanding the caution that was obferved in this inſtance, the whole project was publickly known at Paris pre-vious to Ogé's embarkation, and notice of the fcheme, and even a portrait of Ogé himſelf, were tranfmitted to St. Domingo, long before his arrival in that iſland. He fecretly landed there, from an American floop, on the 12th of October 1790, and found

means

means to convey undifcovered the arms and ammunition which
he had purchafed, to the place which his brother had prepared
for their reception.

THE firft notice which the white inhabitants received of
Ogé's arrival, was from himfelf. He difpatched a letter to the
governor (Peynier) wherein, after reproaching the governor and
his predeceffors with the non-execution of the *Code Noir*, he de-
mands, in very imperious terms, that the provifions of that celebrated ftatute fhould be enforced throughout the colony; he
requires that the privileges enjoyed by one clafs of inhabitants
(the whites) fhould be extended to all perfons without diftinction; declares himfelf the protector of the mulattoes, and an-
nounces his intention of taking up arms in their behalf, unlefs
their wrongs fhould be redreffed.

ABOUT fix weeks had intervened between the landing of
Ogé, and the publication of this mandate; in all which time he
and his two brothers had exerted themfelves to the utmoft in
fpreading difaffection, and exciting revolt among the mulattoes.
Affurances were held forth, that all the inhabitants of the mother country were difpofed to affift them in the recovery of their
rights, and it was added, that the king himfelf was favourably
inclined to their caufe. Promifes were diftributed to fome, and
money to others. But, notwithftanding all thefe efforts, and
that the temper of the times was favourable to his views, Ogé
was not able to allure to his ftandard above 200 followers; and
cf thefe, the major part were raw and ignorant youths, unufed

to

to difcipline, and averfe to all manner of fubordination and order.

HE eftablifhed his camp at a place called *Grande Riviere*, about fifteen miles from Cape François, and appointed his two brothers, together with one Mark Chavane, his lieutenants. Chavane was fierce, intrepid, active, and enterprizing; prone to mifchief, and thirfty for vengeance. Ogé himfelf, with all his enthufiafm, was naturally mild and humane: he cautioned his followers againft the fhedding innocent blood; but little regard was paid to his wifhes in this refpect: the firft white man that fell in their way they murdered on the fpot: a fecond, of the name of Sicard, met the fame fate; and it is related, that their cruelty towards fuch perfons of their own complexion as refufed to join in the revolt was extreme. A mulatto man of fome property being urged to follow them, pointed to his wife and fix children, affigning the largenefs of his family as a motive for wifhing to remain quiet. This conduct was confidered as contumacious, and it is afferted, that not only the man himfelf, but the whole of his family, were maffacred without mercy.

INTELLIGENCE was no fooner received at the town of Cape Francois of thefe enormities, than the inhabitants proceeded, with the utmoft vigour and unanimity, to adopt meafures for fuppreffing the revolt. A body of regular troops, and the Cape regiment of militia, were forthwith difpatched for that purpofe. They foon invefted the camp of the revolters, who made lefs refiftance than might have been expected from men in their defperate circumftances. The rout became general; many of them
were

were killed, and about fixty made prifoners; the reft difperfed themfelves in the mountains. Ogé himfelf, one of his brothers, and Chavane his affociate, took refuge in the Spanifh territories. Of Ogé's other brother no intelligence was ever afterwards obtained.

AFTER this unfuccefsful attempt of Oge, and his efcape from juftice, the difpofition of the white inhabitants in general towards the mulattoes, was fharpened into great animofity. The lower claffes in particular, (thofe whom the coloured people call *les petits blancs)* breathed nothing but vengeance againft them; and very ferious apprehenfions were entertained, in all parts of the colony, of a profcription and maffacre of the whole body.

ALARMED by reports of this kind, and the appearances which threatened them from all quarters, the mulattoes flew to arms in many places. They formed camps at Artibonite, Petit Goaves, Jeremie, and Aux Cayes. But the largeft and moft formidable body affembled near the little town of *Verette.* The white inhabitants collected themfelves in confiderable force in the neighbourhood, and Colonel Mauduit, with a corps of two hundred men from the regiment of Port au Prince, haftened to their affiftance; but neither party proceeded to actual hoftility. M. Mauduit even left his detachment at the port of St. Marc, thirty-fix miles from Verette, and proceeding fingly and unattended to the camp of the mulattoes, had a conference with their leaders. What paffed on that occafion was never publickly divulged. It is certain, that the mulattoes retired to their habitations in confequence of it; but the filence and fecrecy of M. Mauduit, and

* his

his influence over them, gave occasion to very unfavourable suspicions, by no means tending to conciliate the different classes of the inhabitants to each other. He was charged with having traiterously persuaded them not to desist from their purpose, but only to postpone their vengeance to a more favourable opportunity; assuring them, with the utmost solemnity and apparent sincerity, that the king himself, and all the friends of the ancient government, were secretly attached to their cause, and would avow and support it whenever they could do it with advantage; and that the time was not far distant, &c. He is said to have pursued the same line of conduct at Jeremie, Aux Cayes, and all the places which he visited. Every where he held secret consultations with the chiefs of the mulattoes, and those people every where immediately dispersed. At Aux Cayes, a skirmish had happened before his arrival there, in which about fifty persons on both sides had lost their lives, and preparations were making to renew hostilities. The persuasions of M. Mauduit effected a truce; but Rigaud, the leader of the mulattoes in that quarter, openly declared that it was a transient and deceitful calm, and that no peace would be permanent, until one class of people had exterminated the other.

In November 1790, M. Peynier resigned the government to the lieutenant-general, and embarked for Europe;—a circumstance which proved highly pleasing to the major part of the planters:—and the first measure of M. Blanchelande (k), the new commander in chief, was considered as the earnest of a decisive

(k) Guillotined at Paris, 1793.

and

and vigorous adminiſtration. He made a peremptory demand of Ogé and his aſſociates from the Spaniards; and the manner in which it was enforced, induced an immediate compliance therewith. The wretched Ogé, and his companions in miſery, were delivered over, the latter end of December, to a detachment of French troops, and ſafely lodged in the jail of Cape Francois, with the priſoners formerly taken; and a commiſſion was ſoon afterwards iſſued to bring them to trial.

THEIR examinations were long and frequent; and in the beginning of March 1791, ſentence was pronounced. Twenty of Ogé's deluded followers, among them his own brother, were condemned to be hanged. To Ogé himſelf, and his lieutenant Chavane, a more terrible puniſhment was allotted:—they were adjudged to be broken alive, and left to periſh in that dreadful ſituation, on the wheel:—a ſentence, on which it is impoſſible to reflect but with mingled emotions of ſhame ſympathy, indignation, and horror!

THE bold and hardened Chavane met his fate with unuſual firmneſs, and ſuffered not a groan to eſcape him during the extremity of his torture: but the fortitude of Ogé deſerted him altogether. When ſentence was pronounced, he implored mercy with many tears, and an abject ſpirit. He promiſed to make great diſcoveries if his life was ſpared, declaring that he had an important ſecret to communicate. A reſpite of twenty-four hours was accordingly granted; but it was not made known to the publick, at that time, that he divulged any thing of importance. His ſecret, if any he had, was believed to have died with him.

IT

It was difcovered, however, about nine months afterwards, that this moft unfortunate young man had not only made a full confeffion of the facts that I have related, but alfo difclofed the dreadful plot in agitation, and the miferies at that moment impending over the colony. His laft folemn declarations and dying confeffion, fworn to and figned by himfelf the day before his execution, were actually produced; wherein he details at large the meafures which the coloured people had fallen upon to excite the negro flaves to rife into rebellion. He points out the chiefs by name, and relates that, notwithftanding his own defeat, a general revolt would actually have taken place in the month of February preceding, if an extraordinary flood of rain, and confequent inundation from the rivers, had not prevented it. He declares that the ringleaders ftill maintained the fame atrocious project, and held their meetings in certain fubterranean paffages, or caves, in the parifh of La Grande Riviere, to which he offers, if his life might be fpared, to conduct a body of troops, fo that the confpirators might be fecured.

The perfons before whom this confeffion and narrative were made, were the commiffioners appointed for the purpofe of taking Ogé's examination, by the fuperior council of the Northern province, of which body they were alfo members (1). Whether this court (all the members of which were devotedly attached to the ancient fyftem) determined of itfelf to fupprefs evidence of fuch great concern to the colony, or was directed on

(1) Their names were Antoine Etienne Ruotte, and Francois Jofeph de Vertierres.

this

this occafion by the fuperior officers in the adminiftration of the
government, has never been clearly made known.   Suppreffed it
certainly was, and the miferable Ogé hurried to immediate execution; as if to prevent the further communication, and full difclofure of fo weighty a fecret!

CHRISTIAN charity might lead us to fuppofe that the commiffioners by whom Ogé's examination was taken, difregarded
and neglected (rather than fuppreffed) his information; confidering it merely as the fhallow artifice of a miferable man to
obtain a mitigation of the dreadful punifhment which awaited
him, and utterly unworthy of credit.   It does not appear, however, that the commiffioners made this excufe for themfelves;
and the caution, circumfpection, and fecrecy which marked their
conduct, leave no room for fuch a fuppofition.   The planters at
large fcrupled not to declare, that the royalifts in the colony,
and the philanthropick and republican party in the mother
country, were equally criminal; and themfelves made victims to
the blind purpofes, and unwarrantable paffions, of two defperate
and malignant factions.

OF men who openly and avowedly aimed at the fubverfion
of all good order and fubordination, we may eafily credit the
worft; but it will be difficult to point out any principle of rational policy by which the royalifts could have been influenced
to concur in the ruin of fo noble and beautiful a part of the
French empire.   Their conduct therefore remains wholly in-
explicable, or we muft admit they were guided by a fpirit of
Machiavilian policy—a principle of refined cunning, which al-

H   ways

ways defeats its own purpofe. They muft have encouraged the vain and fallacious idea that fcenes of bloodfhed, devaftation, and ruin, in different parts of the French dominions, would induce the great body of the people to look back with regret to their former government, and lead them by degrees to co operate in the fcheme of effecting a counter-revolution; regarding the evils of anarchy, as lefs tolerable than the dead repofe of defpo-tifm. If fuch were their motives, we can only afcribe them to that infatuation with which Providence (as wife men have ob-ferved, and hiftory evinces) *blinds a people devoted to deftruction.*

C H A P.

CHAP. V.

Proceedings in France—Maſſacre of Colonel Mauduit in St. Do-
mingo—and fatal Decree of the National Aſſembly of the 15th
May 1791.

IN detailing the tragical ſtory of the miſerable Ogé, I have
choſen to continue my narrative unbroken: but it is now
time to call the reader homewards, and direct his attention
to the meaſures adopted by the national aſſembly, in conſequence
of advices received from all parts of St. Domingo, concerning
the proceedings of the colonial aſſembly which met at St.
Marc's.

THE eighty-five members, whoſe embarkation for France has
already been noticed, arrived at Breſt on the 13th of September
1790. They were received on landing by all ranks of people, and
even by men in authority, with congratulation and ſhouts of ap-
plauſe. The ſame honours were ſhewn to them as would have
been paid to the national aſſembly. Their expences were defrayed, and ſums of money raiſed for their future occaſions by a
voluntary and very general ſubſcription; but theſe teſtimonies
of reſpect and kindneſs ſerved only to encreaſe the diſappoint-
ment which they ſoon afterwards experienced in the capital;

H 2

where a very different reception awaited them.   They had the mortification to difcover that their enemies had been beforehand with them.   Deputies were already arrived from the provincial affembly of the North, who, joining with the agents of Peynier and Mauduit, had fo effectually prevailed with M. Barnave *(a)*, the prefident of the committee for the colonies, that they found their caufe prejudged, and their conduct condemned, without a hearing.   The national affembly had iffued a peremptory order, on the 21ft of September, directing them to attend at Paris, and wait there for further directions.   Their prompt obedience to this order procured them no favour.   They were allowed a fingle audience only, and then indignantly difmiffed from the bar. They folicited a fecond, and an opportunity of being confronted with their adverfaries : the national affembly refufed their requeft, and directed the colonial committee to haften its report concerning their conduct.   On the 11th of October, this report was prefented by M. Barnave.   It comprehended a detail of all the proceedings of the colonial affembly, from its firft meeting at St. Marc's, and cenfured their general conduct in terms of great afperity; reprefenting it as flowing from motives of difaffection towards the mother country, and an impatience of fubordination to conftitutional authority and good government. The report concluded by recommending, " that all the pre-
" tended decrees and acts of the faid colonial affembly, fhould be
" reverfed, and pronounced utterly null and of no effect; that
" the faid affembly fhould be declared diffolved, and its mem-
" bers rendered ineligible and incapable of being delegated in

(a) Guillotined December 1, 1793.

" future

" future to the colonial affembly of St. Domingo; that tefti-
" monies of approbation fhould be tranfmitted to the Northern
" provincial affembly, to Colonel Mauduit and the regiment of
" Port au Prince, for refifting the proceedings at St Marc's; that
" the king fhould be requefted to give orders for the forming a new
" colonial affembly on the principles of the national decree of
" the 8th of March 1790, and inftructions of the 28th of the
" fame month; finally, that the *ci-devant* members, then in
" France, fhould continue in a ftate of arreft, until the national
" affembly might find time to fignify its further pleafure concern-
" ing them." A decree to this effect was accordingly voted on the
12th of October, by a very large majority; and the king was requefted, at the fame time, to fend out an augmentation of force,
both naval and military, for the better fupporting the regal authority in St. Domingo.

IT is not eafy to defcribe the furprize and indignation which
the news of this decree excited in St. Domingo, except among
the partizans of the former government. By *them* it was regarded as the firft ftep towards the revival of the ancient fyftem;
by moft other perfons it was confidered as a dereliction by the
national affembly of all principle; and the orders for electing a
new colonial affembly were fo little regarded, that many of the
parifhes pofitively refufed to choofe other deputies until the
fate of their former members, at that time in France, fhould be
decided; declaring, that they ftill confidered thofe perfons as the
legal reprefentatives of the colony. One immediate and apparent effect of this decree was, to heighten and inflame the popular refentment againft Mauduit and his regiment. The
reader has already been made acquainted with fome particulars

concerning

concerning this officer; and to what has been said of his general character, and his intemperate zeal for the re-establish-
ment of the regal authority in its fullest extent, it may be added,
that he was the more dangerous, because he was generous in his
disposition, and even profuse in his bounty towards his soldiers.
In return, the attachment of his regiment towards his person
appeared to exceed the usual limits of obedience and duty *(b)*.

THE massacre of this man by those very troops, a short time
after the notification of the aforesaid decree, affords so striking an
instance of that cruel and ungovernable disposition, equally im-
petuous and inconstant, which prevailed, and I am afraid still
continues to prevail, amongst the lower classes of the people
throughout all the French dominions, that I conceive a brief recital of the circumstances attending his murder will not be
thought an unnecessary digression.

I HAVE, in a former place *(c)*, given some account of the proceedings of M. Peynier, the late governor, against certain persons
who composed what was called the committee of the Western
provincial assembly, and of the attempt by M. Mauduit to seize
by force the individuals who composed that committee. This
happened on the 29th of July, 1790; and I observed that the
circumstance of M. Mauduit's carrying off the colours from a
detachment of the national guards on that occasion, ultimately
terminated in his destruction.

(b) After his example they had rejected the national cockade, and wore a white
feather in their hats, the symbol, or avowed signal, of the royal party.

(c) Chap. iii. p. 34.

I

THE cafe was, that not only the detachment from whom their enfign was taken, but the whole of the national guards throughout the colony, confidered this act as the moft outrageous and unpardonable infult that could poffibly be offered to a body of men, who had fworn fidelity to the new conftitution; and nothing but the dread of the fuperior difcipline of the veterans compofing the Port au Prince regiment (which Mauduit commanded) prevented them from exercifing exemplary vengeance on the author of their difgrace. This regiment therefore, being implicated in the crime of their commanding officer, was regarded by the other troops with hatred and deteftation.

On the 3d of March 1791, the frigates Le Fougueux and Le Borée arrived from France, with two battalions of the regiments of Artois and Normandy; and when it is known that thefe troops had been vifited by the crew of the Leopard, it will not appear furprizing that, on their landing at Port au Prince, they fhould have manifefted the fame hoftile difpofition towards Mauduit's regiment, as was fhewn by the national guards. They refufed all manner of communication or intercourfe with them, and even declined to enter into any of their places of refort. They confidered, or affected to confider them, as enemies to the colony, and traitors to their country. This conduct in the new-comers towards the ill-fated regiment foon made a wonderful impreffion on the minds of both officers and privates of the regiment itfelf; and mutual reproach and accufation fpread through the whole corps. The white feather was indignantly torn from their hats, and dark and fullen looks towards

wards their once-loved commander, indicated not only that he
had loſt their confidence, but alſo that he was the object of meditated miſchief.   Mauduit ſoon perceived the full extent of his
danger, and fearing to involve the governor (M. Blanchelande)
and his family, in the ruin which awaited himſelf, with great ge-
neroſity adviſed them to make the beſt of their way to Cape
Francois, while they could do it with ſafety; and Blanchelande,
for which he was afterwards much cenſured, followed this advice.   Mauduit then harangued his grenadiers, to whom he had
always ſhewn great kindneſs, and told them that he was willing,
for the ſake of peace, to reſtore to the national troops the colours
which he had formerly taken from them; and even to carry
them, with his own hands, at the head of his regiment, and de-
poſit them in the church in which they had been uſually lodged;
but he added, that he depended on their affection and duty to
protect him from perſonal inſult, while making this ample apology.   The faithleſs grenadiers declared that they would protect him with their lives.

THE next day the ceremony took place, and Mauduit reſtored
the colours as he had promiſed, before a vaſt croud of ſpectators.
At that moment, one of his own ſoldiers cried aloud, *that he muſt
aſk pardon of the national troops on his knees*; and the whole
regiment applauded the propoſal.   Mauduit ſtarted back with
indignation, and offered his boſom to their ſwords:—it was
pierced with a hundred wounds, all of them inflicted by his own
men, while not a ſingle hand was lifted up in his defence.   The
ſpectators ſtood motionleſs, either through hatred to the man,
or ſurprize at the treachery and cowardice of the ſoldiers.   Such
indeed

indeed was the bafenefs of thefe wretches, that no modern language can defcribe, but in terms which would not be endured,
the horrible enormities that were practifed on the dead body
of their wretched commander. It was referved for the prefent
day to behold, for the firft time, a civilized nation exceeding in
feats of cruelty and revenge the favages of North America. I
grieve to add, that I have many dreadful inftances yet to recite
in confirmation of this remark *(c)*.

WHILE thefe fhameful enormities were paffing in St. Domingo, the fociety of *Amis des Noirs* in the mother country
were but too fuccefsfully employed in devifing projects which
gave birth to deeds of ftill greater horror, and produced fcenes
that transformed the moft beautiful colony in the world into a
field of defolation and carnage.

ALTHOUGH it muft have occurred to every unprejudiced mind,
from the circumftances that have been related concerning the

(c) The following anecdote, though fhocking to humanity, I have thought
too extraordinary to omit. It was communicated to me by a French gentleman who was at St. Domingo at the time, and knew the fact; but decency
has induced me to veil it in a learned language. MAUDUITO *vix mortuo, unus de
militibus, dum cadaver calidum, et cruore adhuc fluente madidum, in pavimentum ec-
clefiæ epifcopalis jacuit, ficam diftringens, genitalia coram populo abfcidit, et membra
truncata in ciftam componens, ad feminam nobilem, quam amicam Mauduito ftatuit, ut
legatum de mortuo attulit.* It may afford the reader fome confolation to find that
the murder of their commanding officer by his own regiment, excited in all the
other troops no other fentiments than thofe of indignation againft his murderers.
They were compelled to lay down their arms, and were fent prifoners to France;
but I fear they efcaped the punifhment due to their crimes.

I   behaviour

behaviour of the mulattoes refident in the colony, that the general body of thofe people were by no means averfe to conciliation with the whites, yet it was found impoffible to perfuade their pretended friends in Europe to leave the affairs of St. Domingo to their natural courfe. Barnave alone (hitherto the moft formidable opponent of the prejudices and pretenfions of the colonifts) avowed his conviction that any further interference of the mother country in the queftion between the whites and the coloured people, would be productive of fatal confequences. Such an opinion was entitled to greater refpect, as coming from a man who, as prefident of the colonial committee, muft be fuppofed to have acquired an intimate knowledge of the fubject; but he was heard without conviction. There are enthufiafts in politicks as well as in religion, and it commonly happens with fanaticks in each, that the recantation of a few of their number ferves only to ftrengthen the errors, and animate the purpofes of the reft. It was now refolved by Gregoire, La Fayette, Briffot, and fome other peftilent reformers, to call in the fupreme legiflative authority of the French government to give effect to their projects; and that the reader may clearly underftand the nature and complexion of the mifchief that was meditated, and of thofe meafures to which the ruin of the French part of St. Domingo is immediately to be attributed, it is neceffary, in the firft place, to recal his attention to the national decree of the 8th of March 1790, of which an account was given in the fecond chapter.

By that decree, as the reader muft have remembered, the national affembly, among other things, difclaimed all right of interference

terference in the local and interior concerns of the colonies; and
it cannot be doubted, that if this declaration had been faithfully
interpreted and acted upon, it would have contributed, in a very
eminent degree, to the restoration of peace and tranquillity in St.
Domingo.   To render it therefore of as little effect as possible,
and to add fuel to the fire which perhaps would otherwise have
become extinguished, it had been insidiously proposed in the national assembly, within a few days after the decree of the 8th of
March had passed, to transmit with it to the governor of St. Domingo, a code, or chapter, of instructions for its due and punctual
observance and execution.   Accordingly, on the 28th of the same
month, instructions which were said to be calculated for that
purpose, were presented and decreed.   They consisted of eighteen
articles, and contained, among other things, a direction " that
" every person of the age of twenty-five and upwards, possessing
" property, or having resided two years in the colony, and paid
" taxes, should be permitted to vote in the formation of the co-
" lonial assembly."

THE friends of the colonists having at that time seats in the
national assembly, opposed the measure chiefly on the ground of
its repugnancy to the decree of the 8th; it being evidently, they
urged, an interference in the local arrangements and interior regulations of the colonial government.   It does not appear (notwithstanding what has since been asserted to the contrary) that
they entertained an idea that the mulatto people were directly
or indirectly concerned.   The framers and supporters of the measure pretended that it went only to the modification of the
privilege of voting in the parochial meetings, which it was well

known

C H A P.
V.

known, under the old government had been conftituted of white perfons only. The coloured people had in no inftance attended thofe meetings, nor fet up a claim, or even expreffed a defire, to take any part in the bufinefs tranfacted thereat. But thefe inftructions were no fooner adopted by the national affembly, and converted into a decree, than its framers and fupporters threw off the mafk, and the mulattoes refident in the mother country, as well as the fociety of *Amis des Noirs*, failed not to apprize their friends and agents in St. Domingo, that the people of colour, not being excepted, were virtually comprized in it. Thefe, however, not thinking themfelves fufficiently powerful to enforce the claim, or, perhaps, doubting the real meaning of the decree, fent deputies to France to demand an explanation of it from the national affembly.

In the beginning of May 1791, the confideration of this fubject was brought forward by the Abbé Gregoire, and the claim of the free mulattoes to the full benefit of the inftructions of the 28th of March 1790, and to all the rights and privileges enjoyed by the white inhabitants, citizens of the French colonies, was fupported with all that warmth and eloquence for which he was diftinguifhed. Unfortunately, at this juncture the news of the miferable death of Ogé arrived at Paris, and raifed a ftorm of indignation in the minds of all ranks of people, which the planters refident in France were unable to refift. Nothing was heard in all companies but declamations againft their oppreffion and cruelty. To fupport and animate the popular outcry againft them, a tragedy or pantomine, formed on the ftory of Ogé, was reprefented on the publick theatres. By thefe and other means,

the

the planters were become fo generally odious, that for a time they dared not to appear in the ftreets of Paris.   Thefe were the arts by which Gregoire, Condorcet, La Fayette, Briffot, and Roberfpierre difpofed the publick mind to clamour for a new and explanatory decree, in which the rights of the coloured people fhould be placed beyond all future doubts and difpute. The friends and advocates of the planters were overpowered and confounded. In vain did they predict the utter deftruction of the colonies if fuch a propofal fhould pafs into a law.   " Perifh the colonies," faid Roberfpierre,. " rather than facrifice one iota of our prin- " ciples."   The majority reiterated the fentiment, and the fa- mous decree of the 15th of May 1791 was pronounced amidft the acclamation and applaufe of the multitude.

By this decree it was declared and enacted, " that the people of colour refident in the French colonies, born of free parents, were entitled to, as of right, and fhould be allowed the enjoyment of, all the privileges of French citizens, and, among others, to thofe of having votes in the choice of reprefentatives, and of *being eligible to feats both in the parochicl and colonial affemblies"*   Thus did the national affembly fweep away in a moment all the laws, ufages, prejudices, and opinions concerning thefe people, which had exifted in the French colonies from their earlieft fettlement, and tear up by the roots the firft principle of a free conftitution : —a principle founded on the cleareft dictates of reafon and juftice, and exprefslv confirmed to the inhabitants of the French Weft Indies by the national decree of the 8th of March 1790; I mean, *the fole and exclufive right of paffing laws for their local and interior regulation and government*   The colonial committee,

of

CHAP.
V.

of which M. Barnave was prefident, failed not to apprize the national affembly of the fatal confequences of this meafure, and immediately fufpended the exercife of its functions. At the fame time, the deputies from the colonies fignified their purpofe to decline any further attendance. The only effect produced by thefe meafures however, on the national affembly, was an order that the three civil commiffioners, who had been appointed in February preceding for regulating the affairs of the colonies on the fpot, fhould immediately repair thither, and fee the national decrees duly enforced. The confequences in St. Domingo will be related in the following chapter *(d)*.

(d) It has been confidently afferted, that *La Fayette*, in order to fecure a majority on this queftion, introduced into the national affembly no lefs than eighty perfons who were not members, but who fat and voted as fuch. This man had formerly been poffeffed of a plantation at Cayenne, with feventy negro flaves thereon, which he had fold, without any fcruple or ftipulation concerning the fituation of the negroes, the latter end of 1789, and from that time enrolled himfelf among the friends of the blacks. The mere Englifh reader, who may be perfonally unacquainted with the Weft Indies, will probably confider the clamour which was raifed on this occafion by the French planters as equally illiberal and unjuft. The planters in the Britifh Weft Indies will perhaps bring the cafe home to themfelves; and I have no hefitation in faying, that, fuppofing the Englifh parliament fhould pafs a law declaring, for inftance, the free mulattoes of Jamaica to be eligible into the affembly of that ifland, fuch a meafure would prove there, as it proved in St. Domingo, the declaration of civil war. On mere abftract reafoning this may appear ftrange and unjuftifiable; but we muft take mankind as we find them, and few inftances occur in which the prejudices of habit, education, and opinion have been corrected *by force*.

CHAP.

CHAP. VI.

Confequences in St. Domingo of the Decree of the 15th of May—Rebellion of the Negroes in the Northern Province, and Enormities committed by them—Revolt of the Mulattoes at Mirebalais—Concordat or Truce between the Inhabitants of Port au Prince and the Men of Colour of the 11th of September—Proclamation by the National Affembly of the 20th of September.

I AM now to enter on the retrofpect of fcenes, the horrors of which imagination cannot adequately conceive nor pen defcribe. The difputes and contefts between different claffes of French citizens, and the violences of malignant factions towards each other, no longer claim attention. Such a picture of human mifery;—fuch a fcene of woe, prefents itfelf, as no other country, no former age has exhibited. Upwards of one hundred thoufand favage people, habituated to the barbarities of Africa, avail themfelves of the filence and obfcurity of the night, and fall on the peaceful and unfufpicious planters, like fo many famifhed tygers thirfting for human blood. Revolt, conflagration and maffacre, every where mark their progrefs; and death, in all its horrors, or cruelties and outrages, compared to which immediate death is mercy, await alike the old and the young, the matron, the virgin, and the helplefs infant. No condition,

age,

age, or fex is fpared. All the fhocking and fhameful enormities, with which the fierce and unbridled paffions of favage
man have ever conducted a war, prevail uncontrouled. The
rage of fire confumes what the fword is unable to deftroy, and,
in a few difmal hours, the moft fertile and beautiful plains in the
world are converted into one vaft field of carnage;—a wildernefs of defolation !

THERE is indeed too much reafon to believe, that thefe miferies would have occurred in St. Domingo, in a great degree,
even if the proceedings of the National Affembly, as related in
the latter part of the preceding chapter, had been more temperate, and if the decree of the 15th of May had never paffed
into a law. The declarations of the dying Ogé fufficiently
point out the mifchief that was meditated, long before that obnoxious decree was promulgated. But it may be affirmed,
with truth and certainty, that this fatal meafure gave life and
activity to the poifon. It was the brand by which the flames
were lighted, and the combuftibles that were prepared fet into
action. Intelligence having been received of it at Cape François on the 30th of June, no words can defcribe the rage and
indignation which immediately fpread throughout the colony;
and in no place did the inhabitants breathe greater refentment than
in the town of the Cape, which had hitherto been foremoft in profeffions of attachment to the mother country, and in promoting
the fpirit of difunion and oppofition in the colonial affembly.
They now unanimoufly determined to reject the civick oath,
although great preparations had been made for a general fede-
ration on the 14th of July. The news of this decree feemed to
unite

1791.

unite the moft difcordant interefts. In the firft tranfports of indignation it was propofed to feize all the fhips, and confifcate the effects of the French merchants then in the harbour. An embargo was actually laid, and a motion was even made in the provincial affembly to pull down the national colours, and hoift the Britifh ftandard in their room. The national cockade was every where trodden under foot, and the governor-general, who continued a forrowful and filent fpectator of thefe exceffes, found his authority, as reprefentative of the parent country, together with every idea of colonial fubordination in the people, annihilated in a moment.

THE fears and apprehenfions which the governor felt on this occafion have been well defcribed by that officer himfelf, in a memorial which he afterwards publifhed concerning his adminiftration. " Acquainted (he obferves) with the genius and " temper of the white colonifts, by a refidence of feven years in " the Windward Iflands, and well informed of the grounds and " motives of their prejudices and opinions concerning the peo- " ple of colour, I immediately forefaw the difturbances and " dangers which the news of this ill-advifed meafure would in- " evitably produce; and not having it in my power to fupprefs " the communication of it, I loft no time in apprizing the " king's minifters of the general difcontent and violent fermen- " tation which it excited in the colony. To my own obferva- " tions, I added thofe of many refpectable, fober, and difpaf- " fionate men, whom I thought it my duty to confult in fo " critical a conjuncture; and I concluded my letter by expref- " fing my fears that this decree would prove the death-warrant

K   " of

" of many thoufands of the inhabitants. The event has mourn-
" fully verified my predictions !"

ON the recommendation of the provincial affembly of the
Northern department, the feveral parifhes throughout the colony now proceeded, without further hefitation, to the election
of deputies for a new general colonial affembly. Thefe deputies, to the number of one hundred and feventy-fix, met at
Leogane, and on the 9th of Auguft declared themfelves *the
general affembly of the French part of St. Domingo.* They tranfacted however but little bufinefs, but manifefted great unanimity and temper in their proceedings, and refolved to hold
their meetings at Cape Francois, whither they adjourned for
that purpofe, appointing the 25th of the fame month for opening the feffion.

IN the mean-while, fo great was the agitation of the publick
mind, M. Blanchelande found it neceffary not only to tranfmit to the provincial affembly of the North, a copy of the
letter which he mentions to have written to the king's minifters,
but alfo to accompany it with a folemn affurance, pledging himfelf *to fufpend the execution of the obnoxious decree, whenever it
fhould come out to him properly authenticated;* a meafure which
too plainly demonftrated that his authority in the colony was at
an end.

JUSTLY alarmed at all thefe proceedings, fo hoftile towards
them, and probably apprehenfive of a general profcription, the
mulattoes throughout the colony began to collect in different

places

places in armed bodies; and the whites, by a mournful fatality, fuffered them to affemble without moleftation. In truth, every man's thoughts were directed towards the meeting of the new colonial affembly, from whofe deliberations and proceedings the extinction of party, and the full and immediate redrefs of all exifting grievances, were confidently expected. M. Blanchelande himfelf declares, that he cherifhed the fame flattering and fallacious hopes. " After a long fucceffion of violent ftorms, " I fondly expected (he writes) the return of a calm and ferene " morning. The temperate and conciliating conduct of the " new affembly, during their fhort fitting at Leogane, the cha- " racters of moft of the individual members, and the neceffity, " fo apparent to all, of mutual conceffion and unanimity on this " great occafion, led me to think that the colony would at " length fee the termination of its miferies; when, alas, the " ftorm was ready to burft, which has fince involved us in one " common deftruction !"

IT was on the morning of the 23d of Auguft, juft before day, that a general alarm and confternation fpread throughout the town of the Cape, from a report that all the negro flaves in the feveral neighbouring parifhes had revolted, and were at that moment carrying death and defolation over the adjoining large and beautiful plain to the North-eaft. The governor, and moft of the military officers on duty, affembled together; but the reports were fo confufed and contradictory, as to gain but little credit; when, as day-light began to break the fudden and fucceffive arrival, with ghaftly countenances, of perfons who had with difficulty efcaped the maffacre, and flown to the town

1791.

K 2

for

for protection, brought a dreadful confirmation of the fatal tidings.

THE rebellion firft broke out on a plantation called *Noé*, in the parifh of *Acul*, nine miles only from the city. Twelve or fourteen of the ringleaders, about the middle of the night, proceeded to the refinery, or fugar-houfe, and feized on a young man, the refiner's apprentice, dragged him to the front of the dwelling-houfe, and there hewed him into pieces with their cutlaffes : his fcreams brought out the overfeer, whom they inftantly fhot. The rebels now found their way to the apartment of the refiner, and maffacred him in his bed. A young man lying fick in a neighbouring chamber, was left apparently dead of the wounds inflicted by their cutlaffes : he had ftrength enough however to crawl to the next plantation, and relate the horrors he had witneffed. He reported, that all the whites of the eftate which he had left were murdered, except only the furgeon, whom the rebels had compelled to accompany them, on the idea that they might ftand in need of his profeffional affiftance. Alarmed by this intelligence, the perfons to whom it was communicated immediately fought their fafety in flight. What became of the poor youth I have never been informed.

THE revolters (confifting now of all the flaves belonging to that plantation) proceeded to the houfe of a Mr. Clement, by whofe negroes alfo they were immediately joined, and both he and his refiner were maffacred. The murderer of Mr. Clement was his own poftillion, a man to whom he had always fhewn great kindnefs. The other white people on this eftate contrived to make their efcape.

AT

At this juncture, the negroes on the plantation of M. Fla-ville, a few miles distant, likewise rose and murdered five white persons, one of whom (the *procureur* or attorney for the estate) had a wife and three daughters. These unfortunate women, while imploring for mercy of the savages on their knees, beheld their husband and father murdered before their faces. For themselves, they were devoted to a more horrid fate, and were carried away captives by the assassins.

The approach of day-light served only to discover sights of horror. It was now apparent that the negroes on all the estates in the plain acted in concert, and a general massacre of the whites took place in every quarter. On some few estates indeed the lives of the women were spared, but they were re-served only to gratify the brutal appetites of the ruffians; and it is shocking to relate, that many of them suffered violation on the dead bodies of their husbands and fathers!

In the town itself, the general belief for some time was, that the revolt was by no means an extensive, but a sudden and par-tial insurrection only. The largest sugar plantation on the plain was that of Monf. Gallifet, situated about eight miles from the town, the negroes belonging to which had always been treated with such kindness and liberality, and possessed so many advan-tages, that it became a proverbial expression among the lower white people, in speaking of any man's good fortune, to say *il est heureux comme un negre de Gallifet* (he is as happy as one of Gallifet's negroes). M. Odeluc, the attorney, or agent, for this plantation, was a member of the general assembly, and being

4

fully

fully perfuaded that the negroes belonging to it would remain firm in their obedience, determined to repair thither to encourage them in oppofing the infurgents ; to which end, he defired the affiftance of a few foldiers from the town-guard, which was granted him. He proceeded accordingly, but on approaching the eftate, to his furprife and grief he found all the negroes in arms on the fide of the rebels, and (horrid to tell !) *their ftandard was the body of a white infant, which they had recently impaled on a ftake !* M. Odeluc had advanced too far to retreat undifcovered, and both he, and a friend that accompanied him, with moft of the foldiers, were killed without mercy. Two or three only of the patrole, efcaped by flight ; and conveyed the dreadful tidings to the inhabitants of the town.

By this time, all or moft of the white perfons that had been found on the feveral plantations, being maffacred or forced to feek their fafety in flight, the ruffians exchanged the fword for the torch. The buildings and cane-fields were every where fet on fire ; and the conflagrations, which were vifible from the town, in a thoufand different quarters, furnifhed a profpect more fhocking, and reflections more difmal, than fancy can paint, or the powers of man defcribe.

CONSTERNATION and terror now took poffeffion of every mind; and the fcreams of the women and children, running from door to door, heightened the horrors of the fcene. All the citizens took up arms, and the general affembly vefted the governor with the command of the national guards, requefting him to give fuch orders as the urgency of the cafe feemed to demand.

ONE

ONE of the firſt meaſures was to ſend the white women and children on board the ſhips in the harbour; and very ſerious apprehenſions being entertained concerning the domeſtick negroes within the town, a great proportion of the ableſt men among them were likewiſe ſent on ſhipboard and cloſely guarded.

THERE ſtill remained in the city a conſiderable body of free mulattoes, who had not taken, or affected not to take, any part in the diſputes between their brethren of colour and the white inhabitants. Their ſituation was extremely critical; for the lower claſs of whites, conſidering the mulattoes as the immediate authors of the rebellion, marked them for deſtruction; and the whole number in the town would undoubtedly have been murdered without ſcruple, if the governor and the colonial aſſembly had not vigorouſly interpoſed, and taken them under their immediate protection. Grateful for this interpoſition in their favour (perhaps not thinking their lives otherwiſe ſecure) all the able men among them offered to march immediately againſt the rebels, and to leave their wives and children as hoſtages for their fidelity. Their offer was accepted, and they were enrolled in different companies of the militia.

THE aſſembly continued their deliberations throughout the night, amidſt the glare of the ſurrounding conflagrations; and the inhabitants, being ſtrengthened by a number of ſeamen from the ſhips, and brought into ſome degree of order and military ſubordination, were now deſirous that a detachment ſhould be ſent to attack the ſtrongeſt body of the revolters. Orders were given accordingly;

cordingly; and M. de Touzard, an officer who had diftinguiſhed himſelf in the ſervice of the North Americans, took the com· mand of a party of militia and troops of the line. With theſe, he marched to the plantation of a M. Latour, and attacked a body of about four thouſand of the rebel negroes. Many were de‑ ſtroyed, but to little purpoſe; for Touzard, finding the number of revolters to encreaſe in more than a centuple proportion to their loſſes, was at length obliged to retreat; and it cannot be doubted, that if the rebels had forthwith proceeded to the town, defence‑ leſs as it then was towards the plain, they might have fired it without difficulty, and deſtroyed all its inhabitants, or compelled them to fly to the ſhipping for refuge.

SENSIBLE of this, the governor, by the advice of the aſſembly, determined to act for ſome time ſolely on the defenſive; and as it was every moment to be apprehended that the revolters would pour down upon the town, the firſt meaſure reſorted to was to fortify the roads and paſſes leading into it. At the eaſtern ex‑ tremity, the main road from the plain is interſected by a river, which luckily had no bridge over it, and was croſſed in ferry boats. For the defence of this paſſage, a battery of cannon was raiſed on boats laſhed together; while two ſmall camps were formed at proper diſtances on the banks. The other principal entrance into the town, and contiguous to it towards the ſouth, was through a mountainous diſtrict, called *le Haut du Cap*. Poſſeſſion was immediately taken of theſe heights, and conſi‑ derable bodies of troops, with ſuch artillery as could be ſpared, were ſtationed thereon. But theſe precautions not being thought ſufficient, it was alſo determined to ſurround the whole of the town,

except

except the fide next the fea, with a ftrong palifade and *chevaux
de frize*; in the erecting and completing of which, all the inhabitants laboured without diftinction or intermiffion. At the
fame time, an embargo was laid on all the fhipping in the harbour; a meafure of indifpenfible neceffity, calculated as well to
obtain the affiftance of the feamen, as to fecure a retreat for the
inhabitants in the laft extremity.

To fuch of the diftant parifhes as were open to communication
either by land or by fea, notice of the revolt had been tranfmitted
within a few hours after advice of it was received at the Cape;
and the white inhabitants of many of thofe parifhes had therefore
found time to eftablifh camps, and form a chain of pofts, which
for a fhort time feemed to prevent the rebellion fpreading beyond the Northern province *(a)*. Two of thofe camps however, one at *Grande Riviere*, the other at *Dondon*, were attacked
by the negroes (who were here openly joined by the mulattoes)
and forced with great flaughter. At Dondon, the whites maintained the conteft for feven hours; but were overpowered by the
infinite difparity of numbers, and compelled to give way, with the
lofs of upwards of one hundred of their body. The furvivors
took refuge in the Spanifh territory.

THESE two diftricts therefore; the whole of the rich and extenfive plain of the Cape, together with the contiguous moun-

(a) It is believed that a general infurrection was to have taken place throughout
the colony on the 25th of Auguft (St. Louis's day); but that the impatience and
impetuofity of fome negroes on the plain, induced them to commence their operations two days before the time.

L

tains,

tains, were now wholly abandoned to the ravages of the enemy, and the cruelties which they exercifed, uncontrouled, on fuch of the miferable whites as fell into their hands, cannot be remembered without horror, nor reported in terms ftrong enough to convey a proper idea of their atrocity.

THEY feized Mr. Blen, an officer of the police, and having nailed him alive to one of the gates of his plantation, chopped off his limbs, one by one, with an axe.

A POOR man named *Robert,* a carpenter by trade, endeavouring to conceal himfelf from the notice of the rebels, was difcovered in his hiding-place; and the favages declared *that he fhould die in the way of his occupation:* accordingly they bound him between two boards, and deliberately fawed him afunder.

M. CARDINEAU, a planter of *Grande Riviere,* had two natural fons by a black woman. He had manumitted them in their infancy, and bred them up with great tendernefs. They both joined in the revolt; and when their father endeavoured to divert them from their purpofe, by foothing language and pecuniary offers, they took his money, and then ftabbed him to the heart.

ALL the white, and even the mulatto children whofe fathers had not joined in the revolt, were murdered without exception, frequently before the eyes, or clinging to the bofoms, of their mothers. Young women of all ranks were firft violated by a whole troop of barbarians, and then generally put to death.
Some

Some of them were indeed reserved for the further gratification of the luft of the favages, and others had their eyes fcooped out with a knife.

In the parifh of *Limbè*, at a place called the Great Ravine, a venerable planter, the father of two beautiful young ladies, was tied down by a favage ringleader of a band, who ravifhed the eldeft daughter in his prefence, and delivered over the youngeft to one of his followers: their paffion being fatisfied, they flaughtered both the father and the daughters.

Amidst thefe fcenes of horror, one inftance however occurs of fuch fidelity and attachment in a negro, as is equally unexpected and affecting. Monf. and Madame Baillon, their daughter and fon-in-law, and two white fervants, refiding on a mountain plantation about thirty miles from Cape François, were apprized of the revolt by one of their own flaves, who was himfelf in the confpiracy, but promifed, if poffible, to fave the lives of his mafter and his family. Having no immediate means of providing for their efcape, he conducted them into an adjacent wood; after which he went and joined the revolters. The following night, he found an opportunity of bringing them provifions from the rebel camp. The fecond night he returned again, with a further fupply of provifions; but declared that it would be out of his power to give them any further affiftance. After this, they faw nothing of the negro for three days; but at the end of that time he came again; and directed the family how to make their way to a river which led to Port Margot, affuring them they would find a canoe on a part of the river which he defcribed. They followed his di-

L 2

rections,

rections; found the canoe, and got safely into it; but were overset by the rapidity of the current, and after a narrow escape, thought it best to return to their retreat in the mountains. The negro, anxious for their safety, again found them out, and directed them to a broader part of the river, where he assured them he had provided a boat; but said it was the last effort he could make to save them. They went accordingly, but not finding the boat, gave themselves up for lost, when the faithful negro again appeared like their guardian angel. He brought with him pigeons, poultry, and bread; and conducted the family, by slow marches in the night, along the banks of the river, until they were within sight of the wharf at Port Margot; when telling them they were entirely out of danger, he took his leave for ever, and went to join the rebels. The family were in the woods nineteen nights.

LET us now turn our attention back to the town of the Cape; where, the inhabitants being at length placed, or supposed to be placed, in some sort of security, it was thought necessary by the governor and assembly, that offensive operations against the rebels should be renewed, and a small army, under the command of M. Rouvray, marched to the eastern part of the plain, and encamped at a place called *Roucrou.* A very considerable body of the rebel negroes took possession, about the same time, of the large buildings on the plantation of M. Gallifet, and mounted some heavy pieces of artillery on the walls. They had procured the cannon at different shipping places and harbours along the coast, where it had been placed in time of war by the government, and imprudently left unprotected; but it was a matter

ter of great furprize by what means they obtained ammunition *(b)*. From this plantation they fent out foraging parties,
with which the whites had frequent fkirmifhes. In thefe en-
gagements, the negroes feldom ftood their ground longer than to
receive and return a fingle volley, but they appeared again the
next day; and though they were at length driven out of their
entrenchments with infinite flaughter, yet their numbers feemed
not to diminifh :—as foon as one body was cut off, another appeared, and thus they fucceeded in the object of haraffing and
deftroying the whites by perpetual fatigue, and reducing the
country to a defert.

To detail the various conflicts, fkirmifhes, maffacres, and
fcenes of flaughter, which this exterminating war produced, were
to offer a difgufting and frightful picture;—a combination of
horrors;—wherein we fhould behold cruelties unexampled in
the annals of mankind; human blood poured forth in torrents;
the earth blackened with afhes, and the air tainted with peftilence. It was computed that, within two months after the revolt firft began, upwards of two thoufand white perfons, of all
conditions and ages, had been maffacred;—that one hundred and
eighty fugar plantations, and about nine hundred coffee, cotton,

(*b*) It was difcovered afterwards, that great quantities of powder and ball were
ftolen by the negroes in the town of Cape François from the king's arfenal, and
fecretly conveyed to the rebels. Moft of the fire-arms at firft in their poffeffion
were fuppofed to have been part of *Ogé's* importation. But it grieves me to add, that
the rebels were afterwards abundantly fupplied, by fmall veffels from North America; the mafters of which felt no fcruple to receive in payment fugar and rum,
from eftates of which the owners had been murdered by the men with whom they
trafficked.

and

and indigo fettlements had been deftroyed (the buildings the on being confumed by fire), and one thoufand two hundred chriftian families reduced from opulence, to fuch a ftate of mifery as to depend altogether for their clothing and fuftenance on publick and private charity. Of the infurgents, it was reckoned that upwards of ten thoufand had perifhed by the fword or by famine; and fome hundreds by the hands of the executioner;—many of them, I grieve to fay, under the torture of the wheel;—a fyftem of revenge and retaliation, which no enormities of favage life could juftify or excufe (c).

HITHERTO, my narrative has applied chiefly to tranfactions in the Northern province; I grieve to relate, that the flames of

(c) Two of thefe unhappy men fuffered in this manner under the window of the author's lodgings, and in his prefence, at Cape François, on Thurfday the 28th of September 1791. They were broken on two pieces of timber placed crofswife. One of them expired on receiving the third ftroke on his ftomach, each of his legs and arms having been firft broken in two places; the firft three blows he bore without a groan. The other had a harder fate. When the executioner, after breaking his legs and arms, lifted up the inftrument to give the finifhing ftroke on the breaft, and which (by putting the criminal out of his pain) is called le coup de grace, the mob, with the ferocioufnefs of cannibals, called out arretez! (ftop) and compelled him to leave his work unfinifhed. In that condition, the miferable wretch, with his broken limbs doubled up, was put on a cart-wheel, which was placed horizontally, one end of the axle-tree being driven into the earth. He feemed perfectly fenfible, but uttered not a groan. At the end of forty minutes, fome Englifh feamen, who were fpectators of the tragedy, ftrangled him in mercy. As to all the French fpectators (many of them perfons of fafhion, who beheld the fcene from the windows of their upper apartments), it grieves me to fay, that they looked on with the moft perfect compofure and fang froid. Some of the ladies, as I was told, even ridiculed, with a great deal of unfeemly mirth, the fympathy manifefted by the Englifh at the fufferings of the wretched criminals.

rebellion

rebellion soon began to break forth alſo in the Weſtern diviſion. Here, however, the inſurgents were chiefly men of colour, of whom upwards of two thouſand appeared in arms in the pariſh of Mirebalais. Being joined by about ſix hundred of the negro ſlaves, they began their operations by burning the coffee plantations in the mountains adjacent to the plain of Cul-de-Sac. Some detachments of the military which were ſent againſt them from Port au Prince were repulſed; and the inſurgents continued to ravage and burn the country through an extent of thirty miles, practiſing the ſame exceſſes and ferocious barbarities towards ſuch of the whites as fell into their hands, as were diſplayed by the rebels in the North. They had the audacity at length to approach Port au Prince, with intention, as it was believed, to ſet it on fire; and ſo defenceleſs was the ſtate of that devoted town, that its deſtruction ſeemed inevitable. Many of the mulatto chiefs, however, finding that their attempts to gain over the negro ſlaves on the ſugar plantations in this part of the country, were not attended with that ſucceſs which they expected, expreſſed an unwillingneſs to proceed to this extremity; declaring that they took up arms not to deſolate the colony, but merely to ſupport the national decree of the 15th of May, and that they were not averſe to a reconciliation. Theſe ſentiments coming to the knowledge of M. de *Jumecourt*, a planter of eminence, he undertook the office of mediator, and through his well-timed and powerful interpoſition, a truce or convention, called the *concordat*, was agreed upon the 11th of September, between the free people of colour, and the white inhabitants of Port au Prince, of which the chief proviſions were an oblivion of the paſt, and an engagement on the part of the whites, to admit in

full

CHAP.
VI.

1791.

full force the national decree of the 15th of May, so often mentioned;—certainly the oftensible, though perhaps not the sole
and original cause of the rebellion.

INSTRUCTED by this example, and softened, it may be pre-
sumed, by the loyal and temperate conduct of the free mulattoes
in the town of Cape François, as before related, the general af-
sembly; by a proclamation of the 20th of September, declared
that they would no longer oppose the operation of the same decree. They even went further, and announced an intention to
grant considerable indulgences towards such free people of colour as were not comprehended in it, meaning those who were
born of enslaved parents. They voted at the same time the
formation of certain free companies of mulattoes, wherein the
men of colour of all descriptions, possessed of certain qualifications, should be allowed to serve as commissioned·officers.

THESE concessions, at an earlier period, would have operated
with powerful effect in the salvation of the colony; but they now
came too late, and produced only a partial truce, a temporary and
fallacious cessation of miseries. The wounds that had been inflicted were yet green and bleeding; and the dark and sullen
passions of disappointed pride, anger, malice, hatred and revenge, were secretly burning in the gloomy minds of all parties. The flames were smothered, not extinguished; soon to
break out again, with aggravated violence and greater fury than
ever.

CHAP.

C H A P. VII.

Of the Motives which induced the People of Colour to join the re-
volted Negroes—Conduct of the British Association for the
Abolition of the Slave Trade, and of the Society in Paris called
Les Amis des Noirs—Letter from Abbé Gregoire to the People
of Colour—Repeal of the Decree of the 15th May 1791—Ef-
fects of that Measure—Civil War with the Mulattoes re-
newed—Port au Prince destroyed by Fire—Cruelties exercised
by both Parties—Arrival at Cape François of the Civil Com-
missioners.

BEFORE I proceed to a renewal of those disgusting scenes
of devastation, slaughter, and ruin, which my duty, as a
faithful historian, calls upon me to describe (happy if they serve
as an impressive lesson to other nations!) it seems necessary to
remove some difficulties which may possibly have arisen in the
mind of the reader, concerning the original and primary cause
of the junction and co-operation of so large a number of the
negro slaves, in this rebellion, with the men of colour. That
the whole body of the latter in St. Domingo had solid ground of
complaint and dissatisfaction, cannot be denied. There is a
point at which oppression sometimes arrives, when forbearance
under it ceases to be a virtue; and I should readily have admitted that the actual situation and condition of the mulattoes
in the French islands would have made resistance a duty, if it

CHAP.
VII.

M   did

did not appear, from what I have already related, that the re-dress of their grievances occupied the very first deliberations of the first general assembly of representatives that ever met in St. Domingo. Certainly, then, no justification can be offered for those pestilent reformers, who could persuade these unfortunate people to seek that relief by rebellion and massacre, which was offered to them by the supreme power of the country, as a spontaneous and voluntary concession;—the homage of enlightened reason on the altar of humanity. Concerning the enslaved negroes, however, it does not appear that the conduct of the whites towards them was in general reprehensible. I believe, on the whole, it was as lenient and indulgent as was consistent with their own safety. It was the mulatto people themselves who were the hard-hearted task-masters to the negroes. The same indignities which they received from the whites, they directed without scruple towards the blacks; exercising over the latter every species of that oppression which they loudly and justly complained of, when exercised on themselves;—and this is a true picture of human nature. By what means, then, it will be asked, were the negroes induced to forget their resentments, and join with those who were the constant objects both of their envy and hatred?

In order to reply to this question, with as much accuracy and precision as the subject will admit, it is necessary to recur to the proceedings of the two associations, of which mention was made in the Second Chapter of this History; namely, the British association for the abolition of the slave trade, which held its meetings in the Old Jewry in London; and the society called

Les

Les Amis des Noirs in Paris. A fhort review of the conduct of thefe focieties will ferve not only to leffen the furprize which may be felt at the revolt of the negroes of St. Domingo, but alfo raife a confiderable degree of aftonifhment that the enflaved negroes in the Britifh iflands had not given them the example.

I HAVE obferved, that the fociety in London *profeffed* to have nothing more in view than to obtain an act of the legiflature for prohibiting the further introduction of African flaves into the Britifh colonies. I have faid, that " they difclaimed all in-" tention of interfering with the government and condition of " the negroes already in the plantations ; publickly declaring " their opinion to be, that a general emancipation of thofe " people, in their prefent ftate of ignorance and barbarity, inftead " of a bleffing, would prove to them the fource of misfortune and " mifery." But although fuch were their oftenfible declarations as a publick body, the leading members of the fociety, in the fame moment, held a very different language ; and even the fociety itfelf (acting as fuch) purfued a line of conduct directly and im-mediately repugnant to their own profeffions. Befides ufing every poffible endeavour to inflame the publick of Great Britain againft the planters, they diftributed at a prodigious expence throughout the colonies, tracts and pamphlets without number, the direct tendency of which was to render the white inhabitants odious and contemptible in the eyes of their own flaves, and ex-cite in the latter fuch ideas of their natural rights and equality of condition, as fhould lead them to a general ftruggle for free-dom through rebellion and bloodfhed. In many of thofe writ-ings, arguments are exprefsly adduced, in language which can-

not

not be mifunderftood, to urge the negroes to rife up and murder their mafters without mercy.—" Refiftance," fay they, " is al- " ways juftifiable where force is the fubftitute of right: *nor is* " *the commiffion of a civil crime poffible in a ftate of flavery.*" Thefe fentiments are repeated in a thoufand different forms; and in order that they might not lofe their effect by abftract reafoning, a reverend divine of the church of England, in a pamphlet addreffed to the chairman or prefident of the fociety, pours forth the moft earneft prayers, in the moft undifguifed ex- preffions, that the negroes would deftroy all the white people, men, women, and children, in the Weft Indies : " Should we " not, (he exclaims) approve their conduct in their violence ? " Should we not crown it with eulogium, if they exterminate " their tyrants with fire and fword ! *Should they even deliberately* " *inflict the moft exquifite tortures on thofe tyrants, would they not* " *be excufable* in the moral judgment of thofe who properly va- " lue thofe ineftimable bleffings, rational and religious li- " berty *(a)* ?"

Befides diftributing pamphlets of this complexion *gratis*, at the doors of all the churches and places of worfhip in the king- dom, and throughout the colonies, the fociety caufed a medal to be ftruck, containing the figure of a naked negro, loaded with

(a) This is a fair extract from a letter addreffed to Granville Sharp, Efq, chair- man of the fociety in the Old Jewry, by the Reverend Percival Stockdale, A. M. Of fuch writers the planters may well exclaim, " *Forgive them, they know not what* " *they do !*" The fame ejaculation I applied to the learned and pious Samuel John- fon, who poffeffed a negro fervant, and before whom he frequently gave as a toaft, " *A fpeedy rebellion of the negroes in Jamaica, and fuccefs to them !*"

chains,

chains, and in the attitude of imploring mercy; thousands of
which also they found means to disperse among the negroes in each
of the sugar islands, for the instruction, I presume, of such of
them as could not read; but, unhappily, this instance of provident
caution was not requisite; for so many negro domesticks return
annually from Europe to the West Indies, as constantly furnish a
sufficient number of living instructors; and certain it is (I pronounce it from my own knowledge respecting Jamaica) that the
labours of the society on their behalf, as well as many of the
most violent speeches in the British parliament, wherein the
whole body of planters were painted as a herd of blood-thirsty
and remorseless tyrants, were explained to the negro slaves, in
terms well adapted to their capacities, and suited, as might have
been supposed, to their feelings. It will be difficult to say what
other measures the Old Jewry associates could have taken to
excite a rebellion, except that of furnishing the objects of their
solicitude with fire arms and ammunition.

HITHERTO, this society had served as a model and exemplar
to that of Paris; but a disposition to stop at half measures con-
stitutes no part of the French character; and the society of
Amis des Noirs resorted, without scruple, to those measures
which their fellow labourers in London still hesitated to adopt:
beginning with the class of free mulattoes, because they found
many of them in France, who became the willing instruments
of their purposes; and who undertook to interpret to the negroes in the French colonies the wishes and good intentions
towards them of their friends in the mother country. Thus an
opening was made towards conciliation and union between the

two

two claffes. The negroes, apprized that it was only through the agency of the mulattoes, and the connections of thofe people in France, they could obtain a regular fupply of arms and ammunition, forgot or fufpended their ancient animofities; and the men of colour, fenfible that nothing but the co-operation of the enflaved negroes (docile, as they fuppofed them to be, from their ignorance, and irrefiftible from their numbers) could give fuccefs to their caufe, courted them with fuch affiduity as gained over at leaft nine-tenths of all the flaves in the Northern province of St. Domingo.

THERE feems however to have been fome apprehenfions entertained by the leading men among the *Amis des Noirs*, that the decree of the national affembly of the 15th of May, confined as the benefits of it were to the people of colour exclufively, (and of thofe, to fuch only as were born of free parents) might give rife to jealoufies and fufpicions, deftructive of that unanimity between the different claffes, the maintenance of which was an object of the laft importance. To obviate any mifapprehenfions on this account, as well as to keep the mulattoes firm to their purpofe, the Abbé Gregoire wrote and publifhed his celebrated circular letter;—a performance which, if the intentions of the writer had been as pure as his expreffions are eloquent, would have reflected luftre on his abilities *(b)*. What effect this diftinguifhed piece of oratory may have had on the rugged and unenlightened minds of favage people,

(b) The reader will find a tranflation of this letter at the end of the prefent Chapter.

I pretend

I pretend not to afcertain. It is certain, that the Abbé Gregoire was confidered by the negroes in St. Domingo as their great advocate and patron; a fort of guardian angel or tutelary deity; of the good effects of whofe benevolent interpofition and friendly offices their mafters unjuftly deprived them, and on whofe fupport and affiftance they might confidently rely, in the attempt, through rebellion and murder, to obtain juftice for themfelves.

Both claffes of people being thus inftructed and prepared, the decree of the 15th of May was the fignal of revolt, the war-hoop of maffacre. From the clamour which it excited amongft all orders of the whites in St. Domingo (the lower claffes efpecially) the people of colour, as I have fhewn, had reafon to apprehend that mifchiefs of an extenfive and alarming nature were meditated againft them. They were thus furnifhed with a plaufible, and, had they meant to have acted folely on the defenfive, a juftifiable caufe for reforting to arms; but, unhappily, the ftrong tide of popular prejudice which prevailed in the mother country againft the planters, and the great majority which voted for the fatal decree in the national affembly, were circumftances that infpired them with fo dangerous a confidence in their own refources, as overpowered all confiderations of prudence, policy, and humanity.

It muft be confidered, at the fame time, that the enflaved negroes (ignorant and depreffed as we fuppofe them to be) could not poffibly be unobfervant of thefe combined and concurring circumftances. They beheld the coloured people in open hoftility
lity

CHAP.
VII.

lity againſt the whites. They were aſſured, that the former had the fulleſt ſupport and encouragement from the ſupreme legiſlature of the mother country. They were taught to believe, that themſelves alſo were become the objects of the paternal ſolicitude of the king and the national aſſembly, who wiſhed to reſcue them from the dominion of their maſters, and inveſt them with their eſtates. It appeared from indiſputable evidence, that aſſurances of this nature were held out to the enſlaved negroes;—aſſurances which could not but excite their attention, awaken their faculties, and rouze them to action. Whoever ſhall calmly deliberate on theſe, and the other facts that have been ſtated, will find no difficulty in accounting for the dreadful extent of this inſurrection; or in aſſigning it to its proper cauſe, and tracing to the fountain-head thoſe rivers of blood which ſtill continue to flow in this unfortunate and devoted colony (c)!

(c) In September 1791, when the author was at Cape François, he dined with a large company, on board the frigate *la Prudente*, commanded by Monſ. *Joyeuſe* (at preſent a diſtinguiſhed admiral in the ſervice of the new republick, by the name of *Villaret*) when, in the midſt of the entertainment, a loud exclamation from the crew announced *that the gunner was returned*. This man, who had been miſſing ſome weeks, was immediately brought forward, and gave the following account of the cauſe of his abſence. He ſaid that, having gone on ſhore, to collect green meat for the pigs, he was ſurrounded by the rebel negroes, who were about putting him to death, when Jean François, the chief, finding that he was an officer in the king's ſervice, ordered that his life ſhould be ſpared, alledging *that the king was their friend*. They detained him however as a priſoner, and compelled him to load and point their artillery in the attack at M. Gallifet's plantation before-mentioned. On the defeat of the rebels in that engagement, he fortunately made his eſcape from them. Some of the ſhocking enormities and cruelties inflicted by the rebels on their white priſoners, as related in the preceding pages, were committed in this man's preſence.

BUT

BUT it is now time to advert to the proceedings which occurred in France, where we left *Gregoire*, *La Fayette*, *Rober-*
fpierre, and the reft of the fociety of *Amis des Noirs*, exulting in
the triumph they had obtained on the 15th of May; and perhaps waiting, in the ardent hope and expectation, that their obnoxious decree of that date, would produce thofe very evils
which actually refulted from it. It was not until the beginning
of September that information arrived at Paris concerning the
reception which the account of this decree had met with in St.
Domingo. The tumults, diforders, and confufions that it produced there, were now reprefented in the ftrongeft colouring,
and the lofs of the colony to France was univerfally apprehended. At this time, however, no fufpicion was entertained
concerning the enflaved negroes; but a civil war, between the
whites and the mulattoes, was believed to be inevitable. The
commercial and manufacturing towns, predicting the ruin of their
trade and fhipping, and the lofs of their capitals from exifting
dangers, prefented remonftrances and petitions to the national
affembly, urging the neceffity of an immediate repeal of all the
decrees by which the rights of the planters were invaded; that
of the 15th of May efpecially. The conftituent national affembly was now on the point of diffolution, and perhaps wifhed to
leave every thing in peace. At the fame time the tide of popular prejudice, which had hitherto ran with fuch violence againft
the colonifts, was beginning to turn. Moft of thofe members
whofe opinions in colonial concerns, a few months before, had
guided the deliberations of the national affembly, were now
either filehtly difregarded, or treated with outrage;—a ftrong
and ftriking proof of the lightnefs and verfatility of the French

N   character.

character. At length, a motion was made to annul the obnoxious decree, and (ſtrange to tell!) on the 24th of September
its repeal was actually voted by a large majority!—At this remarkable change of ſentiment in the ſupreme legiſlature, it is
neceſſary to pauſe, and remind the reader of what was doing at
the ſame time in St. Domingo; where, as we have ſeen, on
the 11th of that very month, the *concordat*, or truce, took place
between the people of colour and the white inhabitants of Port
au Prince; and on the 20th, the colonial aſſembly of Cape
François publiſhed the proclamation mentioned in the latter part
of the preceding Chapter. Thus, almoſt in the very moment
when the juſtice and neceſſity of the decree were acknowledged,
and its faithful obſervance promiſed by the colonial aſſembly, its
repeal was pronounced by the national legiſlature in the mother
country!

To ſuch repugnancy and abſurdity muſt every government be
driven that attempts to regulate and direct the local concerns of
a country three thouſand miles diſtant. Of the two meaſures that
have been mentioned, it is difficult to ſay which produced the
greateſt calamities; the decree of the 15th of May in the firſt
inſtance; or its unexpected repeal, at the time and in the manner
related! Doubts had already ariſen in the minds of the mulattoes of
the ſincerity and good faith of the white people, with reſpect to the
concordat. Their ſuſpicions and apprehenſions had indeed grown
to ſuch a height, as to induce them to inſiſt on a renewal and
confirmation of its proviſions; which were accordingly granted
them, by a new inſtrument or treaty of the 11th of October, and
a ſupplementary agreement of the 20th of the ſame month:
but

but no fooner was authentick information received of the proceedings in France, in the repeal of the decree, than all truft
and confidence, and every hope of reconciliation and amity between the two claffes, vanifhed for ever. It was not poffible to
perfuade the mulattoes that the planters in the colony were innocent, and ignorant of the tranfaction. They accufed the
whites of the moft horrid duplicity, faithlefsnefs and treachery;
and publickly declared that one party or the other, themfelves
or the whites, muft be utterly deftroyed and exterminated:—
There was no longer, they faid, an alternative.

In this difpofition, exafperated to frenzy, the coloured people
throughout the Weftern and Southern provinces flew to arms.
In the Southern province, a body of them became mafters of
Port St. Louis; but the inhabitants of Port au Prince, having
been reinforced, a fhort time before, by the arrival of fome troops
from Europe, were better prepared, and drove the revolters from
the city with great flaughter. They took poft in the parifh of
Croix des Bouquets; but found means, however, before their retreat, to fet fire to the city, and a dreadful conflagration enfued,
in which more than one-third of the buildings were confumed.

Open war, and war in all its horrors, was now renewed.
All the foft workings of humanity—what Shakefpeare calls the
compunctious vifitings of nature—were now abforbed in the raging
and infatiable thirft of revenge, which inflamed each clafs alike.
It was no longer a conteft for mere victory, but a diabolical
emulation which party could inflict the moft abominable cruel-

ties

ties on the other.   The enslaved negroes in the district called *Cul de Sac* having joined the mulattoes, a bloody engagement took place, in which the negroes, being ranged in front, and acting without any kind of discipline, left two thousand of their number dead on the field.   Of the mulattoes about fifty were killed, and several taken prisoners.   The whites claimed the victory; but for want of cavalry were unable to improve it by a pursuit, and contented themselves with satiating their revenge on their captives.   Every refinement in cruelty that the most depraved imagination could suggest, was practised on the persons of those wretched men.   One of the mulatto leaders was unhappily among the number: him the victors placed on an elevated seat in a cart, and secured him in it by driving large spiked nails through his feet into the boards.   In this condition he was drawn a miserable spectacle through the city.   His bones were afterwards broken, and he was then thrown alive into the flames!

THE mulattoes scorned to be outdone in deeds of vengeance, and atrocities shameful to humanity.   In the neighbourhood of *Jeremie* a body of them attacked the house of M. Sejourné, and secured the persons both of him and his wife.   This unfortunate woman (my hand trembles while I write!) was far advanced in her pregnancy.   The monsters, whose prisoner she was, having first murdered her husband in her presence, ripped her up alive, and threw the infant to the hogs.—They then (how shall I relate it!) sewed up the head of the murdered husband in — —!!!
—Such are thy triumphs, philanthropy!

WITH

WITH these enormities terminated the disastrous year 1791. Just before Christmas the three civil commissioners nominated by the national assembly for St. Domingo, arrived at Cape François. Much was expected from their appointment by the friends of peace and good order; but the sequel will shew that they effected very little towards restoring the peace of the country.

Translation of the Letter of ABBE GREGOIRE, *Bishop of the Department of Loire and Cher, Deputy of the National Assembly, to the Citizens of Colour in the French West Indies, concerning the Decree of the 15th of May 1791.*

FRIENDS!

You *were* MEN;—you *are* now CITIZENS. Reinstated in the fulness of your rights, you will in future participate of the sovereignty of the people. The decree which the national assembly has just published respecting you, is not *a favour*; for a favour is *a privilege*: and a privilege to one class of people is an injury to all the rest.—They are words which will no longer disgrace the laws of the French.

IN securing to you the exercise of your political rights, we have acquitted ourselves of *a debt*:— not to have paid it, would have been a crime on our part, and a disgrace to the constitution. The legislators of a free nation certainly could not do less for you than our ancient despots have done.

IT is now above a century that Louis the XIVth solemnly acknowledged and proclaimed your rights; but of this sacred inheritance you have been defrauded by pride and avarice, which have gradually increased your burthens, and embittered your existence.

THE

THE regeneration of the French empire opened your hearts to hope, whose cheering influence has alleviated the weight of your miseries : miseries of which the people of Europe had no idea. While the white planters resident among us were loud in their complaints against *ministerial* tyranny, they took especial care to be silent *as to their own.* Not a hint was suggested concerning the complaints of the unhappy people of mixed blood ; who, notwithstanding, are their own children. It is *we*, who, at the distance of two thousand leagues from you, have been constrained to protect these children against the neglect, the contempt, the unnatural cruelty of their fathers !

BUT it is in vain that they have endeavoured to suppress the justice of your claims. Your groans, notwithstanding the extent of the ocean which separates us, have reached the hearts of the European Frenchmen ;—for *they* have *hearts.*

GOD Almighty comprehends all men in the circle of his mercy. His love makes no distinction between them, but what arises from the different degrees of their virtues. Can laws then, which ought to be an emanation of eternal justice, encourage so culpable a partiality ? Can that government, whose duty it is to protect alike all the members of the same great family, be the mother of one branch, and the step-mother only of the others ?

No, gentlemen :—you could not escape the solicitude of the national assembly. In unfolding to the eyes of the universe the great charter of nature, your titles were traced. An attempt had indeed been made to expunge them ; but happily they are written in characters as indelible as the sacred image of the Deity, which is graven on your countenances.

ALREADY had the national assembly, in the instructions which it prepared for the government of the colonies, on the 28th of March 1790, comprized both the whites and people of colour under one common denomination. Your enemies, in asserting the contrary, have published a forgery. It is incontestibly true, that when I demanded you should be expressly named, a great number of members, among whom were

2   several

several planters, eagerly exclaimed, that you were already comprehended
under the general words contained in those inftructions. M. Barnave
himfelf, upon. my repeated inftances to him on that head, has at length
acknowledged, before the whole affembly, that this was the fact. It
now appears how much reafon I had to apprehend that a falfe con-
ftruction would be put upon our decree !

NEW oppreffions on the part of your mafters,. and new miferies on.
yours, until at length the cup. of affliction is filled even to the brim, have
but too well juftified my apprehenfions. The letters which I have received from you upon this head, have forced tears from my eyes.
Pofterity will learn, with aftonifhment and indignation, that a caufe like
yours, the juftice of which is fo evident, was made the fubject of debate
for no lefs than five days fucceffively. Alas ! when humanity is obliged
to ftruggle fo long againft vanity and prejudice, its triumph is dearly
obtained !

IT is a long time that the fociety of *Amis des Noirs* have employed
themfelves in finding out the means to foften your lot, as well as that
of the flaves. It is difficult—perhaps impoffible, to do good with entire
impunity. The meritorious zeal of this fociety has drawn upon them
much obloquy. Defpicable writers have lanced their poifonous fhafts at
them, and impudent libels have never ceafed to repeat objections and calumnies, which have been a hundred times anfwered and refuted. How
often have we been accufed of being fold to the Englifh, and of being
paid by them for fending you inflammatory writings and arms ? You
know, my friends, the weaknefs and wickednefs of thefe charges. We
have inceffantly recommended to you attachment to your country, re-
fignation and patience, while waiting the return of juftice ! Nothing has
been able to cool our zeal, or that of your brethren of mixed blood who
are at Paris. M. Raimond, in particular, has devoted himfelf moft
heroically to your defence. With what tranfport would you have feen
this diftinguifhed citizen, at the bar of the national affembly, of which he
ought to be a member, laying before it the affecting picture of your

miferies,,

miseries, and strenuously claiming your rights! If that assembly had sacrificed them, it would have tarnished its glory. It was its duty to decree with justice, to explain itself clearly, and cause its laws to be executed with firmness: it has done so; and if (which God forbid!) some event, hidden in the womb of futurity, should tear our colonies from us, would it not be better to have a loss to deplore, than an injustice to reproach ourselves with?

Citizens! raise once more your humiliated countenances, and to the dignity of men, associate the courage and nobleness of a free people. The 15th of May, the day in which you recovered your rights, ought to be for ever memorable to you and to your children. This epoch will periodically awaken in you sentiments of gratitude towards the Supreme Being; and may your accents ascend to the vault of heaven, towards which your grateful hands will be extended! At length you have a country. Hereafter you will see nothing above you but the law; while the opportunity of concurring in the framing it, will assure to you that indefeasible right of all mankind, the right of obeying yourselves only.

You have a country: and it will no longer be a land of exile, where you meet none but tyrants on the one hand, and companions in misfortune on the other; the former distributing, and the latter receiving, contempt and outrage. The groans of your afflictions were punished as the clamours of rebellion; and situated between the uplifted poinard, and certain death, those unhappy countries were often moistened with your tears, and sometimes stained with your blood.

You have a country: and happiness will shine on the seat of your nativity. You will now enjoy in peace the fruits of the fields which you have cultivated without compulsion. Then will be filled up that interval, which, placing at an immense distance from each other, the children of the same father, has suppressed the voice of nature, and broke the bands of fraternity asunder. Then will the chaste enjoyments of conjugal union take place of those vile sallies of debauchery, by which the majesty jefty of moral fentiment has been infulted. By what ftrange perverfion of reafon can it be deemed difgraceful in a white man to marry a black or mulatto woman, when it is not thought difhonourable in him to be connected with her in the moft licentious familiarity!

THE lefs real worth a man poffeffes, the more he feeks to avail him-felf of the appearances of virtue. What can be more abfurd than to make the merit of a perfon confift in different fhades of the fkin, or in a complexion more or lefs fallow? The man who thinks at all muft fome-times blufh at being a man, when he fees his feilow-creatures blinded by fuch ridiculous prejudices; but as unfortunately pride is one of thofe failings we moft unwillingly part with, the empire of prejudice is the moft difficult to fubvert: man appears to be unable to arrive at truth, until he has exhaufted his ftrength in travelling through the different paths of error.

THIS prejudice againft the mulattoes and negroes has however no exiftence in our Eaftern colonies. Nothing can be more affecting than the eulogium made on the people of colour, by the inhabitants of that part of the world, in the inftructions given by them, to thofe they have appointed their deputies to the national affembly. The members of the academy of fciences pride themfelves in reckoning a mulatto of the Ifle of France in the number of their correfpendents. Among ourfelves, a worthy negro is a fuperior officer of the diftrict of St. Hypolite, in the department of Gard. We do not conceive that a difference of colour can be the foundation of different rights among members of the fame political fociety. It is therefore we find no fuch defpicable pride among our brave national guards, who offer themfelves to embark for the Weft Indies to infure the execution of our decrees. Perfectly concurring in the laudable fentiments manifefted by the inhabitants of Bourdeaux, they ac-knowledge with them, that the decree refpecting the people of colour, framed under the aufpices of prudence and wifdom, is an homage ren-dered to reafon and juftice. While the deputies from the colonies have endeavoured to calumniate your intentions, and thofe of the mercantile

CHAP. VII.

O

part

part of the nation, the conduct of those deputies is perfectly contra-dictory. Ardently foliciting their own admiffion among us at Verfailles; fwearing with us in the Tennis Court not to feparate from us, until the conftitution fhould be eftablifhed, and then declaring, when the decree of the 15th of May was paffed, that they could no longer continue to fit with us! This defertion is a defertion of their principles, and a breach of their folemn oaths.

ALL thofe white inhabitants of the colonies who are worthy the name of Frenchmen, have haftened to abjure fuch ridiculous prejudices, and have promifed to regard you in future as brothers and friends. With what delightful fenfations do we cite the words of the citizens of Jacmel. " We fwear to obey, without referve, the decrees of the national affembly " refpecting our prefent and future conftitution, and even fuch of them " as may fubftantially change it!" The citizens of Port au Prince tell the national affembly the fame thing, in different words. " Conde-" fcend, gentlemen," fay they, " to receive the oath which the muni-" cipality has taken to you, in the name of the commons of Port au " Prince, punctually to obey and execute all your decrees, and never to " fwerve from them in any refpect whatfoever."

THUS has philofophy enlarged its horizon in the new world, and foon will abfurd prejudices have no other fupporters than a few inferior ty-rants, who wifh to perpetuate in America, the reign of that defpotifm which has been abolifhed in France.

WHAT would thefe men have faid, if the people of colour had en-deavoured to deprive the whites of *their* political advantages ? With what energy would they not have exclaimed at fuch an oppreffion ! In-flamed into madnefs at finding that your rights have been pointed out to you, their irritated pride may perhaps lead them to make every effort to render our decrees ineffectual. They will probably endeavour to raife fuch difturbances, as, by wrefting the colonies from the mother country, will enable them to defraud their creditors of their juft debts. They have inceffantly alarmed us with threats that St. Domingo will be
lost,

loft, if juftice be rendered to you. In this affertion we have found nothing but falfehood: we pleafe ourfelves in the belief, that our decree
will draw the bands ftill clofer which unite you to the mother country.
Your patriotifm, your intereft, and your affections, will concur in inducing
you to confine your commercial connections to France only; and the
reciprocal tributes of induftry will eftablifh between her and her colonies a conftant interchange of riches and good offices. If you act
unfaithfully towards France, you will be the bafeft and moft abandoned of the human race. But no! generous citizens, you will not
become traitors to your country: you fhudder at the idea. Rallied,
with all other good Frenchmen, around the ftandard of liberty, you
will defend our glorious conftitution. The day fhall arrive, when the
reprefentatives of the people of colour will crofs the ocean to take
their feats with us, and fwear to live and die under our laws. The
day fhall arrive among you when the fun will fhine on none but free-
men; when the rays of light fhall no longer fall on the fetters of flavery.
It is true, the national affembly has not yet raifed the condition of the
enflaved negroes to a level with your fituation; becaufe fuddenly
granting the rights to thofe who are ignorant of the duties of citizens,
might perhaps have been a fatal prefent to them: but forget not, that
they, like yourfelves, are born to freedom and perfect equality. It is
in the irrefiftible courfe of things that all nations, whofe liberty has been
invaded, fhall recover that precious portion of their indefeafible inheritance!

You are accufed of treating your flaves much worfe than the whites:
but, alas! fo various have been the detractions with which you have
been afperfed, that it would be weaknefs in us to credit the charge. If,
however, there be any foundation for what has been advanced on this
head, fo conduct yourfelves in future as to prove it will be a fhameful
calumny hereafter.

Your oppreffors have heretofore endeavoured to hide from their
flaves the lights of chriftianity, becaufe the religion of mildnefs, equa-

O 2   lity,

lity, and liberty, fuits not with fuch blood-thirfty men. May *your* conduct be the reverfe of *theirs*. Univerfal love is the language of the gofpel; your paftors will make it heard among you. Open your hearts to receive this divine fyftem of morality. We have mitigated *your* misfortunes, alleviate, on your part, thofe of the unhappy victims of avarice, who moiften your fields with their fweat, and often with their tears. Let the exiftence of your flaves be no longer their torment; but by your kind treatment of them, expiate the crimes of Europe!

By leading them on progreffively to liberty, you will fulfil a duty: you will prepare for yourfelves the moft comfortable reflections: you will do honour to humanity, and infure the profperity of the colonies. Such will be your conduct towards your brethren, the negroes; but what ought it to be towards your fathers, the whites? Doubtlefs you will be permitted to fhed tears over the afhes of *Ferrand de Baudiere*, and the unfortunate *Ogé*, affaffinated under the forms of law, and dying on the wheel for having wifhed to be free! But may he among you perifh, who fhall dare to entertain an idea of revenge againft your perfecutors! They are already delivered over to the ftings of their own confciences, and covered with eternal infamy. The abhorrence in which they are held by the prefent race of mankind, only precedes the execration of pofterity. Bury then in eternal oblivion every fentiment of hatred, and tafte the delicious pleafure of conferring benefits on your oppreffors. Reprefs even too marked expreffions of your joy, which, in caufing them to reflect on their own injuftice towards you, will make their remorfe ftill more pungent.

Strictly obedient to the laws, teach your children to refpect them. By a careful education, inftruct them in all the duties of morality; fo fhall you prepare for the fucceeding generation virtuous citizens, honourable men, enlightened patriots, and defenders of their country!

How will their hearts be affected when, conducting them to your fhores, you direct their looks towards France, telling them, " be-
" yond thofe feas is your parent country; it is from thence we have
" received

" received juftice, protection, happinefs, and liberty. There dwell our
" fellow citizens, our brethren, and our friends: to them we have
" fworn an eternal friendfhip. Heirs of our fentiments, and of our
" affections, may your hearts and your lips repeat our oaths! Live to
" love them; and, if neceffary, die to defend them!"

" Signed,

GREGOIRE.

Paris, 8th June, 1791.

CHAP.

CHAP. VIII.

Reception and Proceedings of the Civil Commiſſioners, and their Re-
turn to France—National Decree of the 4th of April 1792—
Appointment of a new Governor (Monſ. Deſparbes) and three
other Commiſſioners (Santhonax, Polverel, and Ailhaud)—Their
Embarkation and Arrival, with a ſelect Body of Troops—Their
violent Proceedings—Appointment, by the Executive Council,
of M. Galbaud as Chief Governor, in the Room of Deſparbes—
His Arrival, and Diſputes with the Commiſſioners—Both Par-
ties proceed to Hoſtilities—The revolted Negroes called in to the
Aſſiſtance of the Commiſſioners—A general Maſſacre of the
White Inhabitants, and Conflagration of the Town of Cape
François.

CHAP.
VIII.

January
1792.

THE civil commiſſioners who were to reſtore peace and
ſubordination in St. Domingo, and whoſe arrival there
was noticed in the laſt Chapter, were named Mirbeck, Roome,
and St. Leger. Mirbeck and Roome had formerly been known
as advocates in the parliaments of Paris; and St. Leger, who
was a native of Ireland, had practiſed many years in France as
a ſurgeon. Although the confuſion of the times had elevated
theſe men to power, not one of them was diſtinguiſhed for extraordinary abilities, and their rank in life was not ſuch as to
command any great degree of conſideration from the planters.

† They

They were received however, from refpect to their appointment, with politenefs and fubmiffion, both by the governor and the inhabitants. Military honours were fhewn them, and they were led in publick proceffion to the cathedral, where the bleffing of the Almighty was devoutly implored for fuccefs to their miffion.

THEIR firft proceeding, after announcing the new conftitution and form of government for the mother country, as confirmed by the king, was to publifh the decree of the 24th of September 1791, by which the fatal decree of the 15th of May was annulled. So far all was well: but a few days afterwards they took upon them to proclaim a general amnefty and pardon to fuch people, of all defcriptions, as fhould lay down their arms, and come in, within a certain prefcribed time, and take the oaths required by the new conftitution. This meafure loft them the confidence of all the white inhabitants: a general amnefty to the men of colour and revolted flaves, was confidered as a juftification of the moft horrible enormities, and as holding out a dangerous example to fuch of the negroes as preferved their fidelity; and it loft its effect on the mulattoes, by being accompanied with a repeal of their favourite decree. With what contempt and indignity it was received by the latter, the following circumftance will demonftrate. At *Petit Goave*, the mulattoes were mafters, and held in clofe confinement thirty-four white perfons whom they referved for vengeance. On the publication of this amnefty, they led them to execution: but inftead of putting them to immediate death, they caufed each of them to be broken alive; and in the midft of their tor-

tures,

tures, read to them, in a ftrain of diabolical mockery, the proclamation aloud; affecting to confider it as a pardon for the
cruelties they had juft committed.

THE unlimited and indefinite authority which the commiffioners feemed to claim, alarmed the colonial affembly, who
defired to be informed of the nature and extent of their powers.
To this requeft no fatisfactory anfwer being given, the commiffioners loft ground in the publick opinion daily; and their perfonal conduct, as individuals, contributed by no means to acquire
them refpect. Mirbeck fpent the greateft part of his time in
the practice of low debauchery, giving indulgence to his
vicious propenfities without reftraint or decency. St. Leger
confidered his appointment as an authority to exact money,
in which he was little fcrupulous, and laid the few mulatto
people who remained faithful, under a moft unmerciful contribution. Roome alone conducted himfelf without reproach: he
was a well-meaning inoffenfive man, and attempted, though
without effect, to act the part of mediator between the different
factions which defolated the country. This praife at leaft was
given him—*that if he did no good, he did no harm.*

AFTER a fhort ftay at Cape François, the commiffioners
vifited other parts of the colony; but finding themfelves every
where very lightly regarded, and having no troops to fupport
their authority, they returned feparately to France in the
months of March and April.

TROOPS

Troops however, as I have obferved, had arrived from France to the number in the whole of about four thoufand; but, in the fpirit of the times, they manifefted very little obedience either to the civil commiffioners, or to the governor of the colony; yet they ferved as a check to the revolters, who would otherwife, in all probability, before this time, have become mafters both of Cape François and Port au Prince. In the Northern province, the rebel negroes indeed were fuppofed to be confiderably reduced by difeafe and famine. Having deftroyed all the provifion grounds, and devoured the cattle of all kinds on the plain of the Cape, they had now taken poffeffion of the furrounding mountainous diftricts, and were compelled by their chief leader, *Jean François,* a negro of great fagacity, to plant provifions for their future fubfiftence; a meafure which has kept the flames of rebellion alive to the prefent hour.

In the mean time, the ftate of publick affairs in the mother country was tending to a great and ominous change. Ever fince the flight and feizure of their unhappy king, in the month of June 1791, the faction was hourly increafing in numbers which was foon to lay the kingdom in ruins, and bring the monarch himfelf to the fcaffold. The Jacobin party, headed by a bloodthirfty triumvirate *(a)*, were becoming all-powerful; and the fociety of *Amis des Noirs* had once more acquired a fatal afcendency in the legiflative body. On the 29th of February, one of them, named *Garan de Coulon,* after a long and inflammatory harangue againft the planters in general, propofed the form of a

1792.

(a) Danton, Robefpierre and Marat.

P

decree

decree for abrogating that of the 24th of September, declaring a
general amnesty throughout all the French colonies; and enacting, that new colonial assemblies should be formed, which should
transmit their sentiments not only on the subject of the internal
government of the colonies, *but also on the best method of effecting
the abolition of negro slavery* IN TOTO.

FRANTICK as the new legislature *(b)* had shewn itself on
many occasions since its first meeting, a majority could not at
this time be found to vote for so senseless and extravagant a pro-
position; but in about two months afterwards, this assembly
passed the famous decree of the 4th of April 1792, of which it
is necessary the reader should be furnished with a copy at large;
and it is conceived in the words following:

" THE national assembly acknowledges and declares, that the
people of colour and free negroes in the colonies ought to enjoy
an equality of political rights with the whites; in consequence of
which it decrees as follows:

ARTICLE 1st. Immediately after the publication of the present decree, the inhabitants of each of the French colonies in
the Windward and Leeward Islands shall proceed to the re-
election of colonial and parochial assemblies, after the mode pre-
scribed by the decree of the 8th of March 1790, and the instructions of the national assembly of the 28th of the same month.

2d. THE people of colour and free negroes shall be admitted
to vote in all the primary and electoral assemblies, and shall be

(b) The former assembly is generally known by the name of the *Constituent*
Assembly. The new one met the 1st of October 1791, and called itself the First
Legislative Assembly.

eligible

eligible to the legiflature and all places of truft, provided they poffefs the qualifications prefcribed by the 4th article of the aforefaid inftructions.

3d. THREE civil commiffioners fhall be named for the colony of St. Domingo, and four for the iflands of Martinico, Guadaloupe, St. Lucia, and Tobago, to fee this decree enforced.

4th. THE faid commiffioners fhall be authorized to diffolve the prefent colonial affemblies; to take every meafure neceffary for accelerating the convocation of the primary and electoral affemblies, and therein to eftablifh union, order, and peace: as well as to determine provifionally (referving the power of appeal to the national affembly) upon every queftion which may arife concerning the regularity of convocations, the holding of affemblies, the form of elections, and the eligibility of citizens.

5th. THEY are alfo authorized to procure every information poffible, in order to difcover the authors of the troubles in St. Domingo, and the continuance thereof, if they ftill continue; to fecure the perfons of the guilty, and to fend them over to France, there to be put in a ftate of accufation, &c.

6th. THE faid civil commiffioners fhall be directed for this purpofe to tranfmit to the national affembly minutes of their proceedings, and of the evidence they may have collected concerning the perfons accufed as aforefaid.

7th. THE national affembly authorizes the civil commiffioners to call forth the publick force whenever they may think it neceffary, either for their own protection, or for the execution of fuch orders as they may iffue by virtue of the preceding articles.

8th. THE executive power is directed to fend a fufficient force to the colonies, to be compofed chiefly of national guards.

9th. THE

9th. THE colonial affemblies, immediately after their formation, fhall fignify, in the name of each colony refpectively, their
fentiments refpecting that conftitution, thofe laws, and the adminiftration of them, which will beft promote the profperity
and happinefs of the people; conforming themfelves neverthelefs to thofe general principles by which the colonies and mother
country are connected together, and by which their refpective
interefts are beft fecured, agreeably to the decree of the 8th of
March 1790, and inftructions of the 28th of the fame month.

10th. THE colonial affemblies are authorized to fend home
delegates for the purpofes mentioned in the preceding article, in
numbers proportionate to the population of each colony, which
proportion fhall be forthwith determined by the national affembly, according to the report which its colonial committee is
directed to make.

11th. FORMER decrees refpecting the colonies fhall be in
force in every thing not contrary to the prefent decree."

IT may be fuppofed that the men who (rejecting all pretenfions to confiftency, and defpifing the leffons of experience) firft
propofed this decree, and finally prevailed in carrying it through
the legiflative affembly, had duly confidered of the means for
enfuring its execution in the colonies, and were provided with
fit inftruments for that purpofe. The new commiffioners nominated for St. Domingo were Meffrs. Santhonax, Polverel,
and Ailhaud, all of them among the moft violent of the Jacobin
faction; and it was refolved to furnifh them with fuch a force
as (if properly employed) would, it was alledged, not only eftablifh their authority, but put a fpeedy end to all the difturbances

bances which had fo long afflicted and defolated the colony. Eight thoufand men, felected with great circumfpection, from the national guards, with officers whofe principles were well known to their employers, were accordingly ordered to embark forthwith for St. Domingo. M. Blanchelande, the governor-general, was recalled, and a new commiffion of commander in chief given to a Monf. Defparbes.

THUS appointed and provided, the civil commiffioners and the new governor took their departure from France in the month of July, probably in much the fame difpofition of mind towards the colonifts, as was manifefted by the Duke D'Alva and his Spanifh and Italian troops in 1568, towards the inhabitants of the Low Countries. Inflamed like them with a fpirit of avarice, fanaticifm, and revenge, they meditated on nothing but on the benefits to arife from feizure and confifcation; on fchemes of mifchief and projects of vengeance.

THEY landed at Cape François on the 13th of September, and finding M. Blanchelande at great variance with the colonial affembly, the commiffioners took the fhorteft courfe poffible to terminate the difpute, by forthwith diffolving the affembly and fending the unfortunate Blanchelande a ftate prifoner to France, where, as to be accufed was to be condemned, he foon afterwards perifhed by the guillotine (c).

DISMAY and terror now prevailed throughout the colony. Delegates were fent to the civil commiffioners from all quarters, to

CHAP. VIII.

1792.

1792.

(c) 7th April, 1793.

demand

demand an expofure and explanation of their views and intentions. Sufpicions were already gone forth concerning the project, which the commiffioners afterwards avowed, of declaring a general emancipation of the negro flaves; and all parties, as well among the republicans as the royalifts, concurred on this occafion in re-probating the folly and iniquity of the meafure.   So general was the clamour on this account, that if a firm and extenfive coali-tion of interefts among the planters could at this time have been effected, it is probable the commiffioners might have found that all the force they had brought with them would have proved in-ufficient for the purpofes which they meditated.   Diffimulation therefore was thought neceffary for the prefent.   They declared (and confirmed the declaration with the folemnity of an oath) that they had no wifh or intention to make any change in the fyftem of colonial government concerning the flaves; avowing the fulleft conviction that the emancipation of thofe people, under exifting circumftances, was impracticable.—Their views, they faid, extended no farther than to fee the decree of the 4th of April, in favour of the free people of colour, properly enforced; to reduce the flaves in rebellion to obedience, and to fettle the future government and tranquillity of the colony on a folid and permanent foundation.

THESE, and fimilar, declarations filenced, though they did not fatisfy, the white inhabitants; who foon perceived, with unavailing indignation, that the commiffioners held fecret com-munications with the chiefs of the mulattoes in all parts of the colony.   By the co-operation of thofe people, the commiffion-ers foon found their ftrength fufficient to avow themfelves openly

the

the patrons and protectors of the whole body of the free negroes and mulattoes: and they now made no scruple of seiz-
ing the persons and effects of all such of the whites as opposed
their projects, sending great numbers of them in a state of arrest
to Europe, to answer before the national assembly to the
accusations which they pretended to transmit against them.
Among the persons thus imprisoned and transported to France,
were comprehended the colonel, lieutenant-colonel, and many
other officers of the Cape regiment.

THE white inhabitants now called aloud for the election of a
new colonial assembly, and hoped that the necessity of levying
taxes would induce the commissioners to issue orders for that
purpose; but instead of complying with the publick request,
they substituted what was called *une commission intermediaire*, by
nominating twelve persons, six of whom had been members of
the last assembly, to act as a sort of legislative council: the
other six were mulattoes. To this motley board, the commissioners delegated authority to raise money from the inhabitants;
reserving to themselves, however, the right of appropriating and
expending it, as they alone should think proper.

IN the meanwhile the new governor (Desparbes) began to
manifest some signs of dissatisfaction and impatience. He complained that he was considered as a mere cypher in the government, or rather as an instrument in the commissioners' hands.
His complaints were answered by the arrest of his person, and
he soon afterwards followed his predecessor, M. Blanchelande,
state prisoner to France.

FOUR

FOUR members out of the fix whites that compofed a moiety of the *commiffion intermediaire*, met with fimilar treatment. They ventured to offer their opinion on a meafure of finance, in oppofition to that of M. Santhonax. The commiffioners commended their franknefs, and M. Santhonax invited them to a fupper. The invitation was accepted; but at the hour appointed, they found themfelves furrounded by a detachment of the military, which conveyed them to very forry entertainment in the hold of a fhip, and there left them as ftate prifoners *(d)*.

THE commiffioners, in the next place, fell out among themfelves; and Santhonax and Polverel determined to get quit of their affociate Ailhaud. Prudently judging, however, that the publick degradation of one of their own body would reflect fome degree of ignominy on them all, they perfuaded him to be content with a proportion of the common plunder, and filently quit the country. Ailhaud fubmitted with a good grace to what he could not avoid.

BY thefe, and other means, above all by the practice of beftowing largeffes on the troops, and the acquifition of a defperate band of auxiliaries, compofed of fome of the revolted flaves, and vagabonds of all colours and defcriptions, moftly collected from the jails, Santhonax and Polverel, in the beginning of the year

(d) To one of thefe gentlemen I am indebted for more valuable and extenfive information than I have been able to collect through any other channel. In his voyage to Europe, the fhip in which he was confined was (fortunately for him) captured by an Englifh frigate, which brought him to England, where I had the happinefs to render him fome acceptable fervice.

1793,

1793, found themfelves abfolute mafters of the colony. The lives and properties of all the white inhabitants lay at their mercy, and the dreadful fcenes which were at that time paffing in the mother country, enabled thefe men to profecute their purpofes, and gratify their vindictive and avaricious paffions, without notice or controul from any fuperior.

But the tragedy which was acting in France, was no fooner brought to its cataftrophe, by the foul murder of their amiable and unoffending fovereign, and war declared againft Great Britain and Holland, than the perfons who compofed what was called the executive council, thought it neceffary to pay fome little attention to the fafety of St. Domingo. Not having however leifure or inclination to enter into a full inveftigation of the complaints received from thence, they declined to revoke the powers exercifed by the civil commiffioners, and contented themfelves with appointing a new governor, in the room of M. Defparbes. Their choice fell on a Monf. Galbaud, an officer of artillery, and a man of fair character, whom they directed to embark for his new government without delay, in one of the national frigates, and put the colony into the beft ftate of defence againft a foreign enemy.

Galbaud, with his fuite of attendants, landed at Cape François on the 7th of May, to the great joy of the white inhabitants. At that period, the civil commiffioners, with moft of their troops, were in the Weftern province, endeavouring to quell an infurrection there which their tyranny had created; fo that Galbaud was received with acclamations and fubmiffion by the municipality of the town of the Cape; to whofe place of meet-

1793.

Q

ing

ing he repaired with his attendants, took the neceffary oaths, and entered on his government without oppofition. He declared, at the fame time, that he was not dependent on the civil commiffioners, and not bound to execute, at all events, their proclamations.

A very quick interchange of letters took place between the new governor and the commiffioners. He defired them to repair immediately to the Cape, that he might communicate the inftructions he had received from the executive council. They anfwered that he was an entire ftranger to them; that they had feen no decree of the national convention by which they themfelves were fuperfeded, and that being vefted with authority to fufpend or appoint a governor, as they alone might think proper, he could only be confidered as an agent fubordinate to themfelves:—They added, that they were then affembling an army to fupprefs a rebellion in the town and neighbourhood of Port au Prince; but that as foon as the bufinefs was at an end, they would repair to the Cape, and examine into the validity of his pretenfions.

1793.
On the 10th of June the civil commiffioners, having reduced Port au Prince and Jacmel, arrived at the Cape. The ftreets were lined with troops, and they were received by Galbaud with attention and refpect. A very ferious altercation however immediately took place between them, highly difadvantageous to the governor. There exifted, it feems, a decree of the national affembly, enacting that no proprietor of an eftate in the Weft Indies fhould hold the government of a colony wherein his eftate was fituated; and M. Galbaud was poffeffed of a coffee-plantation in St. Do-
                                                            mingo.

mingo. When therefore he was afked why he had not acquainted the executive council with this circumftance, he was utterly difconcerted and had no reply to make.

On the 13th, the commiffioners ordered M. Galbaud to embark forthwith on board the floop of war La Normande, and return to France. At the fame time they fent inftructions to Monf. de la Salle, whom they had left commandant at Fort au Prince, to repair to the Cape and receive from them, in the name of the French republick, the command of the colony.

The feven following days were fpent on both fides in intrigues and preparations for hoftilities. Galbaud's brother, a man of fpirit and enterprize, had collected from among the inhabitants, the Cape militia, and the feamen in the harbour, a ftrong party to fupport the governor's authority. On the 20th, the two brothers landed at the head of one thoufand two hundred failors, and being joined by a confiderable body of volunteers, immediately marched in array towards the government houfe, in which the commiffioners were ftationed. The latter were defended by the people of colour, a body of regulars, and one piece of cannon. The conflict was fierce and bloody. The volunteers manifefted great firmnefs, but the feamen getting poffeffion of a wine cellar, foon became intoxicated and ungovernable; and the column was obliged to retire to the royal arfenal, where they remained the enfuing night unmolefted.

The next morning many fkirmifhes took place in the ftreets, with various fuccefs, in one of which Galbaud's brother was taken prifoner by the commiffioners' troops; and in another, the

feamen

feamen that were fighting on the part of Galbaud made captive Polverel's fon; and now an extraordinary circumftance occurred. The governor fent a flag propofing to exchange the commiffioner's fon for his brother; but Polverel rejected the propofal with indignation; declaring in anfwer, that his fon knew his duty, and was prepared to die in the fervice of the republick.

BUT a fcene now opens, which, if it does not obliterate, exceeds at leaft, all that has hitherto been related of factious anarchy, and favage cruelty, in this unfortunate colony. On the firft approach of Galbaud with fo large a body of feamen, the commiffioners difpatched agents to call in to their affiftance the revolted negroes; offering them an unconditional pardon for paft offences, perfect freedom in future, and the plunder of the city. The rebel generals, *Jean François* and *Biaffou*, rejected their offers; but on the 21ft, about noon (juft after that Galbaud and moft of his adherents, finding their caufe hopelefs, had retired to the fhips) a negro chief called *Macaya*, with upwards of three thoufand of the revolted flaves, entered the town, and began an univerfal and indifcriminate flaughter of men, women, and children. The white inhabitants fled from all quarters to the fea-fide, in hopes of finding fhelter with the governor on board the fhips in the harbour; but a body of the mulattoes cut off their retreat, and a horrid butchery enfued, a defcription of which every heart fufceptible of humanity muft be unable to bear. Suffice it to fay, that the flaughter continued with unremitting fury from the 21ft, to the evening of the 23d; when the favages, having murdered all the white inhabitants that fell in their way, fet fire to the buildings; and more than half the city was confumed by

x   the

the flames. The commiffioners themfelves, either terrified at beholding the lamentable and extenfive mifchief which they had occafioned, or afraid to truft their perfons with their rebel allies, fought protection under cover of a fhip of the line. The pro-clamations which they publifhed from time to time in pallia-tion of their conduct, manifeft a confcioufnefs of guilt which could not be fuppreffed, and form a record of their villanies, for which the day of retribution awaits, but ftill lingers to overtake them *(f)* !

SUCH was the fate of the once flourifhing and beautiful ca-pital of St. Domingo!—a city which, for trade, opulence, and magnificence, was undoubtedly among the firft in the Weft In-dies,—perhaps in the new world: and here I fhall clofe for the prefent, the difgufting detail of confpiracies, rebellions, crimes, cruelties, and conflagrations (a uniformity of horrors !) through which the nature of my work has compelled me to travel ;— rejoicing that I have at laft

> Efcap'd the Stygian pool, tho' long detain'd
> In that obfcure fojourn ;——

MILTON.

And have the pleafing tafk to perform of rendering due homage to the gallant and enterprizing fpirit of my countrymen in their noble—but alas! hitherto unavailing—endeavours to reftore peace, fubordination, and good government on this theatre of anarchy and bloodfhed. Previous to which, however, it will be a relief and

---

(f) When this was written, the author did not know that Santhonax alone fur-vives. Polverel died in 1794, in fome part of St. Domingo. Santhonax has lately appeared before the national affembly, and been pronounced *guiltlefs !*

fatisfaction

satisfaction to the reader to be prefented with a picture or ftate of the colony, as it exifted in the days of its profperity;—its culture, population, and produce;—its growing importance and commercial value. Hitherto, we have contemplated nothing but fcenes of defolation.—We fhall now behold a pleafing contraft in the bleffings of regular government: due fubordination, focial order, extenfive commerce, peaceful induftry, increafing cultivation, fmiling plenty, and general happinefs! The conclufions to be drawn from the contemplation of fcenes fo different in their nature are of importance to all mankind.

———————————

The Account given above of the Deftruction of the City of Cape François, was drawn up with as much Caution as the Cafe feemed to require, from Information tranfmitted to the Author by Perfons in Jamaica and St. Domingo, fome of whom differed in many effential Circumftances from others. He had afterwards an Opportunity of converfing perfonally on the Subject with a Gentleman of St. Domingo, on whofe Veracity and Honour he could place the fulleft Dependance, by whom he was favoured with the following Notes or Memoranda *in Writing, which he thinks beft to lay before his Readers* verbatim.

Notes sur l'Evenement du Cap.

LE General Galbaud avoit mandé au Cap les commiffaires Santhonax et Polverel, de la maniere la plus imperieufe; les commiffaires fe font déterminés a s'y rendre par terre de S. Marc, d'où ils
font

font partis le 8 Juin, accompagnés de 400 mulâtres et 200 blancs, et compris leurs coupe tête les dragons d'Orleans. Ils ont fait leur entrée au Cap d'une maniere afféz audacieufe pour en impofer.

GALBAUD avait deja indifpofé les habitans du Cap par une addreffe, ou proclamation, qui ordonnait une contribution de 450 mille livres, dont la perception a été faite de la façon la plus violente, et qui tenait plus du pillage que d'une contribution.

LE General Galbaud n'avait fait aucune difpofitions pour fe preferver des refolutions et des entreprifes des commiffaires, qui entrerent cependant d'une maniere menacante.

A LA premiere entrevüe des General Galbaud et des commiffaires, en la maifon de la commiffion (le gouvernement) apres les premiers compliments, il y eut explication fur les pouvoirs du general; les commiffaires lui opoferent un decret qui deffendait qu'aucun proprietaire dans la colonie pût y commander ni y avoir d'autorité; et accuferent M. Galbaud d'avoir diffimulé au confeil executif qu'il avait des proprietés.

PENDANT ce demêlé, qui dura près de deux jours, les agents des commiffaires préparaient les efprits a les laiffer faire, et a ne point fe mêler de la difcution, dans laquelle Santhonax prenait cependant une grande preponderance.

GALBAUD, voyant que perfonne ne s'empreffait a le foutenir, et prevoyant fans doute une chute humiliante, demanda aux commiffaires de s'en retourner en France, préférant la retraite, a des pouvoirs conteftés; ce qui lui fut accordé fur le champ, et il s'embarqua le 14.

LE 17 Galbaud réünit tous les matelots de la rade et ceux des vaiffeaux de guerre, et projette de defcendre a la ville du Cap; il fait fon débarquement le 18, et marche au gouvernement, où logeaient les commiffaires, qui inftruits des mouvemens de Galbaud, réünirent les troupes qui leurs etaient devouées, et particulierement les mulâtres, et les embufquerent derriere les murs du gouvernement, dans toutes les ifües,

fur

fur les terrafles, &c. Auffitôt que les matelots furent a portée de piftolet, on fit des décharges, qui en tuerent et blefferent un grand nombre, néan-moins les mulâtres furent ebranlés deux fois; mais le défordre dans les matelots determina le General Galbaud a faire fa retraite a l'arfenal; là, il fit une proclamation pour inviter les bons citoyens a fe réünir a lui, pour chaffer les commiffaires, qui voulaient ufurper le gouvernement. Dès-lors les commiffaires réünirent aux mulâtres tous les négres de la ville, qui avaient deja pris parti dans l'action en affaffinant dans la ville; toutes les troupes qui leurs avaient fervis a leur expedition, et les placerent par pelotons a chaque coin des rües, et dès qu'un blanc voulait fortir de chéz lui, ou paraiffait aux fenetres, il etait fufillé.

PENDANT ce tems, et dès que les commiffaires eurent appris les mouve-mens de Galbaud, ils avaient depeché des exprès aux chefs des brigands, pour les engager a venir a leur fecours, et leurs offraient le pillage de la ville.

LE 19 Galbaud capitule à l'arfenal, et fe rend abord: il y en mis en etat d'arreftation, ainfi que l'Amiral Cambis, et le Contre-Amiral Sercey, qui font dépouillés de leur commandement.

UNE proclamation des commiffaires avait precedamment a cet' évene-ment, mis a contribution 37 negociants, ou riches particuliers, pour une fomme de 675 mille livres, qui parrait avoir été exigée et payée fur l'heure. Le 19, au foir, le 20, le 21, les brigands entrent de toutes parts dans la ville du Cap, ayant a leur tête leurs chefs, et on affure que M. de Graffe s'y eft trouvé auffi. Le pillage, les maffacrês, les flammes deviennent effroyables; les hommes, les femmes, les enfans font affaffinés, maffacrés, et éprouvent toutes les horreurs imaginables. Ils ont eu la barbarie de renfermer et de brûler dans une maifon plus de 300 perfonnes toutes vives.

LES malheureux de tout fexe, de tout âge, qui cherchaient a fe fauver en gagnant des embarcations, ou a la nage, etaient fufillés même dans l'eau.

IL

Il parrait que dans le massacre les négres ont frapés indistinctement tous les partis, blancs, mulâtres, et que les blancs se font deffendus contre tous avec un grand acharnement ; néanmoins il parrait certain, que la population blanche a été entierement détruite, et qu'il n'a pas resté un seul blanc au Cap ; on estime que, s'il s'est sauvé 12 a 1500 personnes abord, c'est plus qu'on n'ose l'esperer.

Le convoi est sortie du Cap le 23 pour l'Amerique, la majeure partie ayant très peu de vivres, très peu d'eau, et plusieurs sans être préparés a ce voyage, sans mats ni voilles, & ceux qui ont recu les malheureux qui se font sauvés abord, n'y auront trouvé aucune subsistance.

La ville incendiée, détruite, ses habitans massacres, on assuré qu'il ne reste que le gouvernement, une partie des casernes, l'arsenal, et les maisons du Petit Carenage ;—l'église et les fontaines detruites.

Les commissaires ont resté spectateurs tranquilles pendant le carnage et le massacre ; dans leur maison on a vu Santhonax serrer et presser dans ses bras les chefs des brigands, les appeller ses sauveurs, et leur témoigner leur reconnaissance.

Le 23 proclamation des commissaires, qui invite et appelle tous les bons citoyens à se réünir autour d'eux, et de laisser partir les scélerats, qui vont aller subir le juste chatiment de leurs crimes, le convoi en parti le jour même, & la ville fumait encore.

R

CHAP.

C H A P.　IX.

Situation, Extent, and general Defcription of St. Domingo—Origin
of the French Colony, and Topographical Defcription of the fe-
veral Provinces into which the French Poffeffions were divided
—Their Population, and Produce—Shipping and Exports—Com-
pared with the Returns of Jamaica.

THE ifland of St. Domingo is fituated in the Atlantick
Ocean, about three thoufand five hundred miles from
the land's end of England ; the eaftern point lying in north latitude 18° 20', and in longitude 68° 40' W. from Greenwich.
The ifland extends about one hundred and forty miles in the
broadeft part, from north to fouth, and three hundred and
ninety from eaft to weft. In a country of fuch magnitude, di-
verfified with plains of vaft extent, and mountains of prodigious
height, is probably to be found every fpecies of foil which nature
has affigned to all the tropical parts of the earth. In general, it
is fertile in the higheft degree ; every where well watered, and
producing almoft every variety of vegetable nature, for ufe and
beauty, for food and luxury, which the lavifh hand of a bountiful Providence has beftowed on the richeft portion of the globe.
In that part which conftituted the French territory, the quantity of unproductive land bears no manner of proportion to the
whole;

whole; and the liberality of nature was laudably feconded by the induftry of the inhabitants. Until thofe ravages and devafta-tions which I have had the painful tafk of recording, deformed and deftroyed, with undiftinguifhing barbarity, both the bounties of nature, and the labours of art, the poffeffions of France in this noble ifland were confidered as the garden of the Weft Indies; and for beautiful fcenery, richnefs of foil, falubrity and variety of climate, might juftly be deemed *the Paradife of the New World.*

Of the territories which remained exclufively in poffeffion of the original conquerors, the Spaniards, my information is very imperfect. I fhall hereafter give the beft account I have been able to collect concerning them. On the fouthern coaft, more efpecially in the neighbourhood of the ancient city from which the ifland derives its prefent name, the lands are faid to be among the beft, and without doubt a very large proportion of the re-mainder requires only the hand of the cultivator to become very productive. The interior country contains extenfive favannahs, or plains, many of them occupied only by wild fwine, horfes, and horned cattle; for the Spaniards having exterminated the fimple and unoffending natives, fupplied their place with herds of domeftick animals, which running wild, foon multiplied be-yond computation. Thus does the tyranny of man convert the fruitful habitations of his fellow-creatures into a wildernefs for beafts! In the prefent cafe, however, the crime foon brought down its own punifhment;—a punifhment which almoft re-venged the wrongs of the helplefs Americans;—and who does

R 2

CHAP.
IX.

not wifh that avarice, ambition, and cruelty may be thus always entangled in their own projects?

THE reader is doubtlefs apprized that I here allude to the eftablifhment in St. Domingo of that daring and defperate band of adventurers, the *Bucaniers*;—an affociation conftituted of men of all countries and defcriptions, but of whom it may truly be faid that, if felf-prefervation be a law of nature, the hoftilities which they maintained for upwards of fifty years againft their oppreffors, were more juftifiable and legitimate in their origin, than all the wars which the pride and ambition of kingdoms and nations have occafioned, from the beginning of the world to the prefent hour. As the cruelty of the Spaniards firft compelled thefe men, from a fenfe of common danger, to unite their ftrength, fo the blind policy of ftocking with cattle a country of fuch extent, became their fupport; for the flefh of thofe animals fupplied them with food, and they purchafed arms, ammunition, and clothing with the fkins.

OF the rife of thefe people, and the primary caufe of their combining together to make reprifals on the Spanifh fettlements, a fhort account may be neceffary. I have elfewhere treated the fubject more at large *(a)*.—They confifted originally of a body of French and Englifh planters, whom, in the year 1629, a Spanifh armament had expelled from the ifland of St. Chriftopher, with circumftances of outrageous barbarity. Driven from thence, by a force which they could not refift, as the only alternative of

(a) Hift. of the Britifh Colonies, Book ii. C. 2.

efcaping

efcaping from flaughter or flavery, they fled in open boats with their families, and poffeffed themfelves of the fmall unoccupied ifland of *Tortuga*, fituated within a few miles of the northern coaft of St. Domingo. Here they were joined by a confiderable number of Dutch emigrants from *Santa Cruz*, whom the ava-rice and cruelty of the Spaniards had compelled, in like manner, to roam over the ocean for fhelter, after having witneffed the maffacre of many of their number, even to the women and chil-dren. Companions in adverfity, their misfortunes probably taught thefe poor exiles mutual forbearance; for, although they were compofed of three different nations, they appear to have lived for fome years in perfect harmony with each other. Their mode of life contributed to produce the fame beneficial effect: finding a country of immeafurable extent in their neighbourhood abounding in cattle, their time was chiefly occupied in hunting; an employment which left no leifure for diffenfion, and afforded them both exercife and food. The plains of St. Domingo were confidered, however, merely as their hunting grounds: Tortuga continued their home, and place of retreat. Here their women and young people cultivated fmall plantations of tobacco (an herb, of which, in hot and moift climates, the practice of inhaling the fmoke, feems to be pointed out by nature); and as the coaft was rugged, and of difficult approach, they fondly hoped that their obfcurity would protect them from further perfecution.

IF the government of Spain had been actuated at this time by motives of wifdom, it would indeed have left thefe poor people to range over the wildernefs unmolefted. It ought to have known, that the occupation of hunting diverted them from projects of vengeance, and deeds of greater enterprize; but tyranny is without forefight, and the reftlefs and remorfelefs bigotry of the Spanifh nation allowed the fugitives no refpite. An armament was collected, and preparations made to effect their utter extermination; the commanders of which, taking occafion when the ablest of the men had reforted to the larger ifland in their ufual purfuit, landed a body of foldiers at Tortuga, and making captives of the women and children, the old and infirm, caufed them all to be maffacred without mercy.

It does not appear that the miferable people who were thus purfued to deftruction, like beafts of prey, had hitherto been guilty of any outrages or depredations on the fhips or fubjects of Spain, which called for fuch exemplary vengeance. Neither was it imputed to them as a crime that they had poffeffed themfelves of Tortuga, or that they roamed about the defarts of St. Domingo in purfuit of cattle which had no owners. Their guilt confifted in the circumftance of being born out of the Spanifh territories, and prefuming neverthelefs to venture into any part of the New World; for the arrogant prefumption and extravagant felfifhnefs of this bigotted nation, led them to appropriate all the countries of America to themfelves. They claimed even the fole and exclufive right of failing on any fuch part of the main ocean as, in their judgment, conftituted a portion of the newly-difcovered hemifphere; and ftrict orders were iffued to all their commanders, by fea and land, to feize on the fhips and fubjects of all other people that fhould be found within the boundaries which they had prefcribed, and to punifh the intruders with

flavery

flavery or death.—We have feen in what manner thofe orders were executed.

IT is evident, therefore, that no alternative remained to the oc-cupiers of Tortuga, but to turn on their purfuers, and wage offenfive war on thofe who would allow of no peace with them. If the juftice of their caufe be ftill a queftion, let the records of time be confulted; let an appeal be made to that rule of con-duct, which (to ufe an eloquent expreffion of Lord Coke) *is written by the finger of God on the heart of man*; and let hiftory and reafon determine, whether any inftance of hoftility, in the annals of mankind, can be defended on better grounds. To fuch men, in fuch a caufe, no dangers were too formidable, no ob-ftacles too great. Inured by their mode of life to the viciffi-tudes of the climate, united among themfelves, and animated by all the motives and paffions which can inflame the human mind to great exertion, they became the moft formidable antagonifts which the Spaniards had ever encountered, and difplayed fuch deeds of valour and fuccefsful enterprize, as (all circumftances confidered) have never been equalled before or fince.

FROM a party of thefe adventurers (chiefly natives of Nor-mandy) the French colony in St. Domingo derived its origin. By what means they were induced to feparate from their affociates in danger, to relinquifh the gratification of revenge and avarice, and exchange the tumults of war for the temperate occupations of hufbandry, it is neither within my province nor ability to ex-plain. Many of them, without doubt, were men who had been driven from Europe by indigent circumftances and defperate for-tunes;

tunes; fome by the cruelty of creditors; and others, perhaps, by the confcioufnefs of their crimes. Captivated by the renown, and allured by the wealth of the Bucaniers, they joined in their expeditions againft the Spaniards from no better motives than thofe of plunder and rapine; and to fuch men muft be imputed thofe outrages and exceffes which have ftamped the proceedings of the whole affociation with infamy *(b)*. But there is a time

(b) I conceive, however, that thefe have been wonderfully magnified and exaggerated. The narrative called *The Hiftory of the Bucaniers*, publifhed towards the latter end of the laft century, which has been quoted by writers of all defcriptions ever fince, as of unqueftionable authority, was originally written in Dutch, by one John Efquemeling, who confeffes that he had been one of the Bucaniers, and was expelled from their fociety. The reports of fuch a writer ought to have been received with great caution; but there is a ftill ftronger circumftance to excite fufpicion; and it is this: The Englifh work is not taken from the Dutch original, but from *a Spanifh tranflation*; and to fuppofe that a Spaniard would fpeak favourably of the Bucaniers, is the very excefs of human credulity. Not having the original book to refer to, I cannot pronounce with certainty; but I am of opinion, that many of the tragical ftories concerning the torture of the Spanifh prifoners, and the violation of the women, are interpolations of the Spanifh tranflator. I form this conclufion from the malignity difplayed towards the character of the famous Sir Henry Morgan. If we may believe the account given of this gallant commander, he was the moft inhuman monfter that ever exifted. Yet this very man (who by the way acted under a regular commiffion and letters of reprizal from government) after he had quitted the fea, was recommended by the earl of Carlifle to be his fucceffor in the government of Jamaica, and was accordingly appointed lieutenant-governor in the earl's abfence. He afterwards received the honour of knighthood from King Charles II. and paffed the remainder of his life on his plantation in Jamaica. By the kindnefs of a friend in that ifland, I have had an opportunity of perufing fome of Sir Henry Morgan's original private letters; and this I will fay, that they manifeft fuch a fpirit of humanity, juftice, liberality, and piety, as prove that he has either been grofsly traduced, or that he was the greateft hypocrite living; —a character ill-fuited to the frank and fearlefs temper of the man.

for

for all things ; and the change of life in thefe men confirms CHAP.
the obfervation of an elegant writer, " that as there is no foil IX.
" which will not fhew itfelf grateful to culture, fo there is no
" difpofition, no character in mankind, which may not, by
" dexterous management, be turned to the publick advan-
" tage (c)." It was a happy circumftance in the infancy of their
eftablifhment, that while they were too obfcure for the notice of
the government, they had no check given to their induftry by
the chill influence of poverty.   To a fortunate exemption from
the hand of power, and the facility with which they were fupplied with the common neceffaries of life, they were indebted
for their prefervation and profperity.   A mediocrity of condition, and equal freedom, excited the fpirit of emulation among
them ; but oppreffion would have produced difcouragement,
and penury is the parent of floth.

Of the progreffive purfuits of thefe people in extending the
footing which they had obtained, until the French government
accepted their fubmiffion, acknowledged them as faithful fubjects, and availed itfelf of their labours,—and the final ceffion
to France of the weftern part of St. Domingo, by the peace of
Ryfwick, the reader will find an ample account in the hiftory of
this ifland by Pere Charlevoix.   It is therefore unneceffary to
detail what an author fo well informed in the ancient tranfactions of the colony, has written.   All that the Englifh reader will
expect from me, is an account of the political and topographical
ftate of the colony ; its population, produce, and exports at the

(c) European Settlements, Vol. II. p. 109.

S   time

time my History commences; and these particulars will be found in what remains of the present Chapter.

THE possessions of the French in St. Domingo, as I have elsewhere observed, were divided into three great departments, called the Northern, the Western, and the Southern provinces. The Northern province comprehended a line of sea-coast extending about forty leagues, from the river Massacre, to Cape St. Nicholas, and contained (including Tortuga) twenty-five parishes. Its population, in the beginning of 1790, consisted of 11,996 white inhabitants of all ages, and 164,656 negro slaves. The number of sugar plantations was 288, of which 258 made what is called *clayed*, or soft white sugar, and 30 *muscovado*, or new sugar. It reckoned 2,009 plantations of coffee, 66 of cotton, 443 of indigo, and 215 smaller establishments, such as provision-polinks, cacao-groves, tan-pits, potteries, brick-kilns, &c.

OF the towns and harbours in the Northern province, the chief were those of Cape Francois, Fort Dauphin, Port Paix, and Cape St. Nicholas. I shall treat only of the first and the last.

THE town of Cape Francois (which in time of war was the seat of the French government) would have ranked among the cities of the second class, in any part of Europe, for beauty and regularity. It consisted of between eight and nine hundred houses of stone and brick, many of them handsome and commodious, besides shops and warehouses; and it contained two magnificent squares, ornamented each with

a publick

a publick fountain. The chief publick buildings were the church; the Jefuits' college (converted after the revolution into a government-houfe, and place of meeting for the colonial and provincial aſſemblies); a ſuperb barrack for troops; a royal arſenal; a priſon; a play-houſe; and two hoſpitals. The number of free inhabitants of all colours, was eſtimated at eight thouſand, excluſive of the king's troops and ſea-faring people. The domeſtick ſlaves were ſaid to be about twelve thouſand. The ſituation of the town, however, was not to be commended. It was built at the foot of a very high mountain, called *Le Haut du Cap*, which abounds indeed with ſprings of excellent water, and furniſhed a great ſupply of garden vege-tables, but it ſerved as a ſcreen from the land wind, and rever-berated the rays of the ſun. The town aroſe to opulence chiefly from the commodiouſneſs of its harbour, and the ex-treme fertility of the plain adjoining it to the eaſt, a diſtrict fifty miles in length, and twelve in breadth, appropriated ſolely to the cultivation of ſugar (the plantations of which were di-vided from each other only by hedges of citrons and limes) and yielding greater returns than perhaps any other ſpot of the ſame extent in the habitable globe.

THE town of Cape St. Nicholas conſiſts of about 250 houſes, which are chiefly built of American wood. It is ſituated at the foot of a high bluff, called the *Mole*; but having been a free port, it was a place of conſiderable trade, and particularly re-ſorted to by the ſhips of America. It is chiefly known, how-ever, for the ſafety and extent of its harbour, which is juſtly called the key of the Windward paſſage; and the fortifications

towards

CHAP.
IX.

towards the fea are reckoned among the ftrongeft in the Weft Indies. On the fide of the land they are overlooked by the furrounding heights, and hence it is concluded, that although it might be difficult to take the place by an invading armament, it would be ftill more difficult to retain it afterwards, unlefs pof-feffion was obtained alfo of the interior country.

THE Weftern province began at Cape St. Nicholas, and extending along the line of coaft which forms the bight of Leogane, for upwards of one hundred leagues, terminated at Cape Tibu-ron. It contained fourteen parifhes, and five chief towns, namely, Port au Prince, St. Marc, Leogane, Petit Goave, and Jeremie; befides villages, of which thofe of Gonaives, Arcahaye, and Croix des Bouquets, are not inconfiderable. The only good harbours in this great extent of coaft are thofe of Port au Prince and Gonaives. All the other fhipping-places are open roads, fometimes much expofed.

PORT AU PRINCE (except in time of war, when the Governor General was directed to remove to Cape François) was confidered as the metropolis of the colony. It was deftroyed by a dreadful earthquake on the 3d of June 1770, and had never been completely rebuilt. In 1790 it confifted of about 600 houfes, and contained 2,754 white inhabitants (d). The fitu-ation is low and marfhy, and the climate, in confequence, very unhealthy. It is furrounded moreover by hills, which command

(d) The free people of colour were eftimated at 4,000, and the enflaved negroes at about 8,000: but being comprehended in the general return for the whole diftrict, they are no where afcertained with precifion.

both

both the town and the harbour; but both the hills and the vallies are abundantly fertile. To the east is situated the noble plain of Cul de Sac, extending from thirty to forty miles in length by nine in breadth, and it contained one hundred and fifty sugar-plantations, most of which were capable of being watered in times of drought, by canals admirably contrived and disposed for that purpose. The circumjacent mountains were at the same time clothed with plantations of coffee, which extended quite to the Spanish settlements.

THE population and state of agriculture in the Western province were as follow: white inhabitants of all ages 12,798; negroes in a state of slavery 192,961; plantations of clayed sugar 135, of muscovado 222. Plantations of coffee 894, of cotton 489, of indigo 1952, besides 343 smaller settlements.

THE Southern province, extending upwards of sixty leagues from Cape Tiburon, along the southern coast of the island to L'Ance a Pitre, contained ten parishes, and two chief towns, Aux Cayes and Jacmel; two places of which I shall hereafter have occasion to speak. It possesses no safe harbours, and its roads are dangerous. The shipping that load at Aux Cayes take refuge during the hurricane season at La Baye des Flamands.

THE population in this department was composed of 6,037 whites, and 76,812 negro slaves. Its establishments consisted of 38 plantations of white sugar, and 110 of muscovado; 214 coffee-plantations, 234 of cotton, 765 of indigo, and 119 smaller settlements.

THE

THE quantity of land in cultivation throughout all the parishes was 763,923 carreaux *(e)*, equal to 2,289,480 English acres, of which about two-thirds were situated in the mountains; and that the reader may have a state of the agriculture at one view, I shall subjoin a summary of the preceding accounts, from whence it will appear that the French colony contained, the beginning of 1790,

431 plantations of clayed sugar,
362 - - - of muscovado.

Total - 793 plantations of sugar,

3,117 - - - of coffee,
789 - - - of cotton,
3,160 - - - of indigo,
54 - - - of cacao, or chocolate,
623 smaller settlements, chiefly for raising grain, yams, and other vegetable food.

Making - 8,536 establishments of all kinds throughout the colony.

THE population in 1790, on a like summary, appears to have been 30,831 whites of both sexes and all ages (exclusive

(e) The carreau of land in St. Domingo is 100 yards square, of 3½ French feet each; the superficies 122,500 feet. The Paris foot is divided into twelve inches, and each inch into twelve lines; wherefore, if we suppose each line to be divided into 310 parts, the Paris foot will be 1440 parts, the London 1350. These proportions were settled by the Royal Academy of Sciences. The Jamaica acre contains 43,560 English feet superficial measure; which being multiplied by 1,350, and the total divided by 1,440, gives 40,837½, or one-third part of the French carreau.

of

of European troops and fea-faring people), and 434,429 negro CHAP.
flaves. In this account, however, the domeftick flaves, and IX.
negro mechanicks employed in the feveral towns, are not comprehended. They amounted to about 46,000, which made
the number of negro flaves throughout the colony 480,000.

Of the free people of colour, no very accurate account was
obtained. Monf. Marbois, the intendant, reported them in
1787 at about 20,000. In 1790, the general opinion fixed
them at 24,000.

The exterior appearance of the colony, as I have obferved in
another place, every where demonftrated great and increafing
profperity. Cultivation was making rapid advances over the
country. The towns abounded in warehoufes, which were
filled with the richeft commodities and productions of Europe,
and the harbours were crouded with fhipping. There were
freighted, in 1787, 470 fhips, containing 112,253 tons, and na-
vigated by 11,220 feamen. Many of them were veffels of very
large burthen; and the following is an accurate account, from
the intendant's reports, of the general exports, on an average of
the years 1787, 1788, and 1789; viz.

AVERAGE EXPORTS FROM THE FRENCH PART OF
ST. DOMINGO, BEFORE THE REVOLUTION.

				Livres.
Clayed fugar	-	-	lbs. 58,642,214 —	41,049,549
Mufcovado	-	-	lbs. 86,549,829 —	34,619,931
Coffee	-	-	lbs. 71,663,187 —	71,663,187
Cotton	-	-	lbs. 6,698,858 —	12,397,716
Indigo	-	-	Hhds. 951,607 —	8,564,463
Molaffes	-	-	Hhds. 23,061 —	2,767,320
An inferior fort of rum, called taffia	-	-	Hhds. 2,600 —	312,000
Raw hides	-	-	N° 6,500 —	5,2000
Tanned ditto	-	-	N° 7,900 —	118,500

The total value at the ports of fhipping, in
livres of St. Domingo, was   -   -   - 171,544,666

being equal to £. 4,765,129 fterling money of Great Britain.

IF this ftatement be compared by the rule of proportion with
the exports from Jamaica, the refult will be confiderably in favour of St. Domingo, *i. e.* it will be found that the planters of
Jamaica receive fmaller returns from the labours of their negroes,
in proportion to their numbers, than the planters of St. Domingo
have received from theirs. For this difference various caufes have
been affigned, and advantages allowed, and qualities afcribed to the
French planters, which I venture to pronounce, on full enquiry,
had no exiftence. The true caufe arofe, undoubtedly, from the
fuperior fertility of the foil; and, above all, from the prodigious
benefit which refulted to the French planters from the fyftem

§   of

of watering their sugar-lands in dry weather. This is an advantage which nature has denied to the lands in Jamaica, except in a very few places; but has freely bestowed on many parts of St. Domingo; and the planters there availed themselves of it with the happiest success *(f)*.

(f) Having made diligent enquiry into the average produce of the French sugar-lands while on the spot, I venture to give the following estimate, as nearly founded in truth as the subject will admit.

In the North, the districts of Ouanaminthe, Maribaroux, and Quartier Dauphin, generally yielded from six to seven thousand pounds weight of muscovado sugar for each carreau in canes; the average is   -   -   6,500

Jaquizi - - - - - -	7,000
Limonade - - - - - -	9,000
Quartier Morin - - - - -	6,000
Plaine du Nord, Limbé, Petite Anse - -	5,000
	33,500

The average of the whole is 6,700 lbs. each carreau.—This part of St. Domingo was not watered.

In the West—St. Marc, L'Artibonite, and Gonaives, each carreau yielded -   -   -   -   -   -   - 8,500

Vazes, Arcahaye, Boucassin - - - -	10,000
Cul de Sac - - - - - -	9,000
Leogane - - - - - -	6,500
	34,000

The average is 8,500 lbs. the carreau.—All these districts were watered.

In the South—the districts of Grand-Goave, Aux-Cayes, Plaine du Fond, L'Islet, &c. which likewise were watered, yielded -   -   - 7,500

The general average, on the whole, is 7,500 lbs. from each carreau in canes; to which add 8¼ per cent. for the difference between the English and French weights, the total is 8,137 lbs. for every three acres English, or 2,712 lbs. per acre; being nearly two-thirds more than the general yielding of all the land in canes throughout Jamaica.

T

CHAP.
IX.

And fuch, in the days of its profperity, was the French colony in the ifland of St. Domingo. I have now prefented to my readers both fides of the medal. To GREAT BRITAIN, above all other nations of the earth, the facts which I have related may furnifh an important leffon; and it is fuch a one as requires no comment!

CHAP.

CHAP. X.

Emigrations—Overtures to the British Government accepted—Situation and Strength of the Republican Party in St. Domingo, and Difposition of the Inhabitants—Negro Slavery abolifhed by the French Commiffioners—Armament allotted for the Invafion of the Country—Surrender of Jeremie and the Mole at Cape St. Nicholas—Unfuccefsful Attempt on Cape Tiburon—Further Proceedings of the Britifh Army until the Arrival of General Whyte—Capture of Port au Prince.

THE deftruction of the beautiful city of Cape Francois, and the maffacre of moft of the white inhabitants, were the fad events which terminated our hiftorical detail at the clofe of the Eighth Chapter. It was obferved, however, that M. Galbaud and his partizans, among whom were comprehended many refpectable families, had fortunately embarked on the fhips in the harbour, juft before the revolted negroes entered the town. Happy to fly from a country devoted to ruin, they directed their courfe to the united ftates of North America; and to the honour of the human character (debafed as we have beheld it in other fituations) they found there, what great numbers of their unhappy fellow-citizens had found before them, a refuge from the reach of perfecution, and an afylum from the preffure of poverty.

T 2 EMIGRATIONS

EMIGRATIONS from all parts of St. Domingo had indeed prevailed to a very great extent, ever since the revolt of the negroes in the Northern province. Many of the planters had removed with their families to the neighbouring islands: some of them had taken refuge in Jamaica; and it was supposed that not less than ten thousand had transported themselves, at various times, to different parts of the continent of America. Most of these were persons of peaceable tempers, who sought only to procure the mere necessaries of life in safety and quiet. The principal among the planters, having other objects in view, had repaired to Great Britain. It is a circumstance within my own knowledge, that so early as the latter end of 1791 (long before the commencement of hostilities between France and England) many of them had made application to the King's ministers, requesting that an armament might be sent to take possession of the country for the king of Great Britain, and receive the allegiance of the inhabitants. They asserted (I am afraid with much greater confidence than truth) that all classes of the people wished to place themselves under the English dominion, and that, on the first appearance of a British squadron, the colony would surrender without a struggle. To these representations no attention was at that time given; but at length, after the national assembly had thought proper to declare war against Great Britain, the English ministry began to listen, with some degree of complacency, to the overtures which were again made to them, to the same effect, by the planters of St. Domingo. In the summer of 1793, a M. Charmilly (one of those planters) was furnished with dispatches from the secretary of state to General Williamson, the lieutenant-governor and commander in

chief

chief of Jamaica, fignifying the king's pleafure (with allowance of great latitude however to the governor's difcretion) that he fhould accept terms of capitulation from the inhabitants of fuch parts of St. Domingo as folicited the protection of the Britifh government; and for that purpofe the governor was authorized to detach, from the troops under his command in Jamaica, fuch a force as fhould be thought fufficient to take and retain poffeffion of all the places that might be furrendered, until reinforcements fhould arrive from England. M. Charmilly, having thus delivered the orders and inftructions with which he was entrufted, fent an agent without delay to *Jeremie (a)*, a fmall port and town in the diftrict of *Grand Ance*, to which he belonged, to prepare the loyal inhabitants for a vifit from their new allies and protectors the Englifh.

But, before we proceed to detail the operations which followed this determination of the Britifh cabinet, it feems neceffary, as well for the fatisfaction of the reader, as in juftice to the gallantry and good conduct of the officers and men who were afterwards fent to St. Domingo, that fome account fhould be given of the difficulties which were to arife, and the force that was to be encountered in this attempt to annex fo great and valuable a colony to the Britifh dominion. I am well apprized that I am here treading on tender ground; but if it fhall appear, as unhappily it will, that the perfons at whofe inftance and entreaty the project was adopted, either meant to deceive, or were themfelves grofsly deceived, in the reprefentations which they made to the Englifh government on this occafion, it is my province and my

(a) It is fituated juft within the Bight of-*Leogane*.

duty

duty to place the failure which has enſued to its proper account. The hiſtorian who, in ſuch caſes, from fear, favour, or affection, ſuppreſſes the communication of facts, is hardly leſs culpable than the factious or venal writer, who ſacrifices the intereſts of truth, and the dignity of hiſtory, to the prejudices of party.

THE republican commiſſioners, as the reader has been informed, had brought with them from France ſix thouſand choſen troops; which, added to the national force already in the colony, and the militia of the country, conſtituted a body of fourteen or fifteen thouſand effective whites; to whom were joined the greateſt part of the free negroes and mulattoes, beſides a motley but deſperate band of all complexions and deſcriptions, chiefly ſlaves which had deſerted from their owners, and negroes collected from the jails. All theſe, amounting in the whole to about twenty-five thouſand effectives, were brought into ſome degree of order and diſcipline; were well armed, and, what is of infinite importance, were, in a conſiderable degree, inured to the climate. Being neceſſarily diſperſed, however, in detachments throughout the different provinces, they were become on that account leſs formidable to an invading enemy. Aware of this circumſtance, the commiſſioners, on the firſt intimation of an attack from the Engliſh, reſorted to the moſt deſperate expedient to ſtrengthen their party, that imagination can conceive. They declared by proclamation all manner of ſlavery aboliſhed, and pronounced the negro ſlaves to be from thenceforward a free people, on condition of reſorting to their ſtandard. From this moment it might have been foreſeen that the colony was loſt to Europe; for though but few of the negroes, in proportion to the whole, joined the commiſſioners, many thouſands chooſing

3

to

to continue flaves as they were, and participate in the fortunes of CHAP. their mafters, yet vaft numbers in all parts of the colony (appre- X. henfive probably that this offer of liberty was too great a favour to be permanent) availed themfelves of it to fecure a retreat to the mountains, and poffefs themfelves of the natural faftneffes which the interior country affords. Succeffive bodies have fince joined them, and it is believed that upwards of 100,000 have eftablifhed themfelves, in thofe receffes, into a fort of favage republick, like that of the black Charaibes of St. Vincent, where they fubfift on the fpontaneous fruits of the earth, and the wild cattle which they procure by hunting; prudently declining offen- five war, and trufting their fafety to the rocky fortreffes which nature has raifed around them, and from which, in my opinion, it will be no eafy undertaking to diflodge them *(b)*.

Of the revolted negroes in the Northern province, many had perifhed of difeafe and famine; but a defperate band, amounting as it was fuppofed to upwards of 40,000, inured to war, and practifed in devaftation and murder, ftill continued in arms. Thefe

(b) The proclamation alluded to, was iffued at Port au Prince the latter end of Auguft, and was figned by Polverel alone, Santhonax being at that time in the Northern province. It begins by declaring, that neither himfelf nor Santhonax are recalled or difgraced. That, in order to encourage the negro flaves to affift in op- pofing the meditated invafion of the Englifh, all manner of flavery is abolifhed; and the negroes are thenceforward to confider themfelves as free citizens. It then expatiates upon the neceffity of labour, and tells the negroes that they muft engage to work as ufual, from year to year; but that they are at liberty to make choice of their refpective mafters. That one third of the crop fhall be appropriated annually to the purchafe of clothing and provifions for their maintenance; and that in the month

Thefe were ready to pour down, as occafion might offer, on all nations alike; and, inftead of joining the Englifh on their landing, would rejoice to facrifice both the victors and the vanquifhed, the invaders and invaded, in one common deftruction.

Concerning the white proprietors, on whom alone our dependence was placed, a large proportion, as we have feen, perhaps more than one half of the whole, had quitted the country. Of thofe that remained, *fome* there were, undoubtedly, who fincerely wifhed for the reftoration of order, and the bleffings of regular government; but the greateft part were perfons of a different character: they were men who had nothing to lofe, and every thing to gain, by confufion and anarchy: not a few of them had obtained poffeffion of the effects and eftates of abfent proprietors. From people of this ftamp, the moft determined oppofition was neceffarily to be expected; and unfortunately, among thofe of better principle, I am afraid but a very fmall number were cordially attached to the Englifh. The majority feem to have had nothing in view but to obtain by any means the reftoration of their eftates and poffeffions. Many of them, under their ancient government, had belonged to the

month of September in each year they are at liberty to make a new choice, or to confirm that of the preceding year. Such, to the beft of my remembrance (for I fpeak from memory) are the chief provifions of this celebrated proclamation, which I think extended only to the Weftern and Southern provinces; Santhonax being empowered to make what other regulations he might think proper for the Northern province. The whole appears to have been a matchlefs piece of abfurdity; betraying a lamentable degree of ignorance concerning the manners and difpofitions of the negroes, and totally impracticable in itfeif.

lower

lower order of *nobleſſe*, and being tenacious of titles and honours, in proportion as their pretenſions to real diſtinction were
diſputable; they dreaded the introduction of a ſyſtem of laws
and government, which would reduce them to the general level
of the community. Thus, as their motives were ſelfiſh, and
their attachment feeble, their exertions in the common cauſe
were not likely to be very ſtrenuous or efficacious. I do not
find that the number of French in arms, who joined us at
any one period (I mean of white inhabitants) ever exceeded
two thouſand. It were unjuſt, however, not to obſerve, that
among them were ſome diſtinguiſhed individuals, whoſe fidelity was above ſuſpicion, and whoſe ſervices were highly
important. Such were the Baron de Montalembert, the Viſ-
count de Fontagnes, Monſ. Deſources, and perhaps a few
others *(c)*.

FROM this recapitulation it is evident, that the invaſion of
St. Domingo was an enterprize of greater magnitude and diffi-

(*c*) A few men of colour alſo diſtinguiſhed themſelves in the common cauſe;
viz. Monſieur *Le Point*, Lieutenant-Colonel of the St. Marc's legion, who, with
about 300 Mulattoes under his command, kept the pariſh of L'Arcahaye in complete ſubjection for a conſiderable time. 2. *Boucquet*, Major of the *Milice Royale*
of Verettes, a perſon much attached to the Engliſh. 3. *Charles Savory*, who
commanded a very important poſt in the plain of Artibonite, upon the river
D'Eſterre. Great confidence was placed in this man by Colonel Briſbane, and
never was it abuſed. All theſe men were well educated, and nouriſhed deep reſentment againſt the French planters, on account of the indignities which the
claſs of coloured people had received from them. At Cape Tiburon, three or
four hundred blacks were embodied very early, under a black general named Iean
Kina, who ſerved well and faithfully.

U   culty

culty than the British government seem to have imagined.
Considering the extent and natural strength of the country,
it may well be doubted, whether all the force which Great
Britain could have spared, would have been sufficient to reduce it to subjection, and restore it at the same time to such
a degree of order and subordination, as to make it a colony
worth holding. The truth seems to have been, that General
Williamson, to whom, as hath been observed, the direction
and distribution of the armament was entrusted, and whose
active zeal in the service of his country was eminently con-
spicuous, was deceived, equally with the King's ministers, by
the favourable accounts and exaggerated representations of
sanguine and interested individuals, concerning the disposition of
their countrymen, the white planters remaining in St. Domingo.
Instead of the few hundreds of them which afterwards resorted
to the British standard, the Governor had reason to expect the
support and co-operation of at least as many thousands. In
this fatal confidence, the armament allotted for this important
expedition was composed of only the 13th regiment of foot,
seven companies of the 49th, and a detachment of artillery,
altogether amounting to about eight hundred and seventy, rank
and file, fit for duty. Such was the force that was to annex
to the crown of Great Britain, a country nearly equal in extent, and in natural strength infinitely superior, to Great Britain itself ! Speedy and effectual reinforcements from England
were, however, promised, as well to replace the troops which
were removed from Jamaica, as to aid the operations in St.
Domingo.

In

IN the meantime, the firſt diviſion, conſiſting of ſix hundred and ſeventy-ſeven rank and file, under the command of Lieutenant-Colonel Whitelocke, ſailed from Port Royal the 9th of September, and arrived at Jeremie on the 19th of the ſame month. They were eſcorted by Commodore Ford, in the Europa, accompanied by four or five frigates.

As the propoſitions, or terms of capitulation, had been previ-ouſly adjuſted between the people of Jeremie, by their agent Mr. Charmilly, and General Williamſon, it only remained for the Britiſh forces to take poſſeſſion of the town and harbour. Accordingly, the troops diſembarked early the next morning; the Britiſh colours were hoiſted at both the forts, with royal ſalutes from each, which were anſwered by the Commodore and his ſquadron, and the oaths of fidelity and allegiance were taken by the reſident inhabitants, with an appearance of great zeal and alacrity.

AT the ſame time information was received, that the gar-riſon at the Mole of Cape St. Nicholas, were inclined to ſur-render that important fortreſs in like manner. As this was a circumſtance not to be neglected, the Commodore immediately directed his courſe thither, and, on the 22d, took poſſeſſion of the fortreſs and harbour, and received the allegiance of the officers and privates. The grenadier company of the 13th regiment, was forthwith diſpatched from Jeremie to take the command of the garriſon; which was ſoon afterwards ſtrengthened by the arrival of the ſecond diviſion of the armament ordered from Jamaica, conſiſting of five companies of forty men each.

U 2 THE

THE voluntary furrender of thefe places raifed expectations in the people of England, that the whole of the French colony in St. Domingo would fubmit without oppofition; but the advantages hitherto obtained, feem to have been greatly overvalued.   The town of Jeremie is a place of no importance.—It contains about one hundred very mean houfes, and the country in the vicinage is not remarkably fertile; producing nothing of any account but coffee.   At the Mole of Cape St. Nicholas, the country is even lefs productive than in the neighbourhood of Jeremie; but the harbour is one of the fineft in the new world, and the fortifications vie with the ftrongeft in the Weft Indies : unfortunately, from the elevation of the furrounding heights, the place is not tenable againft a powerful attack by land.   The garrifon confifted only of the regiment of Dillon, which was reduced by ficknefs or defertion to about one hundred and fifty men. The town of St. Nicholas adjoining, was in the higheft degree hoftile : moft of the inhabitants, capable of bearing arms, left the place on the arrival of the Englifh, and joined the republican army.

ZEALOUS, however, to promote the glory of the Britifh name, Colonel Whitelocke determined that his little army fhould not continue inactive at Jeremie.   It was reprefented to him, that the acquifition of the neighbouring poft of Tiburon would prove of the utmoft importance towards the fecurity of Grand Ance, and a M. Duval pledging himfelf to raife five hundred men to co-operate in its reduction, an expedition was undertaken for that purpofe, and Colonel Whitelocke, with moft of
the

the Britiſh force from Jeremie, arrived in Tiburon Bay on the
4th of October.

BUT, on this occaſion, as on almoſt every other, the Engliſh
had a melancholy proof how little dependence can be placed on
French declarations and aſſurances. Duval never made his appearance, for he was not able to collect fifty men; the enemy's
force was found to be far more formidable than had been repre
ſented, and the gallantry of our troops proved unavailing againſt
ſuperiority of numbers. They were compelled to retreat, with
the loſs of about twenty men killed and wounded.

THE defeat and diſcouragement ſuſtained in this attack
were the more grievouſly felt, as ſickneſs began to prevail
to a great extent in the army. The ſeaſon of the year
was unfavourable in the higheſt degree for military operations in a tropical climate. The rains were inceſſant; and
the conſtant and unuſual fatigue, and extraordinary duty to
which the ſoldiers, from the ſmallneſs of their number, were
neceſſarily ſubject, co-operating with the ſtate of the weather,
produced the moſt fatal conſequences. That never-failing attendant on military expeditions in the Weſt Indies, the yellow
or peſtilential fever, raged with dreadful virulence, and ſo many,
both of the ſeamen and ſoldiers, periſhed daily, that the ſurvivors were ſtricken with aſtoniſhment and horror at beholding
the havock made among their comrades!

GENERAL WILLIAMSON, with his uſual humanity, exerted
himſelf to give them all the relief in his power. Unhappily he
had

had no alternative but either to withdraw the troops altogether from St. Domingo, leaving our allies and new fubjects, the French planters who had fworn allegiance to our government, to the mercy of their enemies, or to fend, from an already ex- haufted army, a fmall reinforcement of men, to perifh probably in the fame manner as thofe had done whofe numbers they were fcarcely fufficient to replace.

THE latter meafure was adopted : in truth, the circum- ftances of the cafe admitted of no other. The remainder of the 49th regiment, the 20th, and the royals, amounting altogether to feven or eight hundred men, were therefore difpatch- ed with all poffible expedition ; and the fafety of Jamaica was at length entrufted to lefs than four hundred regular troops.

THE fudden appearance in St. Domingo of a reinforcement, though fmall in itfelf, produced however a confiderable effect among the French planters, by inducing a belief that the Britifh government was now ferioufly refolved to follow up the blow. In the beginning of December, the parifhes of Jean Rabel, St. Marc, Arcahaye, and Boucaffin furrendered on the fame con- ditions as had been granted to Jeremie ; and their example was foon afterwards followed by the inhabitants of Leogane. All the former parifhes are fituated on the north fide of the Bight : Leogane on the fouth.

THE Britifh commanders now directed their views once more towards the capture of Tiburon. The defeat which our troops
had

had fuſtained in the late attack of that important poſt, ſerved only to animate them to greater exertions; but a conſiderable time unavoidably elapſed before the expedition took place; the interval being employed in ſecuring the places which had ſurrendered. On the 21ſt of January, however, the Commodore touched at Jeremie with the ſquadron, and received the troops on board; and the whole arrived off Cape Tiburon on the evening of the 2d of February.

THE enemy appeared in conſiderable force, and ſeemed to wait the arrival of the Britiſh with great reſolution; but a few broadſides from the ſhips ſoon cleared the beach. They came forward however again, as the flank companies approached the ſhore, and directed a general diſcharge of muſquetry at the boats; but our troops landed and formed in an inſtant, routed their line with great ſlaughter, and immediately took poſſeſſion of the poſt. The gallantry of Major Spencer who commanded, and of the officers and men who compoſed, the flank companies, was particularly conſpicuous. It ſeems, indeed, to have been a ſpirited and well conducted enterprize throughout; and it was happily effected with the loſs of only three of the Engliſh killed, and ſeven wounded. Of the enemy, one hundred and fifty ſurrendered priſoners of war; and their magazines were found replete with ammunition.

By the poſſeſſion of this poſt on the ſouth, and that of the Mole at Cape St. Nicholas on the north-weſtern part of the iſland, the Britiſh ſquadron commanded the navigation of the

the whole of that extensive bay which forms the Bight of Leogane, and the capture of the forts, shipping, and town of Port au Prince (the metropolis of the French colony) seemed more than probable, on the arrival of a large armament now daily expected, with much anxiety, from England.

IN the mean while (the reduced state and condition of the troops not admitting of great enterprize) the commander in chief conceived an idea of obtaining possession of the town of Port Paix, an important station to the eastward of Cape St. Nicholas, *by private negociation.* The town was commanded by Lavaux, an old general in the French service, to whom Colonel Whitelocke addressed himself by letter, which he sent with a flag, ana offered five thousand pounds to be paid to him in person, on his delivering up the post. Colonel Whitelocke seems, however, to have mistaken the character of Lavaux, who was not only a man of distinguished bravery, but of great probity. His answer is remarkable: " You " have endeavoured (said he) to dishonour me in the eyes of " my troops, by supposing me so vile, flagitious, and base, as to " be capable of betraying my trust for a bribe: this is an affront " for which you owe me personal satisfaction, and I demand it " in the name of honour. Wherefore, previous to any general " action, I offer you single combat until one of us falls; leaving " to you the choice of arms, either on foot or horseback. Your " situation, as my enemy on the part of your country, did not give " you a right to offer me a personal insult; and as a private

8   " person,

" perſon, I aſk ſatisfaction for an injury done me by an indi-
" vidual *(d)*."

THIS attempt therefore proving abortive, it was determined
(now that the ſeaſon was favourable) in order that the troops
might not continue inactive, as well as to facilitate the meditated reduction of Port au Prince, to attack *L'Acul*, an important fortreſs in the vicinity of Leogane. Accordingly, on the
19th of February, the flank companies, a detachment of the
royal artillery, and of the 13th regiment, with ſome colonial
troops, having two five half-inch howitzers and two four-
pounders, marched from thence under the command of Colonel Whitelocke, at four in the morning. Baron de Montalembert, with about two hundred colonial troops, and a
few of the Britiſh artillery, were previouſly embarked on
tranſports, and ordered to land and attack the fort at an hour
appointed. Captain Vincent, with the light infantry of the
49th, and about eighty of the colonial troops, took a mountain
road, while Colonel Whitelocke moved forward on the great
road, and took poſt juſt out of cannon ſhot, waiting the united
attacks of the Baron and Captain Vincent's detachments. The
enemy began to cannonade about ſeven o'clock, and continued

(d) Colonel Whitelocke, I ſuppoſe, rejected the challenge; but the officer
who was ſent by him with the letter to Lavaux, had a ſervice of danger:
for Lavaux, having ſilently read the letter, compelled him to declare, upon the
honour of a ſoldier, whether he knew the contents of it. The officer, as the fact
was, anſwered in the negative. The French general thereupon read the letter
aloud to the people who ſurrounded him, and told the Britiſh officer, that if he
had brought him ſuch a propoſal *knowingly*, he would inſtantly have cauſed him to
be executed on a gibbet.

it with intervals till eleven, when Colonel Whitelocke ordered Captain Smith, with the howitzers and cannon, to advance and fire upon the fort, fupported by the light infantry of the royals and 13th regiments, under the command of Major Spencer, in order to give time for the Baron's people to land. Unfortunately, from the mifmanagement of one of the tranfports, the troops under the orders of the Baron de Montalembert could not be landed. Colonel Whitelocke, therefore, finding he had nothing to expect from them, the day being confiderably advanced, now came to the determination of attacking the fort by ftorm; and detached Major Spencer, with the grenadiers of the 49th regiment, and light infantry of the 13th, to join Captain Vincent, and approach the fort by the mountain road, while he himfelf marched by the great road for the fame purpofe. At half paft four or five o'clock, the two columns moved forward, and the moment the enemy difcovered the march of Colonel Whitelocke's divifion, they commenced a very heavy fire of cannon and mufquetry. Orders were immediately given for the column to advance and gain the fort, which orders were gallantly and rapidly executed. At this inftant, Lieutenant M'Kerras of the engineers, and Captain Hutchinfon of the royals, were both wounded; but they continued their exertions, notwithftanding, till the fort was in quiet poffeffion of the victors. Our lofs was not great; but Captain Morfhead (who had before received a fhot in the body, when gallantly mounting the hill) with Lieutenant Tinlin of the 20th grenadiers, Lieutenant Caulfield of the 62d regiment, and fome privates, were unfortunately blown up from an explofion which took place after the fort was taken; for the officer who commanded, finding he could no longer defend it,

placed

placed a quantity of powder and other combuftibles in one
of the buildings, which was fired by an unfortunate brigand,
who perifhed in the explofion. Captain Morfhead died the
next day, and was interred with military honours, attended by
the Britifh garrifon ; Lieutenant Caulfield lingered fome time
longer, and then followed him to the grave ; but Lieutenant
Tinlin recovered.

THE next enterprize of our gallant little army had a lefs favourable termination. It was directed againft a ftrong poft and
fettlement at a place called *Bompard*, about fifteen miles from
Cape St. Nicholas, where a hardy race of people, chiefly a
colony of Germans, had eftablifhed themfelves, and lived in un-
ambitious poverty. A detachment of two hundred men, from
the different corps, were ordered on this fervice in two divifions,
one of which was commanded by Major Spencer, the brave and
active officer already mentioned, the other by Lieutenant-Colonel Markham. Of their proceedings during the attack, and
their retreat afterwards, I have not been furnifhed with the particulars. All that is known to the publick with certainty is,
that our troops were repulfed by fuperior numbers, with the
lofs of forty men, but without any diminution of the national
character. It was allowed, even by the enemy, that they fought
bravely. They were defeated, not difmayed, by circumftances
probably which they did not forefee, and againft which human
prudence could not provide.

THIS afflicting lofs was but ill compenfated, by the very
diftinguifhed honour which was foon afterwards acquired by the

few

few Britifh troops that had been left in poffeffion of Cape Ti-buron, who were attacked on the 16th of April, by an army of brigands amounting to upwards of two thoufand. The enemy's force was led on by Andrew Rigaud, a man of colour, who commanded at Aux Cayes, and was compofed of revolted negroes, and defperadoes of all defcriptions, rapacious after plunder, and thirfting for blood. This favage horde furrounded the fort about three o'clock in the morning. It was defended with much fpirit until a quarter before nine, when the befieged, quitting the fort, affailed the affailants, and routed the befiegers with great flaughter, one hundred and feventy of their number being left dead on the field; but when it was difcovered that no lefs than twenty-eight of our gallant foldiers had loft their lives, and that one hundred and nine others were feverely wounded in this bloody conteft, the fhouts of triumph were fuppreffed by gloomy reflections on the forlorn condition of the army, it being mournfully evident that a few more fuch victories would annihilate the victors!

THE whole of the Britifh force at this time in all parts of St. Domingo did not, I believe, amount to nine hundred effective men, a number by no means fufficient to garrifon the places in our poffeffion; and the rapid diminution which prevailed among them, could not fail to attract obfervation among all claffes of the French inhabitants; to difpirit our allies, and encourage our enemies. Such of the planters as had hitherto ftood aloof, now began to declare themfelves hoftile; and defertions were frequent from moft of the parifhes that had furrendered. At Jean Rabell, a place which, a few months before, had voluntarily

tarily declared for the Britifh government, the garrifon, confifting of two hundred and fifty of our fuppofed allies, rofe on their officers, and compelled them to deliver up the poft to Lavaux, the French general, and it was greatly apprehended that, unlefs a very powerful reinforcement fhould fpeedily arrive to ftrengthen the Britifh army, many other places would follow their example.

EIGHT months had now elapfed fince the furrender of May 1794 Jeremie, and in all that interval, not a foldier had arrived from Great Britain; and the want of camp-equipage, provifions, and neceffaries, was grievoufly felt. The army feemed devoted to inevitable deftruction, and difappointment and difmay were ftrongly marked in the countenance of every man. At length, however, on the 19th of May, when expectation was nearly loft in defpair, it was announced that his Majefty's fhips the Belliqueux and the Irrefiftible, with the Fly floop, had caft anchor in the harbour of Cape St. Nicholas, having on board the 22d, 23d, and 41ft regiments of infantry, under the command of Brigadier General Whyte. This event, as may well be imagined, afforded infinite relief and fatisfaction to the haraffed and worn-out troops on fhore; and their animation on this occafion was heightened by the confident hope and expectation that Port au Prince would be the object of an immediate attack. It was known that its harbour was crowded with fhips, moft of which were fuppofed to be laden with the richeft productions of the colony; and although the regiments newly arrived did not exceed fixteen hundred men in the whole (of whom two hundred and fifty were fick and convalefcent) the deficiency of numbers was no longer the fubject of complaint. Every one anticipated

†   to

to himfelf the poffeffion of great wealth from the capture; and juftly concluded that his fhare of the prize money would augment or diminifh in an inverfe proportion to the number of captors.

The belief that Port au Prince would be the firft object of attack, was well founded; and the road of Arcahaye was fixed on as the place of rendezvous for the men of war and tranfports. Accordingly, General Whyte, having landed his fick at Cape St. Nicholas, and taken one hundred and fifty of the garrifon in their room, proceeded on the 23d to the place appointed, to concert meafures with Commodore Ford, and receive on board fuch of the colonial troops as were to co-operate with the Britifh in this enterprize. On the 30th the fquadron failed from Arcahaye, and caft anchor off Port au Prince on the evening of the fame day. It was compofed of four fhips of the line, the Europa, the Belliqueux, the Irrefiftible and the Sceptre, three frigates, and four or five fmaller veffels; the whole under the immediate command of Commodore Ford; and the land forces, under the orders of General Whyte, confifted of 1,465 rank and file fit for duty.

The whole force being thus collected, and the neceffary preparations made, a flag was fent, early the next morning, to demand the furrender of the place; but the officer charged with the difpatch, was informed that no flag would be admitted, and the letter was returned unopened. It was now determined to commence operations by the cannonade of Fort Bizotton, a fortrefs fituated on a commanding eminence, well adapted to guard the approach to the harbour, and defended by five hundred

dred men, eight pieces of heavy cannon, and two mortars. Two
line of battle ships were ordered to attack the sea-front, and
a frigate was stationed close to the shore, to flank a ravine to
the eastward. From these vessels a brisk and well-directed fire
was maintained for several hours; but no great impression appearing to be made, Major Spencer, with three hundred British,
and about five hundred of the colonial troops, was put on
shore in the evening, within a mile of the fort, with orders to
commence an attack on the side of the land. On their arrival
at a small distance from the scene of action, about eight o'clock
at night, a most tremendous thunder-storm arose, accompanied with a deluge of rain, of which, as it overpowered the
found of their approach, the advanced guard, commanded by
Captain Daniel, of the 41ft, determined to take advantage.
These brave men, sixty only in number, accordingly rushed forward, and finding a breach in the walls, entered with fixed
bayonets, and became instantly masters of the fortress; the be-
sieged every where throwing down their arms and calling for
mercy. So rapid were the movements of this gallant band, and
so unexpected was their success, that Major Spencer, the commander, had his fears for the safety of the whole party, of
whose situation he was unapprized for some hours. I grieve
to add, that Captain Daniel, who so gallantly led the advanced
guard on this occasion, received a severe wound in the attack,
while his brave associate, Captain Wallace, the second in command, was most unfortunately killed on the glacis.

THE possession of Fort Bizotton determined the fate of the
capital, which was evacuated by the enemy on the 4th of June;

and

and the Britifh commanders were fo fortunate as to preferve, not only the town itfelf, but alfo the fhipping in the harbour, from conflagration, although the republican commiffioners had given orders and made preparations for fetting fire to both. The commiffioners themfelves, with many of their adherents, made their efcape to the mountains.

THUS was achieved the conqueft of Port au Prince; an event which has proved not lefs profitable than honourable to fuch of the officers and foldiers by whom it was effected, as have lived to enjoy the fruits of their victory; for there were captured in the harbour, two-and-twenty top-fail veffels, fully laden with fugar, indigo, and coffee, of which thirteen were from three to five hundred tons burthen, and the remaining nine, from one hundred and fifty to three hundred tons; befides feven thoufand tons of fhipping in ballaft; the value of all which, at a moderate computation, could not be far fhort of £. 400,000 fterling.

CHAP.

CHAP. XI.

Sickness among the Troops, and the Causes thereof.—Reinforcement.—Dreadful Mortality.—General Whyte is succeeded by Brigadier General Horneck.—Leogane taken by the Rebels.—Temporary Successes of Lieutenant-Colonel Brisbane at Artibonite.—Revolt of the Mulattoes at St. Marc.—Attack of Fort Bizotton.—Preparations by Rigaud for a second Attempt on Tiburon.—The Post attacked on Christmas Day, and carried.—Gallant Defence and Escape of the Garrison, and melancholy Fate of Lieutenant Baskerville.—Lieutenant-Colonels Brisbane and Markham killed.—Observations and Strictures on the Conduct of the War.

FROM the success which attended the British arms in the conquest of Port au Prince, it might have been hoped that we were now to enter on the survey of brighter prospects than those which have hitherto presented themselves to our contemplation ; but a melancholy reverse of fortune was soon to await the conquerors ; for, immediately after possession was taken of the town, the same dreadful scourge—disease, exasperated to contagion, which had been so fatally prevalent among our troops, in the preceding autumn, renewed its destructive progress ; and, on this occasion, it is not difficult to trace the proximate causes of so terrible a calamity. The situation of

Y   the

CHAP. the town of Port au Prince has already been noticed. Un-
XI.   healthy in itself, it is furrounded by fortified heights, which
command both the lines and the harbour; and thefe heights are
again commanded by others. Here, the enemy, on their retreat
from the town, made their ftand, in the well-founded confidence of receiving regular fupplies of men, ammunition, and
neceffaries from Aux Cayes, a fea-port on the fouthern coaft,
diftant only from Port au Prince by a very eafy road, about
forty miles *(a)*. No part of St. Domingo poffeffes a more ready
communication with the French Iflands to windward, or with
the ftates of America, than the port laft mentioned; and from
both thofe fources, reinforcements were conftantly poured into
the enemy's camp. On this account the Britifh commanders
found it indifpenfibly neceffary to ftrengthen the lines, and raife
additional intrenchments and works on that fide of the town
which fronts the mountains. Thus a moft fevere and unufual
burthen was impofed on the foldiers. They were compelled,
with but little intermiffion, to dig the ground in the day, and
to perform military duty in the night; expofed, in the one cafe,
to the burning rays of the fun; in the other, to the noxious
dews and heavy rains of the climate. Such extraordinary and

(a) The harbour of Aux Cayes was guarded by two fmall forts, each of which
was furnifhed with only fix pieces of cannon, and a fmaller battery, which
mounted only five pieces. The number of white inhabitants belonging to the
town were computed at eight hundred; but the people of colour had taken poffeffion
of it the latter end of 1792, and Andrew Rigaud, a Mulatto, was made commander in chief and governor-general of the fouth fide of the French part of St.
Domingo. His power was abfolute, and his brother, of the fame colour, was appointed next in command. Thefe men were invefted with this authority by the
two commiffioners, Polverel and Santhonax.

3   exceffive

excessive labour imposed on men, most of whom had been actually confined six months on ship-board, without fresh provisions or exercise, co-operating with the malignancy of the air, produced its natural consequences. They dropt like the leaves in autumn, until at length the garrison became so diminished and enfeebled, that deficiencies of the guards were oftentimes made up from convalescents, who were scarcely able to stand under their arms *(b)*.

IT is true, that a reinforcement came from the Windward Islands, soon after the surrender of the town;—but, by a mournful fatality, this apparent augmentation of the strength of the garrison, contributed in an eminent degree to the rapid encrease and aggravation of its miseries. On the 8th of June, eight flank companies belonging to the 22d, 23d, 35th, and 41st regiments, arrived at Port au Prince, under the command of Lieutenant-Colonel Lenox. They consisted, on their embarkation, of about seventy men each, but the aggregate number, when landed, was not quite three hundred. The four grenadier companies, in particular, were nearly annihilated. The frigate in which they were conveyed, became *a house of pestilence*. Upwards of one hundred of their number were buried in the deep, in the short passage between Guadaloupe and Jamaica, and one hundred and fifty more were left in a dying state at Port Royal. The wretched remains of the whole de-

(b) It was fortunate for the British army, that the French troops suffered by sickness almost as much as our own: Port au Prince would otherwise have been but a short time in our possession.

Y 2

tachment

tachment difcovered, on their landing at Port au Prince, that they came—not to participate in the glories of conqueft, but—to perifh themfelves within the walls of an hofpital! So rapid was the mortality in the Britifh army, after their arrival, that no lefs than forty officers and upwards of fix hundred rank and file met an untimely death, without a conteft with any other enemy than ficknefs, in the fhort fpace of two months after the furrender of the town.

GENERAL WHYTE, his health much impaired, and hopelefs, it may be prefumed, of further triumphs, with an army thus reduced and debilitated, now folicited and obtained permiffion to return to Europe. He was fucceeded in the chief command by Brigadier-General Horneck, who arrived from Jamaica about the middle of September; and if the requifite qualifications for fuch a ftation—firmnefs without arrogance, and conciliating manners without weaknefs, could always enfure fuccefs to the poffeffor, General Horneck would have brought good fortune with him. But the difficulties which the former commander would have had to encounter, had he remained in his ftation, devolved with aggravated weight on his fucceffor. The only reinforcement which followed General Horneck, confifted of fifty men from Jamaica. Whatever troops were promifed or expected from Great Britain, none arrived, until the expiration of feven months after General Horneck had taken the command. Inftead, therefore, of attempting new achievements, he was compelled, by irrefiftible neceffity, to act chiefly on the defenfive. The rebel Mulattoes, under Rigaud, even became mafters of Leogane, and fatiated their vengeance by

putting

1794.

Oct. 1794.

putting to death all fuch of the French planters, our allies, as unfortunately fell into their power.

On the other hand, the judicious exertions and rapid fuc-ceffes of Lieutenant-Colonel Brifbane on the plain of Artibo-nite, had been for fome time the fubject of much applaufe, and had given birth to great expectation. The French inhabitants of the town and neighbourhood of St. Marc, had been all along more heartily difpofed to co-operate with the Englifh, than any of their countrymen. Mr. Brifbane had not above four-fcore Britifh under his command. The reft of his little army was compofed of the remains of Dillon's regiment, the St. Marc's legion, the militia of the neighbouring parifhes, and a body of about three hundred reluctant Spaniards from Verette; the whole not exceeding twelve hundred men in arms. With this force, properly diftributed, he had routed the republican troops and rebel negroes in every quarter; and even brought the negro chiefs to folicit permiffion to capitulate. Eight or ten thoufand of thefe deluded wretches, had actually fubmitted unconditionally, and many returned, of their own accord, to the plantations of their mafters. But thefe promifing ap-pearances were of fhort continuance. While Colonel Brifbane was following up his fucceffes in a diftant part of Artibonite, the men of colour in the town of St. Marc, feduced by the promifes of the French commiffioners, and finding the town itfelf without troops, had violated their promifes of neutra-lity, and on the 6th of September taken up arms on the part of the republick; putting to death every man that fell in their way, whom they confidered as an enemy to the French commiffioners.

commiffioners.—The garrifon, confifting of about forty Britifh convalefcents, threw themfelves into a fmall fort on the fea-fhore, which they gallantly defended for two days, when a fri-gate came to their relief from the Mole of Cape St. Nicholas.—The triumph of the Mulattoes, however, was tranfient. Colonel Brifbane attacked them on the fide of the land, and recovered the town; making upwards of three hundred of the infurgents prifoners, and driving the reft over the Artibonite river; but the advantages which he had obtained on the plain, were loft in the interim. The negro chiefs no longer folicited to capitulate, but appeared in greater force than ever. Being joined by the fugitive Mulattoes, they foon repaffed the river; and having, in the beginning of October, obtained poffeffion of two out-pofts (St. Michael and St. Raphael) they had procured plenty of arms and ammunition, and now threatened fo for-midable an attack on the town of St. Marc, as to excite the moft ferious apprehenfions for its fafety.

Such was the fituation of affairs in the weftern parts of St. Domingo about the period of General Horneck's arrival. The northern province (the Mole of St. Nicholas and the town of Fort Dauphin excepted) was entirely in poffeffion of the rebel negroes; and unhappily, in all other parts of the colony, the weaknefs of the Britifh was fo apparent, as not only to invite attacks from the enemy, but alfo to encourage revolt and con-fpiracy in the pofts in our poffeffion (c). Rigaud, who commanded

(c) Colonel Brifbane had fcarcely driven the Mulattoes from St. Marc, and reftored order and tranquillity in the town, before a dark confpiracy was agitated
among

manded in the fouth, now determined to make a bold effort for the recovery of Fort Bizotton, in which, if he had fucceeded, the lofs of the whole of the Britifh army at Port au Prince would have been inevitable. The fort was attacked early in the morning of the 5th of December, by three columns of the enemy, amounting in the whole to about two thoufand men; but they were defeated with great flaughter on their part, and with little lofs on ours. Captain Grant, however, and both his lieutenants, Clunes and Hamilton, were feverely wounded early in the attack; yet they continued their efforts, and nobly fucceeded; and General Williamfon bore teftimony to their good conduct and valour.

BAFFLED in this attack, Rigaud refolved to make another, and a more formidable attempt, for the recovery of Tiburon. His intentions were known, and his project might have been defeated, if any one Englifh fhip of war could have been fpared to watch his motions off the harbour of Aux Cayes, from whence he conveyed his artillery, ammunition, and provifions. He proceeded, however, without interruption in his

among fome of the French inhabitants under the Britifh protection to cut him off; but it was happily difcovered and defeated before it broke out into action. This happened the beginning of January 1795; and a ftill more daring and dangerous plot was carried on a month afterwards in Port au Prince, to feize on the garrifon, and put all the Englifh to death. This confpiracy alfo was fortunately difcovered, and twenty of the confpirators being brought to trial before a council of war, compofed of the principal commanders by fea and land (among whom were five French field officers) they were all adjudged to fuffer death, and fifteen of them were accordingly fhot on the 18th of February.

preparations

preparations for the attack; and his armament failed from Aux Cayes on the 23d of December. His naval force confifted of one brig of fixteen guns, and three fchooners of fourteen guns each, and he commanded a body of near three thoufand men, of all colours and defcriptions. The attack commenced on Chriftmas day. The garrifon, confifting of only four hundred and eighty men, made a vigorous defence for four days, when, having loft upwards of three hundred of their number, and finding the poft no longer tenable, the furvivors, headed by their gallant commander, Lieutenant Bradford, of the 23d regiment, with unexampled bravery fought their way for five miles through the enemy, and got fafe to Irois. Lieutenant Bafkerville was the only officer who, by fome unfortunate circumftance, was unable to join his companions in their retreat; and this high-fpirited young man, with a refolution which, though a Chriftian muft condemn it, a Roman would have approved, to defeat the triumph of his favage enemy, who would probably have made him fuffer a fhameful death, put a period to his own exiftence, as Rigaud entered the fort.

WITH this difaftrous occurrence terminated the year 1794 *(d)*, and here I fhall clofe my account of the military tranfactions of

(d) Major General Williamfon, the latter end of the year, was appointed governor-general and commander in chief of his Majefty's poffeffions in St. Domingo; and was foon afterwards honoured with the order of the Bath—a diftinction which he had nobly earned. He arrived at Port au Prince, and took upon him the government, in May 1795.

the

the Britiſh army in St. Domingo; for, although hoſtilities are ſtill continued in this ill-fated country, it is, I think, ſufficiently apparent, that all hopes and expectations of ultimate ſucceſs are vaniſhed for ever! The hiſtorian who ſhall recount the events of 1795, will have to lament the mournful and untimely deaths of many brave and excellent young men who periſhed in this fruitleſs conteſt. Among the foremoſt of theſe was Lieutenant-Colonel Thomas Briſbane, of whom honourable mention is made in the foregoing pages, and whoſe gallantry and good conduct were not more the ſubject of univerſal admiration, than his untimely fate of univerſal regret. He was killed on a reconnoitring party in February. By his death, his country was deprived, at a moſt critical juncture, of an able, indefatigable, and intelligent officer, who had gained the affections of moſt of the various deſcriptions of people under his command by his kindneſs, and the confidence of all by his courage (e). The ſame fate, a month afterwards, awaited Lieutenant-Colonel Markham, who periſhed in attacking an out-poſt of the enemy's forces which were at that time laying ſiege to Fort Bizotton. The out-poſt was carried; the colours of the enemy, and five pieces of their cannon, were taken, and upwards of ſix hundred of their number ſlain on the ſpot; but the victory was dearly obtained by the loſs of ſo enterprizing and accompliſhed a leader. Yet it affords ſome conſolation to reflect, that theſe brave young men, though cut off in the bloom of life, fell in the field of glory, nobly exerting them-

(e) He was a captain in the 49th regiment, and lieutenant colonel of the colonial corps called the St. Marc's Legion.

Z

ſelves

CHAP.
XI.

felves in the caufe of their country, and dying amidft the bleffings and applaufes of their compatriots. Alas, how many of their youthful affociates, in this unhappy war, might have envied them fo glorious an exit! What numbers have perifhed—not in the field of honour—but on the bed of ficknefs!—not amidft the fhouts of victory—but the groans of defpair!—condemned to linger in the horrors of peftilence ; to fall without a conflict, and to die without renown (f)!

THESE reflections, and the obfervations which I have made in the preceding pages, on the infufficiency of the means to the

(f) The difeafe in which fo many gallant men have perifhed, is commonly known by the name of the *yellow fever*. Two writers of great ability (Dr. Rufh of Philadelphia, and Dr. Benjamin Mofeley of Pall Mall, London) have treated fully of this dreadful calamity. The picture which the latter has given of an unhappy patient of his in the Weft Indies, a young officer of great merit, in the laft ftage of this difeafe, after four days illnefs, is drawn by the hand of a mafter. " I arrived at the lodgings of this much-efteemed young man (fays the doctor) about four hours before his death. When I entered the room, he was vomiting a black muddy cruor, and was bleeding at the nofe. A bloody ichor was oozing from the corners of his eyes, and from his mouth and gums. His face was befmeared with blood, and, with the dulnefs of his eyes, it prefented a moft diftreffing contraft to his natural vifage. His abdomen was fwelled, and inflated prodigioufly. His body was all over of a deep yellow, interfperfed with livid fpots. His hands and feet were of a livid hue. Every part of him was cold excepting about his heart. He had a deep ftrong hiccup, but neither delirium nor coma; and was, at my firft feeing him, as I thought, in his perfect fenfes. He looked at the changed appearance of his fkin, and expreffed, though he could not fpeak, by his fad countenance, that he knew life was foon to yield up her citadel, now abandoning the reft of his body. Exhaufted with vomiting, he at laft was fuffocated with the blood he was endeavouring to bring up, and expired."

Mofeley on Tropical Difeafes, 3d edit. p. 459.

objects

objects in view, are not written in the spirit of accusation against men in authority; nor (if I know myself) is there any bias of party zeal on my judgment. I am far from asserting, that the situation and resources of Great Britain were such as to afford a greater body of troops for service in St. Domingo, at the proper moment, than the number that was actually sent thither. I presume not to intrude into the national councils, and am well apprized that existing alliances and pre-engagements of the state, were objects of important consideration to his Majesty's ministers. Neither can I affirm, that the delays and obstructions, which prevented the arrival at the scene of action of some of the detachments, until the return of the sickly season, were avoidable. A thousand accidents and casualties continually subvert and overthrow the best laid schemes of human contrivance. We have seen considerable fleets detained by adverse winds, in the ports of Great Britain for many successive months, and powerful armaments have been driven back by storms and tempests, after many unavailing attempts to reach the place of their destination. Thus much I owe to candour; but, at the same time, I owe it also to truth to avow my opinion, that in case no greater force could have been spared for the enterprize against St. Domingo, the enterprize itself ought not to have been undertaken *. The

* If, from the ill success which has attended the attack of St. Domingo, a justification of the original measure shall be thought necessary, it ought not to be overlooked, that General Williamson, among other motives, had also strong reason to believe, that attempts were meditated by the republican commissioners on the island of Jamaica. He therefore, probably thought, that the most certain way of preventing the success of such designs, was to give the commissioners sufficient employment at home.—I write this note in justice to a distinguished officer, than whom no man living has deserved better of his country.

Z 2

object

CHAP.
XI.

object of the Britifh minifters was avowedly to obtain poffeffion of the whole of the French part of the country. That they placed great dependence on the co-operation of the French inhabitants, and were grofsly deceived by agents from thence, I believe and admit; but they ought furely to have forefeen, that a very formidable oppofition was to be expected from the partizans and troops of the republican government; and they ought alfo to have known, that no confiderable body of the French planters could be expected to rifk their lives and fortunes in the common caufe, but in full confidence of protection and fupport. In my own judgment, all the force which Great Britain could have fent thither, would not have been fufficient for the complete fubjugation of the colony. It is afferted by competent judges, that not lefs than fix thoufand men were neceffary for the fecure maintenance of Port au Prince alone; yet I do not believe that the number of Britifh, in all parts of St. Domingo, at any one period, previous to the month of April 1795, exceeded two thoufand two hundred, of whom, except at the capture of Port au Prince, not one half were fit for active fervice; and during the hot and fickly months of Auguft, September, and October, not one third *(g)*.

                                                    PERHAPS

(g) The following returns are authentick.

Return of the provincial troops in the fervice of the Britifh government at St. Domingo, 1ft January 1795.

	Rank and file fit for duty.	Sick.	Total.
At Port au Prince	496 —	48 —	544
Mole St. Nicholas	209 —	38 —	247
St. Marc	813 —	321 —	1134
	1518	407	1925

                                                    Return

PERHAPS the moſt fatal overſight in the conduct of the whole expedition, was the ſtrange and unaccountable neglect of not ſecuring the town and harbour of Aux Cayes, and the little port of Jacmel on the ſame part of the coaſt, previous to the attack of Port au Prince. With thoſe places, on the one ſide of the peninſula, and the poſt of Acul in our poſſeſſion on the other, all communication between the Southern and the two other provinces would have been cut off; the navigation from the Windward Iſlands to Jamaica would have been ſecure, while the poſſeſſion of the two Capes which form the entrance into the Bight of Leogane (Cape Nicholas and Tiburon) would have protected the homeward trade in its courſe through the Windward Paſſage. All this might have been accompliſhed and ſecured; and I think it is all that, in ſound policy, ought to have been attempted. As to Port au Prince, it would have been for-

Return of the Britiſh forces in the iſland of St. Domingo, 1ſt January 1795.

				Rank and file effective.	Sick.	Total.
Port au Prince	-	-	-	366 —	462 —	828
Mole St. Nicholas		-	-	209 —	166 —	375
Jeremie	-	-	-	-	95 —	59 —	154
Tiburon	-	-	-	-	34 —	18 —	52
St. Marc	-	-	-	-	48 —	33 —	81
				752 —	738 —	1490

The next reinforcement from Europe arrived the latter end of April 1795, and conſiſted of about fourteen hundred men (the 81ſt and 96th regiments): a further reinforcement (the 82d regiment) landed in Auguſt following. All theſe corps, the laſt eſpecially, from its landing at ſo unfavourable a ſeaſon, ſuffered prodigiouſly. The 82d landed nine hundred and eighty men, of whom ſix hundred and thirty were buried within ten weeks. In one of the companies, three rank and file only were able to do duty.

tunate

tunate if the works had been deftroyed, and the town evacuated immediately after its furrender.

THE retention by the enemy of Aux Cayes and Jácmel,
not only enabled them to procure reinforcements and fupplies, but alfo moft amply to revenge our attempts on their
coafts, by reprifals on our trade. It is known that upwards
of thirty privateers, fome of them of confiderable force, have
been fitted out from thofe ports, whofe rapacity and vigi-
lance fcarce a veffel bound from the Windward Iflands to Jamaica can efcape. The prizes which they made, in a few fhort
months, abundantly compenfated for the lofs of their fhips at
Port au Prince *(h)*.

AFTER

(h) The following is a lift of veffels bound to Jamaica, which were taken and
carried into Aux Cayes, between June 1794 and June 1795, moft of them laden
with dry goods, provifions, and plantation ftores, and many of them of great value.

			From
The Edward - - -	Wᵐ Marfhall -	{ 13th June 1794, }	Briftol.
Fame - - -	Robᵗ Hall - -	July - - -	L. and Cork.
Bellona - -	Thoˢ White -	- - - - -	Liverpool.
Hope - - -	Wᵐ Swan.		
Molly - - -	Peter Mawdfley -	5thMar.1795,	Africa, 300 negroes.
Hodge - - -	Geo. Brown -	19th Ditto,	Liverpool.
William - - -	Thoˢ Calloine -	20th Ditto.	
Bell - - - -	Archᵈ Weir -	Ditto,	Greenock.
Buftler - - -	Sewell -	- - - - -	a tranfport.
Druid - - -	Wilfon -	14th March,	Leith.
Martha - - -	Wᵐ Reid - -	31ft March,	London.
Alexander - -	Benjᵃ Moor -	17th April,	Glafgow.
Lovely Peggy -	Peter Murphy.		
Swallow - - -	Lachlan Vafs -	10th May.	

a

Dunmore

AFTER all, though I have afferted nothing which I do not believe to be true, I will honeftly admit, that many important facts and circumftances, unknown to me, very probably exifted, an acquaintance with which is indifpenfably neceffary to enable any man to form a correct judgment on the meafures which were purfued on this occafion.   To a writer, fitting with compofure in his clofet, with a partial difplay of facts before him, it is no difficult tafk to point out faults and miftakes in the conduct of publick affairs; and even where miftakes are difcovered, the wifdom of after-knowledge is very cheaply acquired. It is the lot of our nature, that the beft concerted plans of human policy are fubject to errors which the meaneft obferver will fometimes detect. " The hand (fays an eminent writer) that " cannot build a hovel, may demolifh a palace."

BUT, a new fcene now opens for contemplation and reflection, arifing from intelligence received fince I began my work, that the Spanifh government has formally ceded to the republick of

Dunmore	- -	Stephen Conmick	26th May,	London.
Maria	- - -	Wilkinfon	- - - -	Ditto.
Minerva	- - -	Robertfon	4th June,	Africa, 450 negroes.
General Mathew	Tho' Douglas	8th Ditto,	London.
A fchooner, name forgot - -	Adam Walker -	22d Ditto,	Glafgow.
Hope	- - -	Hambleton	Ditto,	Ditto.
Caledonia	- -	Hunter -	25th Ditto,	Leith, laft from London.
Molly	- - -	Simpfon -	27th Ditto,	Glafgow.
Refolution	- -	Taunton -	29th Ditto,	Hull.

And feveral veffels belonging to Kingfton, names forgot.

France

France the whole of this great and noble ifland in perpetual fovereignty! So extraordinary a circumftance will doubtlefs give birth to much fpeculation and enquiry, as well concerning the value and extent of the territory ceded, as the prefent difpofition and general character of the Spanifh inhabitants. Will they relifh this transfer of their allegiance from a monarchical to a republican government, made, as it confeffedly is, without their previous confent or knowledge; or may reafonable expectations be encouraged, that they will now cordially co-operate with the Englifh, in reducing the country to the Britifh dominion? Will fuch affiftance effect the re eftablifhment of fubordination and good government among the vaft body of revolted negroes? Thefe are deep queftions, the inveftigation of which will lead to enquiries of ftill greater magnitude; for, whether we confider the poffeffion, by an active and induftrious people, of fo vaft a field for enterprize and improvement on the one hand, or the triumph of fuccefsful revolt and favage anarchy on the other, it appears to me that the future fate and profitable exiftence of the Britifh territories in this part of the world, are involved in the iffue. On all thefe, and various collateral fubjects, I regret that I do not poffefs the means of giving much fatisfaction to the reader. Such information, however, as I have collected on fome of the preceding enquiries, and fuch reflections as occur to me on others, will be found in the enfuing chapter, which concludes my work.

C H A P.

CHAP. XII.

Ancient State of the Spanish Colony.—The Town of St. Domingo established by Bartholomew Columbus in 1498.—Pillaged by Drake in 1586.—Conjectures and Reflections concerning its present Condition, and the State of Agriculture in the interior Country.—Numbers and Character of the present Inhabitants.—Their Animosity towards the French Planters, and Jealousy of the English.—Conjectures concerning the future Situation of the whole Island; and some concluding Reflections.

THE Spanish colony in Hispaniola (the name St. Domingo being properly applicable to the chief city only) was the earliest establishment made by the nations of Europe in the new world; and, unhappily, it is too notorious to be denied, that it was an establishment founded in rapacity and cemented with blood! The sole object of the first Spanish adventurers was to ransack the bowels of the earth for silver and gold; in which frantick pursuit, they murdered at least a million of the peaceful and inoffensive natives! As the mines became exhausted, a few of the more industrious entered on the cultivation of cacao, ginger, and sugar; but the poverty of the greater part of the inhabitants, and the discovery of new mines in Mexico, occasioned a prodigious emigration;—the experience of past disappointments not proving sufficiently powerful to cure the rage for acquiring wealth by a shorter course than that of patient industry. In less than a century, therefore, Hispaniola was nearly deserted, and nothing preserved it as a co-

A a
lony,

CHAP.
XII.
lony, but the eftablifhment of archiepifcopal government in its chief city, St. Domingo, and its being for many years the feat of civil and criminal jurifdiction, in cafes of appeal, from all the territories of Spain in this part of the world (a).

THE settlement of the French in the weftern part of the ifland, of the origin of which I have already given an account, though the primary caufe of hereditary and irreconcilable enmity between the two colonies, was however productive of good even to the Spaniards themfelves. As the French fettlers increafed in number, and their plantations became enlarged, they wanted oxen for their markets, and horfes for their mills. Thefe, their neighbours were able to fupply without much exertion of labour; and thus an intercourfe was created, which has continued to the prefent day; the Spaniards receiving, through the French, the manufactures of Europe, in exchange for cattle. The example too, before their eyes, of fuccefsful induftry and growing profperity, was not wholly without its effect. The cultivation of fugar, which had diminifhed nearly to nothing, was revived in different parts of the Spanifh territory, and plantations were eftablifhed of cacao, indigo, ginger, and tobacco. The quantity of fugar exported in the beginning of the prefent century, is faid to have amounted yearly to 15,000 chefts each of 7 cwt.

THE country itfelf being evidently more mountainous in the central and eaftern than in the weftern parts, it is probable, that the Spanifh territory is, on the whole, naturally lefs fer-

(a) The adminiftration of juftice throughout Spanifh America is at prefent divided into twelve courts of *audience*, one only of which is at St. Domingo.

tile

tile than that of the French; but much the greater portion of the ifland remained, until the late treaty, under the Spanifh dominion; and of that, by far the major part continues at this hour an unproductive wildernefs. On the northern coaft, the line of divifion began at the river Maffacre, and, croffing the country fomewhat irregularly, terminated on the fouthern fide, at a fmall bay called *Les Ances à Pitre*; leaving about two-thirds of the whole ifland in the poffeffion of Spain. Proceeding eaftward along the fhore from the boundary on the north, the firft place of note is Monte Chrifti, a town which formerly grew to importance by contraband traffick with North America, but is now reduced to a miferable village, the abode of a few fifhermen, and the furrounding country exhibits a melancholy profpect of neglect and fterility. The river St. Jago runs into the fea at this place; on the banks of which, at fome diftance inland, are grafs farms of confiderable extent. From the mouth of this river, for the fpace of fifteen leagues, to Punta Ifabella (the fcite of the firft fettlement eftablifhed by Chriftopher Columbus) the foil, though capable of improvement, exhibits no fign of cultivation. From Ifabella to old Cape François (with the exception of Puerto de Plata) the coaft feems entirely deferted; nor, after paffing the bay of Samana, does a much better profpect offer, until coafting round the eaftern extremity, we reach a vaft extent of level country called *Los Llanos*, or the Plains; at the weft end of which, on the banks of the river Ozama, ftands the metropolis.

THIS city, which was long the moft confiderable in the new world, was founded by Bartholomew Columbus, in the year 1498, and named after a faint of great renown in thofe days, St.

A a 2

Dominick.

Dominick.   There is preferved in Oviedo, a Spanifh hiftorian,
who refided here about thirty years after its firft eftablifhment,
an account of its ftate and population at that period, which being equally authentick and curious, I fhall prefent to the reader
at length.

     " But nowe (fays the Hiftorian) to fpeake fumwhat of the;
" principall and chiefe place of the iflande, whiche is the citie
" of *San Domenico :* I faye, that as touchynge the buildynges,,
" there is no citie in Spaine, fo muche for fo-muche (no not
" *Barfalona,* whiche I have oftentymes feene) that is to bee
" preferred before this generallye.   For the houfes of San Do-
" menico are for the mofte parte of ftone, as are they of
" Barfalona.   The fituation is muche better tha that of *Bar-*
" *falona,* by reafon that the ftreates are much larger and playner,
" and without comparyfon more directe and ftrayght furth.
" For beinge buylded nowe in our tyme, befyde the commo-
" ditie of the place of the foundation, the ftreates were alfo
" directed with corde compafe and meafure; werein it excelleth
" al the cities that I have fene.   It hath the fea fo nere, that
" of one fyde there is no more fpace betwen the fea and the
" citie, then the waules.   On the other parte, hard by the
" fyde and at the foote of the houfes, paffeth the ryver *Ozama,*
" whiche is a marveylous porte; wherein laden fhyppes ryfe
" very nere to the lande, and in manner under the houfe wyn-
" dowes.   In the myddeft of the citie is the fortreffe and
" caftle; the port or haven alfo, is fo fayre and commodious
" to defraight or unlade fhyppes, as the lyke is founde but in
" fewe places of the worlde.   The chymineis that are in this citie
" are about fyxe hundreth in number, and fuch houfes as I have
                                              " fpoken

" fpoken of before; of the which fum are fo fayre and large
" that they maye well receave and lodge any lorde or noble
" manne of Spayne, with his trayne and familie; and efpecially
" that which Don *Diego Colon,* viceroy under your majeftie,
" hath in this citie, is fuche that I knowe no man in Spayne that
" hath the lyke, by a quarter, in goodneffe, confyderynge all the
" commodities of the fame. Lykewyfe the fituation thereof as
" beinge above the fayde porte, and altogyther of ftone, and
" havynge many faire and large roomes, with as goodly a pro-
" fpect of the lande and fea as may be devyfed, feemeth unto
" me fo magnifical and princelyke, that your majeftie may bee
" as well lodged therein as in any of the mofte exquifite build-
" ed houfes of Spayne. There is alfo a cathedrall churche
" buylded of late, where, aswell the byfhop accordyng to his
" dygnitie, as alfo the canones, are wel indued. This church
" is well buylded of ftone and lyme; and of good woorkeman-
" fhyppe. There are further-more three monafteries bearyng
" the names of Saynt Dominike, Saynt Frances, and Saynt
" Mary of Mercedes; the whiche are well buylded, although
" not fo curiouflye as they of Spayne. There is alfo a very
" good hofpitall for the ayde and fuccour of pore people,
" whiche was founded by Michaell Paffamont, threafurer to
" your majeftie. To conclude, this citie fro day to day in-
" creafeth in welth and good order, as wel for that the fayde
" admyrall and viceroy, with the lorde chaunceloure and coun-
" fayle appoynted there by your majeftie, have theyr conti-
" nuall abydynge here, as alfo that the rycheft men of the
" ilande refort hyther, for thyre mofte commodious habitation
" and trade of fuch merchaundies as are eyther brought owt of
                                                    " Spayne,

" Spayne, or fent thyther from this iland, which nowe fo
" abundeth in many thynges, that it ferveth Spayne with
" many commodities, as it were with ufury requityng fuch
" benefites as it fyrft receaved from thenfe *(b)*.

IT is probable that St. Domingo had now attained the fummit
of its profperity. About fixty years afterwards (1ft January
1586) it was attacked by Sir Francis Drake; a narrative
of whofe expedition, by an eye-witnefs, is preferved in
Hakluyt's Collection; from which it appears, that it was, even
then, a city of great extent and magnificence; and it is fhocking to relate, that, after a month's poffeffion, Drake thought
himfelf authorized, by the laws of war, to deftroy it by fire.
" We fpent the early part of the mornings (fays the hiftorian
of the voyage) in fireing the outmoft houfes; but they being
built very magnificently of ftone, with high loftes, gave us no
fmall travell to ruin them. And albeit, for divers dayes together, we ordeined ech morning by day-break, until the heat
began at nine of the clocke, that two hundred mariners did
nought els but labour to fire and burn the faid houfes, whilft
the fouldiers, in a like proportion, ftood forth for their guard;
yet did we not, or could not, in this time, confume fo much
as one third part of the towne; and fo in the end, wearied with
firing, we were contented to accept of five and twenty thoufand
ducats, of five fhillings and fixpence the peece, for the ranfome
of the reft of the towne *(c)*."

OF

(b) From a tranflation by Richard Eden, printed, London 1555, in black
letter.

(c) The following anecdote, related by the fame author, is too ftriking to be
overlooked. I fhall quote his own words: During the ftay of the Englifh army
in

OF the prefent condition of this ancient city, the number of its inhabitants, and the commerce which they fupport, I can obtain no account on which I can depend. That it hath been long in its decline, I have no doubt ; but that it is wholly depopulated and in ruins, as Raynal afferts, I do not believe. The cathedral and other publick buildings are ftill in being, and were lately the refidence of a confiderable body of clergy and lawyers. The city continued alfo, while under the Spa-nifh government, the diocefe of an archbifhop, to whom, it is faid, the bifhops of St. Jago in Cuba, Venezuela in New Spain, and St. John's in Porto Rico, were fuffragans. Thefe circumftances, added to the fecurity, commodioufnefs, and ex-tent of the port or harbour, containing throughout not lefs than

in the city, " it chanced that the general fent on a meffage to the Spanifh governor, a negro boy with a flag of white, fignifying truce, as is the Spanyards ordinarie manner to do there, when they approch to fpeak to us ; which boy unhappily was firft met withall by fome of thofe who had been belonging as officers for the king in the Spanifh galley, which, with the towne, was lately fallen into our hands, who, without all order or reafon, and contrary to that good ufage wherewith wee had intertained their meffengers, furioufly ftrooke the poor boy thorow the body, with which wound the boy returned to the general, and, after he had declared the manner of this wrongfull crueltie, died forthwith in his prefence ; wherewith the generall being greatly paffion'd, commanded—the provoft martiall to caufe a couple of friers, then prifoners, to be carried to the fame place where the boy was ftroken, and there prefently to be hanged ; difpatching, at the fame inftant, another poor prifoner, with the reafon wherefore this execution was done, and with this further meffage, that untill the party who had thus murdered the general's meffenger, were delivered into our hands to receive condigne punifhment, there fhould no day paffe wherein there fhould not two prifoners be hanged, until they were all confumed which were in our hands. Whereupon the day following, hee that had been captaine of the king's galley, brought the offender to the towne's end, offering to deliver him into our hands ; but it was thought to be a more honourable revenge to make them there, in our fight, to performe the execution themfelves, which was done accordingly."

three

CHAP.
XII.

three fathoms of water, and protected by a bar over which the largeſt veſſels may paſs with ſafety, have hitherto ſaved St. Domingo from entire decay, and may poſſibly continue to ſave it. With this very defective information the reader muſt be content. As little ſeems to be known concerning the ſtate of agriculture in the Spaniſh poſſeſſions in this iſland, as of their capital and commerce. A few planters are ſaid to cultivate cacao, tobacco, and ſugar, for their own expenditure; and, perhaps ſome ſmall quantities of each are ſtill exported for conſumption in Spain. The chief article of exportation, however, continues to be, what it always has been ſince the mines were abandoned, *the hides of horned cattle*; which have multiplied to ſuch a degree, that the proprietors are ſaid to reckon them by thouſands; and vaſt numbers (as I believe I have elſewhere obſerved) are annually ſlaughtered ſolely for the ſkins †.

IT ſeems therefore extremely probable, that the cultivation of the earth is almoſt entirely neglected throughout the whole of the Spaniſh dominion in this iſland; and that ſome of the fineſt tracts of land in the world, once the paradiſe of a ſimple and innocent people, are now abandoned to the beaſts of the field, and the vultures which hover round them *(d)*.

OF this deſcription, probably, is the country already mentioned, called Los Llanos, which ſtretches eaſtward

† It is ſaid that a Company was formed at Barcelona in 1757, with excluſive privileges, for the re-eſtabliſhment of agriculture and commerce in the Spaniſh part of St. Domingo: I know not with what ſucceſs.

(d) The *Gallinazo*, or American vulture, a very ravenous and filthy bird that feeds on carrion. Theſe birds abound in St. Domingo, and devour the carcaſſes of the cattle as ſoon as the ſkins are ſtripped off by the hunters.

from

from the capital upwards of fourscore British miles in length, by twenty or twenty-five in width; and which, abounding in rivers throughout, may be supposed adapted for the growth of every tropical production in the greatest perfection: It seems capable also of being artificially flooded in dry weather.

NEXT to Los Llanos in magnitude, but superior, it is believed, in native fertility, is the noble valley to the north, called *Vega Real*; through the middle of which flows the river *Yuna*, for the space of fifty miles, and disembogues in Samana bay to the east. Perhaps it were no exaggeration to say, that this and the former districts are alone capable of producing more sugar, and other valuable commodities, than all the British West Indies put together.

THESE plains, however, though in contiguity the largest, are not the only parts of the country on which nature has bestowed extraordinary fertility. Glades abundantly rich, easy of access, and obvious to cultivation, are every where found even in the bosom of the mountains; while the mountains themselves contribute to fertilize the vallies which they encircle.

IN beholding the gifts of a bountiful Creator, thus lying useless and unimproved, and remembering at what an expence of human blood, and by what inexpiable guilt the Spanish nation obtained the possession of these countries from the rightful possessors, it is scarce possible to abstain from very gloomy and

B b

desponding

defponding reflections, or to fupprefs the exclamation, *how in-*
fcrutable are the ways of Divine Providence!

THUS fcanty and uninterefting is the beft account I have to
give of the territory itfelf; nor is my information much more
perfect concerning the number and condition of the people by
whom it is at prefent inhabited.   The earlieft detachments
from Old Spain were undoubtedly numerous.   Herrera, an
accurate and well-informed hiftorian, reckons that there
were, at one period, no lefs than 14,000 Caftillians in Hifpaniola.   Such was the renown of its riches, that men of all
ranks and conditions reforted thither, in the fond expectation of fharing in the golden harveft.   Its mines, indeed, were
very productive.   Robertfon relates, that they continued for
many years to yield a revenue of 460,000 pefos *(e)*.   In contrafting this fact, with an anecdote which I have elfewhere †
recorded, that the inhabitants, at the time of Drake's invafion, were fo wretchedly poor, as to be compelled to ufe, in
barter among themfelves, *pieces of leather* as a fubftitute for money, we are furnifhed with a ftriking proof, that the true way to
acquire riches, is not by digging into the bowels, but by improv-
ing the furface, of the earth.   Not having any manufactures, nor
the productions of agriculture, to offer in exchange for the neceffaries and conveniencies of life, all their gold had foon found
its way to Europe; and when the mines became exhaufted, their

(e) Upwards of £. 100,000 fterling.

† Hiftory of the Britifh Weft Indies, vol. i.

penury

penury was extreme; and floth, depopulation, and degeneracy, were its neceffary confequences (f).

THE introduction into this ifland of negroes from Africa, of which I have elfewhere traced the origin and caufe (g), took place at an early period. This refource did not, however, greatly contribute to augment the population of the colony; for fuch of the whites as removed to the continent, in fearch of richer mines and better fortune, commonly took their negroes with them; and the fmall pox, a few years afterwards, deftroyed prodigious numbers of others. In 1717, the whole number of inhabitants under the Spanifh dominion, of all ages and conditions, enflaved and free, were no more than 18,410, and fince that time, I conceive, they have rather diminifhed than increafed. Of pure whites (in contradiftinction to the people of mixed blood) the number is undoubtedly very inconfiderable; perhaps not 3,000 in the whole.

(f) The grofs ignorance of confidering gold and filver as *real* inftead of *artificial* wealth, and the folly of neglecting agriculture for the fake of exploring mines, have been well expofed by Abbé Raynal; who compares the conduct of the Spaniards in this refpect, to that of the dog in the fable, dropping the piece of meat which he had in his mouth, to catch at the fhadow of it in the water.

(g) Hift. of the Britifh Weft Indies, Book iv. c. 2. A curious circumftance was, however, omitted. When the Portuguefe firft began the traffick in negroes, application was made to the Pope to fanctify the trade by a bull, which his Holinefs iffued accordingly. In confequence of this permiffion and authority, a very confiderable flave-market was eftablifhed at Lifbon, infomuch, that about the year 1539, from 10 to 12,000 negroes were fold there annually.

THE

THE hereditary and unextinguifhable animofity between the Spanifh and French planters has already been noticed. It is probable, however, that the knowledge of this circumftance created greater reliance on the co-operation of the Spaniards with the Britifh army than was juftified by fubfequent events. At the earneft and repeated folicitations of Lieutenant Colonel Brifbane, in 1794, orders were indeed tranfmitted from the city of St. Domingo to the Commandant at Verettes, Don Francifco de Villa Neuva, to join the Englifh with the militia of that part of the country; the Britifh garrifon at St. Marc undertaking to fupply them with provifions and ammunition: but thefe orders were ill obeyed. Not more than three hundred men were brought into the field, and even thofe were far from being hearty in the common caufe. The French loyalifts appeared in greater numbers in the neighbourhood of St. Marc than in any other diftrict; and the Spaniards detefted the French colonifts of all defcriptions. It was evident, at the fame time, that they were almoft equally jealous of the Englifh; betraying manifeft fymptoms of difcontent and envy, at beholding them in poffeffion of St. Marc, and the fertile plains in its vicinage. They proceeded, however, and took the town and harbour of Gonaive; but their fubfequent conduct manifefted the bafeft treachery, or the rankeft cowardice. The town was no fooner attacked by a fmall detachment from the revolted negroes, than the Spaniards fuffered themfelves to be driven out of it, in the moft unaccountable manner; leaving the French inhabitants to the fury of the favages, who maffacred the whole number (as their

2　　　　　　　　　　　　　　　　　　　　comrades

comrades had done at Fort Dauphin) and then reduced the town itself to afhes *(h)*.

ON the whole, there is reafon to fuppofe that a great proportion of the prefent Spanifh proprietors in St. Domingo are a debafed and degenerate race ; a motley mixture from European, Indian, and African anceftry ; and the obfervation which has been made in another place *(i)*, concerning the Spanifh inhabitants of Jamaica, at the conqueft of that ifland in 1655, will

(h) In the northern province of the French colony, the inhabitants of Fort Dauphin, a town fituated on the Spanifh borders, having no affiftance from the Englifh, and being apprehenfive of an attack from the rebel negroes, applied for protection, and delivered up the town, to the Spanifh government. The Spanifh commandant, on accepting the conditions required, which were chiefly for perfonal fafety, iffued a proclamation, importing, that fuch of the French planters as would feek refuge there, fhould find fecurity. Seduced by this proclamation, a confiderable number repaired thither ; when, on Monday the 7th of July 1794, *Jean François*, the negro general, and leader of the revolt in 1791, entered the town with fome thoufands of armed negroes. He met not the fmalleft refiftance, either at the advanced pofts, or at the barriers occupied by the Spanifh troops ; the inhabitants keeping their houfes, in the hope of being protected by the commandant. In an inftant, every part of the city refounded with the cry of " Long live the king of Spain ! Kill all the French ; but offer no violence to the Spaniards;" and a general maffacre of the French commenced, in which no lefs than 771 of them, without diftinction of fex or age, were murdered on the fpot : the Spanifh foldiers ftanding by, fpectators of the tragedy. It is thought. however, that if the Spaniards had openly interpofed, they would have fhared the fate of the French. It is faid that Mont-Calvos, commander of the Spanifh troops, moved by compaffion towards fome French gentlemen of his acquaintance, admitted them into the ranks, dreffing them in the Spanifh uniform for their fecurity ; others were fecretly conveyed to the fort, and fent off in the night to Monte Chrifti, where they got on board an American veffel belonging to Salem.

(i) Hiftory of the Britifh Weft Indies, vol. i.

equally

equally apply to thefe. They are neither polifhed by focial in-tercourfe, nor improved by education; but pafs their days in gloomy languor, enfeebled by floth, and depreffed by poverty. From fuch men, therefore, great as their antipathy is to the French nation, and however averfe they may be to a change of laws and government, I am afraid that no cordial co-operation with the Britifh can ever be expected. The beft families among them, rather than fubmit to the French dominion, will probably remove to Cuba, or feek out new habitations among their countrymen on the neighbouring continent; while thofe which remain will neceffarily fink into the general mafs of coloured people, French and Englifh; a clafs that, I think, in procefs of time, will become mafters of the towns and culti-vated parts of the ifland on the fea-coaft; leaving the interior country to the revolted negroes. Such, probably, will be the fate of this once beautiful and princely colony; and it grieves me to fay, that the prefent exertions of Great Britain on this blood-ftained theatre, can anfwer no other end than to haften the cataftrophe!

I MIGHT here expatiate on the wonderful difpenfations of Divine Providence, in raifing up the enflaved Africans to avenge the wrongs of the injured aborigines: I might alfo indulge the fond but fallacious idea, that as the negroes of St. Domingo have been eye-witneffes to the benefits of civilized life among the whites;—have feen in what manner, and to what ex-tent, focial order, peaceful induftry, and fubmiffion to laws, contribute to individual and general profperity (advantages which were denied to them in their native country;) fome fupe-rior

rior spirits may hereafter rise up among them, by whose encouragement and example they may be taught, in due time, to
discard the ferocious and sordid manners and pursuits of savage
life; to correct their vices, and be led progressively on to civilization and gentleness, to the knowledge of truth, and the
practice of virtue. This picture is so pleasing to the imagination, that every humane and reflecting mind must wish it may
be realized; but I am afraid it is the mere creation of the
fancy—" the fabrick of a vision!" Experience has demonstrated, that a wild and lawless freedom affords no means
of improvement, either mental or moral. The Charaibes of St.
Vincent, and the Maroon negroes of Jamaica, were originally
enslaved Africans; and *what they now are*, the freed negroes of
St. Domingo *will hereafter be*; savages in the midst of society—
without peace, security, agriculture, or property; ignorant of
the duties of life, and unacquainted with all the soft and en-
dearing relations which render it desirable; averse to labour,
though frequently perishing of want; suspicious of each other;
and towards the rest of mankind revengeful and faithless, remorseless and bloody-minded; pretending to be free, while
groaning beneath the capricious despotism of their chiefs, and
feeling all the miseries of servitude, without the benefits of
subordination!

IF what I have thus—not hastily, but—deliberately predicted,
concerning the fate of this unfortunate country, shall be verified
by the event, all other reflections must yield to the pressing
consideration how best to obviate and defeat the influence
which so dreadful an example of successful revolt and triumphant

phant anarchy may have in our own iflands. This is a fubject which will foon force itfelf on the moft ferious attention of Government; and I am of opinion, that nothing lefs than the co-operation of the Britifh parliament with the colonial legiflatures can meet its emergency. On the other hand, if it be admitted that the object is infinitely too important, and the means and refources of France much too powerful and abundant, to fuffer a doubt to remain concerning the ultimate accomplifhment of her views, in feizing on the whole of this extenfive country: if we can fuppofe that (convince at length, by painful experience, of the monftrous folly of fuddenly emancipating barbarous men, and placing them at once in all the complicated relations of civil fociety) fhe will finally fucceed in reducing the vaft body of fugitive negroes to obedience; and in eftablifhing fecurity, fubordination, and order, under a conftitution of government fuited to the actual condition of the various claffes of the inhabitants:—if fuch fhall be her good fortune, it will not require the endowment of prophecy to foretel the refult. The middling, and who are commonly the moft induftrious, clafs of Planters, throughout every ifland in the Weft Indies, allured by the cheapnefs of the land and the fuperior fertility of the foil, will affuredly feek out fettlements in St. Domingo; and a Weft Indian empire will fix itfelf in this noble ifland, to which, in a few fhort years, all the tropical poffeffions of Europe will be found fubordinate and tributary. Placed in the centre of Britifh and Spanifh America, and fituated to windward of thofe territories of either nation which are moft valuable, while the commerce of both muft exift only by its good pleafure, all the riches of Mexico will be wholly at its difpofal.

Then

Then will the humbled Spaniard lament, when it is too late, the thoughtlefs and improvident furrender he has made, and Great Britain find leifure to reflect how deeply fhe is herfelf concerned in the confequences of it.   The dilemma is awful, and the final iffue known only to that omnifcient Power, in whofe hand is the fate of empires !   But whatever the iffue may be,—in all the varieties of fortune,—in all events and circumftances, whether profperous or adverfe,—it infinitely concerns both the people of Great Britain, and the inhabitants of the Britifh colonies,—I cannot repeat it too often,—to derive admonition from the ftory before us.   To Great Britain I would intimate, that if, difregarding the prefent example, encouragement fhall continue to be given to the peftilent doctrines of thofe hot-brained fanaticks, and deteftable incendiaries, who, under the vile pretence of philanthropy and zeal for the interefts of fuffering humanity, preach up rebellion and murder to the contented and orderly negroes in our own territories, what elfe can be expected, but that the fame dreadful fcenes of carnage and defolation, which we have contemplated in St. Domingo, will be renewed among our countrymen and relations in the Britifh Weft Indies ?   May God Almighty, of his infinite mercy, avert the evil !   To the refident Planters I addrefs myfelf with ftill greater folicitude ; and, if it were in my power, would exhort them, " with more than mortal voice," to rife above the foggy atmofphere of local prejudices, and, by a generous furrender of temporary advantages, do that which the Parliament of Great Britain, in the pride and plenitude of imperial dominion, cannot effect, and ought not to attempt.   I call on them, with the fincerity and the affection of a brother, of them-

felves

felves to reftrain, limit, and finally abolifh the further introduction of enflaved men from Africa;—not indeed by meafures of
fudden violence and injuftice, difregarding the many weighty
and complicated interefts which are involved in the iffue; but
by means which, though flow and gradual in their operation,
will be fure and certain in their effect.   The Colonial Legiflatures, by their fituation and local knowledge, are alone competent
to this great and glorious tafk : and this example of St. Domingo,
and the dictates of felf-prefervation like the hand-writing againft
the wall, warn them no longer to delay it!   Towards the poor
negroes over whom the ftatutes of Great Britain, the accidents
of fortune, and the laws of inheritance, have invefted them with
power, their general conduct for the laft twenty years (notwithftanding the foul calumnies with which they have been loaded)
may court enquiry and bid defiance to cenfure. A perfeverance
in the fame benevolent fyftem, progreffively leading the objects of
it to civilization and mental improvement, preparatory to greater
indulgence, is all that humanity can require; for it is all that
prudence can dictate. Thus will the Planters prepare a fhield of
defence againft their enemies, and fecure to themfelves that fere-
nity and elevation of mind, which arife from an approving confcience; producing affurance in hope, and confolation in adverfity.   Their perfecutors and flanderers in the meantime will be
difregarded or forgotten; for calumny, though a great is a temporary evil, but truth and juftice will prove triumphant and
eternal !

TABLEAU

Du Commerce et des Finances de la partie Françoise

de S<small>T</small>. DOMINGUE

1791.

☞ The firſt Four of the following TABLES were drawn up by order of the Legiſlative Aſſembly of FRANCE, which met the 1ſt of October 1791, and ſeem to have been framed in the view of aſcertaining the actual ſtate of the Colony, and its Commerce, immediately before the breaking out of the rebellion of the Negroes in the Month of Auguſt of that Year. The totals will be found to differ, in ſome of the particulars, from the ſtatement which has been given in the preceding pages. The difference ariſes partly from the actual change of circumſtances, in the courſe of two years which intervened between the periods when each ſtatement was made up, and partly, I am afraid, from errors and omiſſions of my own.

No. I.

Etat Général des Cultures et des Manufactures de la Partie Françoise de St Domingue. 1791.

CHEFS LIEUX OU JURISDICTIONS.	QUARTIERS OU PAROISSES.	Sucreries. En blanc.	En brut.	Cafeteries.	Cotonneries.	Indigoteries.	Tanneries.	Guildiveries.	Cacaoteries.	Fours a Chaux.	Briqueries et Poteries.	Nombre de Nègres.
Partie du Nord. — Le Cap	Le Cap et dépendances	1	—	2	—	—	1	3	—	2	1	21,613
	La petite Ance et la plaine du Nord	43	7	37	1	5	2	3	—	4	2	11,122
	L'acul, Limonade et Ste Suzanne	52	4	157	3	6	—	9	—	1	1	19,876
	Morin et la Grande Rivière	35	1	255	2	1	—	5	5	7	—	18,554
	Le Dondon et Marmelade	—	—	216	1	—	—	1	1	32	2	17,376
	A' Limbé et Port Margot	22	3	272	5	11	—	7	1	2	2	15,978
	Plaisance et le Borgne	—	—	324	2	4	—	—	—	3	5	15,018
Le Fort Dauphin	Le Fort Dauphin	29	7	71	2	10	—	4	—	3	8	10,004
	Ouanaminthe et Valhere	25	2	151	—	2	—	4	—	—	3	9,987
	Le Terrier rouge et le trou	56	1	123	1	37	—	5	—	4	1	15,476
Le Port de Paix	Le Port de Paix le petit St Louis / Jean Rabel et le gros Morne	6	2	218	9	369	—	4	18	26	4	29,540
Le Mole	Le Mole et Bombarde	—	—	31	14	15	—	—	—	—	—	3,183
Partie de l' Ouest. — Port au Prince	Port au-Prince et la Croix des Bouquets	65	75	151	22	15	—	29	1	20	1	42,848
	L'Arcahaye	11	36	62	24	48	—	14	—	23	5	18,553
	Mirebalais	3	—	27	19	322	—	—	2	5	—	10,902
Léogane	Léogane	27	39	58	18	78	—	25	1	14	1	14,896
St Marc	St Marc, la petite Rivière / Les Verettes et les Gonaives	22	21	298	315	1,184	—	10	1	71	12	67,216
Le petit Goave	Le petit Goave, le grand Goave, et le fonds des Négres	11	16	52	25	31	—	11	2	9	—	18,829
	L'Anse a Veau et le petit trou	6	11	11	7	185	—	7	1	9	2	13,229
Jérémie	Jérémie et le Cap Dame Marie	3	5	105	30	44	—	6	25	14	—	20,774
Partie du Sud. — Les Cayes	Les Cayes et Torbeck	24	86	69	76	175	—	18	2	32	8	30,937
Le Cap Tiburon	Le Cap Tiburon et les Coteaux	1	1	24	12	169	—	4	7	1	—	8,153
St Louis	St Louis, Cavaillon et Aquin	9	23	39	28	157	—	8	2	18	1	18,785
Jacmel	Jacmel, les Cayes, et Baynel	—	1	57	89	129	—	—	3	7	1	21,151
Total	51 Paroisses	451	341	2,810	705	3,097	3	173	69	313	61	453,000

No. II.

Etat des Denrées de St. Domingue exportées en France depuis le 1er Janvier 1791 au 31 Décre inclusivement.

Départemens.	Sucre. Blanc. Livres.	Sucre. Brut. Livres.	Café. Livres.	Coton. Livres.	Indigo. Livres.	Cuirs. en Poil. Banettes.	Cuirs. Tannés. Côtes.	Sirop. Boucauts.	Tafia. Barique.
Partie du Nord.									
Le Cap - - -	43,864,552	1,517,489	29,367,382	—	195,099	2,006	6,975	10,654	
Le Fort Dauphin -	8,609,258	1,639,900	2,321,610	1,200	2,005	1,134	160	2,731	
Le Port de Paix -	473,800	824,500	1,829,754	38,752	61,472	120	—	272	25
Le Mole - - -	22,500	105,680	294,550	29,236	6,294	31	—	84	6
Partie de l'Ouest.									
Le Port au Prince -	7,792,219	53,648,923	14,584,023	1,370,021	176,918	1,601	752	8,350	36
Léogane - - -	1,492,983	7,688,537	1,786,484	154,084	12,520	112	—	95	45
Saint Marc - -	3,244,673	6,993,966	5,521,237	3,008,163	357,530	—	—	73	49
Le Petit Goave - -	218,866	855,237	1,395,690	84,865	320	—	—	206	6
Jérémie - - -	19,804	476,445	4,453,331	189,194	1,075	100	—		
Partie du Sud.									
Les Cayes - -	4,375,627	18,984,425	1,843,403	720,770	105,456	67	—	6,938	136
Le Cap Tiburon -	63,150	278,500	305,740	34,325	1,954	—	—	99	
St Louis - - -	2,000	9,600	90,706	42,497	2,064				
Jacmel - - -	48,266	67,910	4,357,270	613,019	7,309	15			
Total - - -	70,227,708	93,177,512	68,151,180	6,286,126	930,016	5,186	7,887	29,502	303

Valeur

No. II *continued.*

Valeur commune des Exportations et des Droits perçus dans la Colonie fur toutes les Denrées.

Indication de la nature des Denrées.	Quotité en nature.	Eftimation en raifon du prix Commun.		Du 1er Janvier 1791 au 31'Xbre de la même année.		Vendus en France.
				Valeur Commune.	Droits perçus.	
Sucre { Blanc ou terré	70,227,708	Livres - à —	12	67,670,781	2,528,197	65,142,584
{ Brut	93,177,512	Livres - à —	6	49,941,567	1,677,195	48,264,372
Café	68,151,180	Livres - à —	16	51,890,748	1,226,720	50,664,028
Coton	6,286,126	Livres - à 2 —		17,572,252	785,766	16,786,486
Indigo	930,016	Livres - à 7	10	10,875,120	465,008	10,410,112
Cacao	150 000	Livres - à —	16	120,000		120,000
Sirop	29,502	Boucauts - à 66 —		1,947,132	221,275	1,725,857
Tafia	303	Bariques - à 72 —		21,816	1,821	19,995
Cuirs Tannés	7,887	Cotés - à 10 —		78,870	10,377	68,493
Cuirs en poil	5,186	Banettes - à 18 —		93,348	7,807	85,541
Caret (tortoife fhell)	5,000	Livres - à 10 —		50,000	—	50,000
Gayac, Acajou, et Campêche.	1,500,000	Livres - à Eftimés		40,000	—	40,000
Total de la Valeur commune de toutes les Denrées - - - - -				200,301,634	6,924,166	193,377,468

Obfervation effentielle.

Toutes les fommes dont il eft queftion dans ce tableau font Argent des Colonies. Le change y eft à 33 ½, et la Livre Tournois comptée pour une livre dix fous.

1er Exemple.

Le montant des Exportations s'éleve Argent des Colonies à la fomme de - - - - - - 200,301,634
Réduite Argent de France à - - - 133,534,423

Différence fur cet Article de - - 66,767,211

2me Exemple.

La totalité des denrées exportées, et vendues en France montant enfemble à la fomme de - - - 193,377,468
Reduite en Livres Tournois à - - 128,918,312

Différence fur cet Article de - - 64,459,156

On obtiendra le même réfultat article par article ayant l'attention de reduire le tiers fur chaque fomme.

No. III.

Apperçu des Richeffes territoriales des habitations en grande Culture de la Partie Françoife de St. Domingue.

Indication de la Nature des Capitaux.	Nombre.	Eftimation particulière de chaque Objet en raifon du prix moyen.	Evaluation des Capitaux.		Totalité de la Valeur Générale.
			En Terres, Bâtimens, et Plantations.	En Négres et animaux employés à l'exploitation.	
Sucreries { en Blanc	451	à - 230,000	103,730,000	—	103,730,000
en Brut	341	à - 180,000	61,380,000	—	61,380,000
Cafeteries	2,810	à - 20,000	56,200,000	—	56,200,000
Cotonneries	705	à - 30,000	21,150,000	—	21,150,000
Indigoteries	3,097	à - 30,000	92,910,000	—	92,910,000
Guildiveries	173	à - 5,000	865,000	—	865,000
Cacaotières	69	à - 4,000	275,000	—	275,000
Tanneries	3	à - 160,000	480,000	—	480,000
Fours à Chaux, Briqueries et Poteries	374	à - 15,000	5,510,000		5,510,000
Nègres anciens et nouveaux, grands et petits	455,000	à - 2,500		1,137,500,000	1,137,500,000
Chevaux et Mulets	16,000	à - 400		6,400,000	6,400,000
Bêtes à cornes	12,000	à - 120		1,440,000	1,440,000
Total des Richeffes employées à la Culture			342,500,000	1,145,340,000	1,487,840,000

No. IV.

RECETTES ET DEPENSES, &c.

RECETTES.

DESIGNATION DES OBJETS.		Sommes.
Caiffe de la Marine.		
1. Reftant en Caiffe au 31 Décembre 1790		935,160
2. Droits perçus fur les Denrées exportées de la Colonie en France pendant l'anneé 1789 — 6,924,166		
A déduire les appointemens des Réceveurs de l'Octroi et frais de Bureaux — 34,200		6,889,966
3. Impofition pour la capitation des Efclaves — 581,035		
A déduire les remifes et modérations en faveur des Contribuables, cy — 25,286		555,749
4. Droits de 2 ½ pour Ct. fur les loyers des maifons —		376,143
5. Reçu de divers Débiteurs au Roi —		229,403
6. Loyers des Halles et maifons au profit de Sa Majefté —		30,453
7. Objets vendus dans les magazins des divers Départements —		139,324
8. Reçu de divers pour journées employées à l'Hôpital —		13,295
9. Rembourfemens des avances faites à divers —		149,930
10. Dépôt à charge de rembourfemens —		465,820
11. Montant des Lettres de change tirées fur les Tréforiers et Munitionnaires Généraux —		1,053,100
		10,838,348
Caiffe Générale.		
1. Reftant en Caiffe au 31 Décembre 1790 —		159,886
2. Reçu de divers Comptables en exercife et à valoir fur les débits pendant les années 1787, 1788, et 1789 —		178,756
3. Révenu de la ferme du bac du Cap. —		87,500
4. Révenu de la ferme des Poftes —		161,847
5. Reçu des anciens Comptables, Fermiers, &c. —		150,716
6. Remboursement d'un Prêt fait à la Caiffe Municipale —		30,000
7. Remboursement de celui fait à la Caiffe de la Marine —		49,042
8. Loyer de la Salle de Spectacle au Port au Prince —		2,000
9. Rembourfemens par divers Réceveurs des Droits domaniaux —		30,400
10. Reçu des Curateurs aux Succeffions vacantes —		321,143
		1,171,290

D d

DESIGNATION

No. IV. *continued.*

DESIGNATION DES OBJETS.	Sommes.

Caiſſe des Libertés.

1. Reſtant en Caiſſe au 31 Décembre 1790	51,642	
2. Il a eté verſé dans cette Caiſſe pour l'affranchiſſement de 297 Eſclaves pendant l'année 1790	547,892	654,906
3. Rembourſemens de divers Débiteurs a cette Caiſſe	33,830	
4. A compte ſur le produit de la vente de divers Comeſtibles	21,542	

Caiſſe des Droits Domaniaux.

1. Montant des Amandes	143,010	
2. Négres épaves vendus au profit du Roi	152,634	
3. Succeſſions à titre d'Aubaines, Bâtardiſes, &c.	318,444	780,300
4. Confiſcations	51,343	
5. Droits de 2 pour C. ſur le montant des ventes judiciaires	114,869	

Caiſſe de l'Entrepôt.

1. Droit d'un pour C. impoſé ſur les marchandiſes qui ſont importées et exportées par le Commerce étranger	112,397	
2. Droit de 3ll Tournois par quintal ſur le bœuf ſalé introduit dans la Colonie par le Commerce étranger	42,378	459,078
3. Droits additionels impoſés par arrêt du Conſeil de l'année 1786 et 1787	304,303	

Caiſſe des Conſignations.

1. Reſtant en Caiſſe au 31 Décembre 1790	82,500	
2. Conſigné par divers; dans la caiſſe du Tréſorier principal des Colonies pendant le cours de l'année 1789, pour la ſureté de 68 Eſclaves embarqués pour France	102,000	184,500

Invalides et fonds d'Armemens.

1. Recettes faites pendant l'année 1790 au profit des Invalides de la Marine	153,620	
2. Montant des gages acquis aux équipages dont les bâtimens ont été deſarmés dans la Colonie pendant les 9 derniers mois de 1789, et pendant l'année 1790	430,972	584,592

| Total de la Recette | 14,673,014 | 14,673,014 |

DEPENSES.

DESIGNATION DES OBJETS.	Sommes.

Caisse de la Marine.

1. Traitemens et Appointemens des Officiers de l'Etat Major général, et particuliers des Places - - -	580,000^{ll}	
2. Officiers de l'Administration - - -	670,000	
3. Conseils et Jurisdictions - - -	710,000	
4. Officiers de Santé - - -	183,547	
5. Appointemens et Soldes des Troupes - -	1,206,003	
6. Subsistences et Fournitures rélatives aux Troupes -	293,656	
7. Journées d'Hôpital - - -	606,478	
8. Fortifications et entretiens des Bâtimens publics -	917,560	
9. Achâts des matériaux nécessaires à la construction des Edifices publics - - - -	851,193	9,448,168
10. Entretiens des Bâtimens de Mer sur l'isle de la Gonave -	90,635	
11. Aux Entrepreneurs des Hôpitaux - -	196,000	
12. A divers pour fournitures de Riz et de Biscuit -	120,000	
13. Dépenses pour les chemins de communication -	586,102	
14. A divers Entrepreneurs de maçonnerie, charpente, &c. -	235,061	
15. Frais de voyages et avaries de mer. - -	142,064	
16. Remboursemens à la Caisse générale des Invalides -	511,520	
17. A divers pour loyers des maisons, magasins, &c. -	233,679	
18. Dépense faite par les vaisseaux de S. M. en Station dans la Colonie -	1,204,650	
19. Frais de transports, journées d'Ouvriers, &c. -	119,720	

Caisse Générale.

1. Traitemens et gages assignés sur cette Caisse - -	202,775	
2. A divers Entrepreneurs des Canaux, Fontaines, &c. -	229,403	
3. Payé aux Héritiers et Créanciers des Successions vacantes -	192,794	1,131,656
4. Payé à la décharge de la Caisse des Biens domaniaux -	397,109	
5. Indemnités et gratifications à divers - -	109,575	

Caisse des Libertés.

1. Pensions aux Peres et Meres de 10 a 12 enfans -	71,765	
2. Dépense pour l'achévement des remblais du quay du Roi -	72,731	
3. Travaux rélatifs au chemin de Jacmel -	86,621	
4. Jardin du Roi au Port au Prince et Plantes d'Asie -	50,912	
5. Travaux faits au Cap - - -	70,464	651,354
6. Entretiens et constructions des Fontaines publiques -	101,896	
7. Abrévoirs et Lavoirs publics -	65,058	
8. A divers pour transports des comestibles -	90,951	
9. Dons et gratifications assignées sur cette Caisse -	40,956	

No. IV. *continued.*

DESIGNATION DES OBJETS.	Sommes.
Caiffe des Droits domaniaux.	
1. Traitemens et gages des employés, rembourfemens des amandes, taxations de Témoins, et frais de voyages - - 482,550	
2. Réclamation des Epaves vendus au profit du Roi - - 46,521	
3. Frais de juftice applicables au produit des Succeffions vacantes - 160,848	702,380
4. Payé aux dénonciateurs, fur le produit des confifcations pour fait de Commerce interlope - - - - 12,461	
Caiffe de l'Entrepôt.	
1. Traitemens des Directeurs, Receveurs et Employés des Bureaux - 112,397	
2. Rembourfemens à divers pour les marchandifes ré-exportées - 2,028	459,070
3. Verfé dans la Caiffe de la Marine à titre de Dépôt - - 344,653	
Caiffe des Confignations.	
1. Rembourfemens à divers confignataires pour le rétour dans la Colonie de 53 Efclaves embarqués pour la France - - 79,500	81,000
2. Frais rélatifs à cette comptabilité - - - - 1,500	
Invalides et Fonds d'Armemens.	
1. Montant des remifes à faire à la Caiffe Générale des Invalides - 153,620	
2. Remifes faites dans les differents Ports, pour les gages acquis aux équipages pour les Défarmemens - - - 433,972	584,592
.Montant des Fonds non confommés au 31 Décembre 1791.	
Par la Caiffe de la Marine - - - - 1,493.674	
Par la Caiffe Générale - - - - - 39,634	1,614,886
Par la Caiffe des Libertés - - - - 3,659	
Par la Caiffe des Droits domaniaux - - - 77,919	
Somme pareille à la Recette - - - -	
14,673,014	14,673,014

No. IV. *continued.*

Rélévé Général des Dettes actives et paffives de St. Domingue au 31 X^{bre} 1791.

Dettes actives en faveur des diverfes Caiffes.

Indication de la nature des Créances.	Montant de la Créance publique.	Recouvremens faits en 1789.	en 1790.	Sommes dues en 1791.
1. Sommes dues à la Caiffe de la Marine par pro-meffes, obligations, &c. - - - -	6,576,838	633,221	229,403	5,714,214
2. Sommes dues par divers Contribuables -	2,514,465	483,701	376,143	1,654,621
3. Avances faites par la Colonie en faveur des Troupes et des Efcadres alliées - -	3,385,917	3,182,804	—	203,113
4. Débits de comptes ou arrerages des Fermes -	1,471,511	546,433	103,618	821,460
5. Sommes dues par divers particuliers - -	978,299	101,579	73,999	802,721
Total de la Créance publique de la Colonie -	14,927,030	4,947,738	783,163	9,196,129

Dettes paffives à la charge de diverfes Caiffes.

Indication de la nature des Dettes.	Montant de la Dette publique.	Payemens faits en 1789.	en 1790.	Sommes à payer en 1791
1. Il eft dû à l'Entrepreneur des Travaux du Roi dans la Partie du Nord - - -	3,141,265	1,446,814	334,451	1,360,000
2. Il eft dû à divers Fourniffeurs, Entrepreneurs, Pro-piétaires et autres, tant pour Soldes d'entre-prifes, que pour avances par eux faites dans la partie de l'Oueft - - - -	1,140,530	1,070,072	70,458	
3. Il eft dû à divers Entrepreneurs, Fourniffeurs, &c. dans la Partie du Sud - - -	543,220	533,889	7,395	1,936
4. Il eft dû aux Etats Majors des divers Bâtimens du Roi - - - - -	117,401	88,341	29,060	
Total de la Dette publique de la Colonie -	4,942,416	3,139,116	441,364	1,361,936

ADDITIONAL TABLES, containing Information not comprehended in the preceding; collected by the Author when at Cape Francois.

No. V.

TRADE of the French Part of St. Domingo with Old France.

IMPORTS for the Year 1788.

Quantity.	Nature of Goods.	Amount in Hispaniola Currency.
		Liv.
186,759	Barrels of Flour, — —	12,271,247
1,366	Quintals of Biscuit, — —	38,684
3,309	Ditto - - Cheese, — —	217,450
2,044	Ditto - - Wax Candles, —	602,010
27,154	Ditto - - Soap, — —	1,589,985
16,896	Ditto - - Tallow Candles, —	1,479,510
20,762	Ditto - - Oil, — —	1,973,750
1,359	Ditto - - Tallow, —	55,770
121,587	Casks of Wine, — —	13,610,960
7,020	Cases of D°, — —	584,770
5,732	Casks of Beer, — —	328,175
6,174	Hampers of Beer, — —	157,380
10,375	Cases of Cordials, — —	340,070
6,937	Ankers of Brandy, — —	140,238
2,284	Ditto of Vinegar, — —	23,784
19,457	Baskets of Aniseed Liquor, —	254,398
5,999	Quintals of Vegetables, —	322,130
14,613	Cases of preserved Fruit, —	320,477
2,486	Quintals of Cod Fish, — —	85,607
1,308	Ditto - - Salt Fish, — —	26,700
17,219	Ditto - - Butter, — —	1,650,150
24,261	Ditto - - Salt Beef, —	998,300
14,732	Ditto - - Salt Pork, —	1,101,395
4,351	Ditto - - Ditto, — —	376,560
1,627	Ditto - - Hams, — —	177,340
	Dry Goods, viz. Linens, Woollens, Silks, Cottons, and Manufactures of all kinds, — —	39,008,600
	Sundry other Articles, valued at -	8,685,600
	Amount of all the Goods imported	86,414,040

No. V. *continued.*

Thefe Importations were made in 580 Veffels, meafuring together 189,679 Tons, or by Average 325 ½ Tons each Veffel; *viz.*

224	from Bourdeaux.	3	from Harfleur.
129	from Nantes.	2	from Cherbourg.
90	from Marfeilles.	2	from Croific.
80	from Havre de Grace.	1	from Dieppe.
19	from Dunkirk.	1	from Rouen.
11	from St. Malo.	1	from Granville.
10	from Bayonne.	1	from Cette.
5	from La Rochelle.	1	from Rhedon.

Add to the 580 Veffels from France, 98 from the Coaft of Africa, and the French Part of Hifpaniola will be found to have employed 678 Veffels belonging to France in the year 1788.

No. VI.

Foreign TRADE in 1788 (exclufive of the Spanifh.)

Imported by Foreigners (Spaniards excepted) to
the Amount of - - - - 6,821,707 Livres.
Exported by the fame - - - 4,409,922

Difference - - - 2,411,785

N B. This Trade employed 763 fmall Veffels, meafuring 55,745 Tons. The Average is 73 Tons each. Veffels from North America (American built) are comprehended in it; but there were alfo employed in the North American Trade 45 French Veffels, meafuring 3,475 Tons (the Average 77 Tons each), which exported to North America Colonial Products, Value -   525,571 Livres. And imported in return Goods to the Amount of   465,081

Difference - - - 60,490

No. VI. *continued.*

Spanish TRADE in 1788.

259 Spanish Vessels, measuring 15,417 Tons, or 59 Tons each, imported to the Amount of (chiefly Bullion) - 9,717,113
And exported Negro Slaves, and Goods, chiefly
European Manufactures, to the Amount of - 5,587,515

Difference - - - 4,129,598

N. B. This is exclusive of the inland Trade with the Spaniards, of which there is no Account.

No. VII.

AFRICAN TRADE.

NEGROES imported into the French Part of HISPANIOLA, in 1788.

Ports of Importation.	Men.	Women.	Boys.	Girls.	Amount.	Num. of Vessels.
Port au Prince	4,732	2,256	764	541	8,293	24
St. Marc - -	1,665	645	230	60	2,600	8
Léogane - -	1,652	798	469	327	3,246	9
Jérémie - -	88	75	23	18	204	1
Cayes - -	1,624	872	1,245	849	4,590	19
Cape François	5,913	2,394	1,514	752	10,573	37
	15,674	7,040	4,245	2,547	29,506	98

In 1787, 30,839 Negroes were imported into the French Part of St. Domingo.

The 29,506 Negroes imported in 1788, were sold for 61,936,190 Livres (Hispaniola Currency) which on an average is 2,099 liv. 2s. each, being about £. 60. sterling.

ADDITIONAL NOTES

AND

ILLUSTRATIONS.

CHAP. I. p. LI.

THIS applies equally to all the European Colonies in America, and accordingly the actual condition of the Negroes in all those colonies, to whatever nation they belong, is, I believe, nearly the same, &c.

CHAP. I. p. II.

THIS is meant, however, rather as a *general* obfervation, than a precife and accurate ftatement applicable to all cafes. *Habit* alone has fo great an influence in national manners, as on fome occafions to counteract the plaineft dictates of felf-intereft. The Dutch, for inftance, are, as I have heard, *habitually* a cruel and unfeeling people. The ftate of flavery, therefore, in Surinam, differs probably, in many refpects, from the fame condition of life both in the Britifh and Spanifh Weft Indies. Among the Spaniards the fuperftitious obfervances of the Romifh Church co-operate with the flothful difpofition of the white inhabitants, to produce a great relaxation of difcipline. On the other hand, the Dutch difregard all religious feftivals, and abhor idlenefs. Thefe cafes, however, are the oppofite extremes.

E e

CHAP.

CHAP. II. p. 16.

The Society in France called Amis des Noirs, *was, I believe, originally formed on the model of a similar Affociation in London, &c.*

SINCE the foregoing fheets were printed, I have met with a work publifhed this prefent year (1796) at Paris, entitled, *Reflexions fur la Colonie de St. Domingue;* the following paffage from which is given, as a ftriking illuftration of the foregoing obfervation: fpeaking of the difcuffions which arofe in the Britifh Parliament about the year 1789, concerning the Slave Trade, the author continues thus: Les idées Anglaifes furent un brandon lancé au milieu de matiéres combuftibles, et elles furent accueillies en France avec aùtant de fureur qu'on en mettait précédemment à adopter fes ridicules et la forme de fes vêtemens. Toute raifon de convenance et d'intérêt national fut foulée aux pieds; on fe précipita dans le piége groffier tendu à l'ignorance et à la prefomption, et l'on ne parut plus animé que par la crainte d'être précédé par fes rivaux dans ce nouveau champ de gloire. Soit que les imaginations malades ou fortement ébranlées, fe repaiffent plus volòntiérs de chiméres que de realité, foit que des agens fecrets fuffent chargés de dohneroune direction á l'amour violent de la nouveauté, les cœurs refterent fecs & infenfibles au fpectacle de la mifère dont les yeux etoient journellement frappés, pour ne s'occupér exclufivement que de

                                                              maux

maux imaginaires ou eloignés, et fur lefquels on n'avoit que des
idées vagues. Tous les maux de l'humanité furent l'ouvrage
des intrigans, de ces hommes mille fois plus funeftes a là fociété
que les brigands le plus feroces, &c.

Reflexions fur la Colonie de St. Domingue, tom. i. p. 72.

CHAP. III. p. 31.

*All that can be urged in extenuation, feems to be that the cir-
cumftances of the cafe were novel, and the Members of the Colonial
Affembly unexperienced in the bufinefs of legiflation, &c.*

A MOST able and elaborate defence of the Colonial Affembly
was drawn up by one of its Members (Mr. de Pons) and publifhed at Paris in November 1790, wherein (as far as general
rules will admit) the relation in which the Colony ftood to the
Mother Country, and the rights that diftinctly appertained to
each party, confiftently with that due fubordination which was
due from the child to the parent, was clearly, and (with one
or two exceptions) I think very accurately defined. I fhall
prefent the reader with an extract from this performance, not
only as illuftrating the cafe of St. Domingo, but as furnifhing
fome hints which the government and colonies of Great Britain may not find unworthy attention, if unhappily difputes fhall
hereafter arife between them, concerning the extents of jurifdiction on the one hand, and the obligation to obedience on the
other.

Un

Un principe d'où font émanés tous les travaux de l'Affemblée de la Colonie, fut généralement adopté par tous fes Membres, c'eft que les Colonies ne doivent intéreffer la Métropole, qu'en proportion des avantages qu'elles lui procurent. Cette confidération dût acquérir, dans l'efprit de tous les Colons, un caractère de légalité à tous les moyens qui pouvoient affurer la profpérité de la Colonie, & augmenter fes rapports avec la mère-patrie.

Il auroit été fans doute à fouhaiter, & il le feroit bien plus encore, qu'une même Loi pût convenir à tous les climats, à toute efpèce de mœurs, à toutes les populations; mais malheureufement les hommes ne font pas les mêmes par-tout; telle Loi qui convient dans un endroit, feroit nuifible dans un autre.

L'Affemblée générale envifagea donc la Conftitution de Saint-Domingue fous trois rapports, toujours dirigés d'après fon intérêt de refter unie à la Métropole, & d'après la révolution de l'empire.

1°. Comme faifant partie intégrante de l'empire François.

2°. Comme obligée de concourir par fes productions à la profpérité de l'Etat.

3°. Comme affujettie par la diffemblance de fon climat, de fes mœurs & de fa population, à des befoins particuliers & différens de ceux de la Métropole.

4

DIVISION DE LA CONSTITUTION DE SAINT-DOMINGUE.

CES divers rapports firent divifer la Conftitution convenable
à Saint-Domingue,

En Loix générales ;

En Loix communes,

Et en Loix particulières.

LOIX GENERALES.

LES Loix générales de l'empire, celles qui intéreffent tous les
François, dans quelque coin de la terre qu'ils foient placés, furent confidérées comme obligatoires pour les Colonies, fans
aucun examen, fans aucune reftriction.

Ces Loix font : la forme du Gouvernment, le fort de la
Couronne, la réconnoiffance du Monarque, les Déclarations de
guerre, les Traités de paix, l'organifation générale de la Police
& de la Juftice, &c. &c. L'intérêt des Colonies fe trouvant à
cet égard confondu avec celui de toute la Nation, l'Affemblée
Nationale a feule le droit de décréter ces Loix.

LOIX COMMUNES.

LES Loix communes font celles qui ont rapport aux rélàtions
de la Métropole avec les Colonies ; c eft un contrat par lequel
la France s'oblige de protéger & défendre les Colonies contre
les puiffances étrangères, de l'ambition defquelles elles devien-
droient l'objet. Cette protection ne devant ni ne pouvant être

F f

gratuite,

gratuite, les Colonies doivent en dédommager l'Etat par les avantages du Commerce. Délà, le régime prohibitif dans les fers duquel la deftinée les a condamnés à refter toujours ; & quel que foit le degré de liberté dont jouiffe la Nation, les Colonies feront toujours efclaves du Commerce. C'eft une pofition politique abfolument inhèrente à leur pofition phyfiquè, elles n'en laiffent pas échapper le moindre murmure ; elles favent bien que leur qualité de Francois ne leur donne pas de droit fur les déniers de l'Etat ; elles confentent donc à ne récévoir que de la France tous les objets de confommation que fes Manufactures & fon fol peuvent fournir ; elles foufcrivent encore à l'obligation de n'envoyer leurs denrées qu'en France. Ce qu'elles demandent, ce qu'on ne peut leur réfufer, c'eft qu'en confacrant ces conventions fondamentales, les abus que le régime prohibitif entraîne àprès lui foient détruits.

Loix particulieres ou regime interieur.

Les Loix particulières font celles qui n'intéreffent que les Colonies. De grands motifs ont porté la Colonie de Saint-Domingue à s'en réferver la formation : 1 . il eft bien reconnu que les Loix de Saint-Domingue ne peuvent être faites ailleurs que dans fon fein ; cette vérité fondamentale a échappé à fon ennemi le plus cruel.   M. la Luzerne, dans fon mémoire préfenté à l'Affemblée Nationale, le 27 Octobre 1789, (N°. 2.) difoit que les Colonies n'ont jamais pu être régies par les mêmes Loix que le Royaume, & qu'il a fallu toujours conférer le pouvoir à deux Adminiftrateurs de faire les Loix locales, parce qu'il

eft

eſt une infinité de convenances qu'on ne peut connoître que ſur les lieux.

Ce que l'Aſſemblée générale s'eſt réſervée n'eſt donc que la portion du pouvoir légiſlatif qui réſidoit, contre le droit des hommes, dans les mains de deux ſatrapes, que la Colonie n'in-téreſſe que par les richeſſes qu'ils en retirent pendant leur triennat.

2°. Il eſt contraire aux principes conſtitutionnels, que celui qui fait la Loi n'y ſoit point aſſujetti.

Tous les hommes ont le droit de concourir à la formation de la Loi à laquelle ils ſont aſſujettis ; mais nul ne peut con-courir à la formation de celle qui ne l'aſſujettit pas.

Ce principe, ſeul égide de la liberté individuelle, ſeul garant de la bienfaiſance de la Loi, n'a pas permis aux Colons de Saint-Domingue de douter que l'Aſſemblée Nationale, diſpenſatrice des bienfaits régénérateurs, n'approuvât cette diſpoſition qui aſ-ſure la proſpérité de Saint-Domingue.

En effet, il ne peut pas en être des Loix locales des Sections éloignées de l'Empire, comme des Loix qui n'intéreſſent que la France.

La Loi décrétée pour le Royaume eſt la même pour tous les Cantons. L'univerſalité des Députés de l'Aſſemblée Nationale eſt intéreſſée à en examiner ſcrupuleuſement tous les rapports, à en conſidérer tous les avantages & tous les inconvéniens. De ſorte que l'intérêt que tous ont à ce que la Loi, du vice de la-

F f 2

quelle

quelle ils feroient eux-mêmes les victimes, ne foit que le fruit d'une longue méditation, & de réflexions longuement & foigneufement difcutées, en affure la fageffe.

Les Loix particulières de Saint-Domingue n'affujettiffant que les habitans qui y réfident ou qui y ont leurs fortunes, n'intéreffent dans l'Affemblée Nationale que les douze Députés des Colonies.

3 . Une des conditions effentielles, à la bonté de la Loi, eft que celui qui la fait, connoiffe parfaitement les rapports qui doivent la conftituer. Or, nul ne peut connoître les particularités locales que celui qui eft fur les lieux, parce que ces mêmes particularités changent & varient ; & il faut que la Loi foit faite, d'après ces changemens, d'après ces variations.

4 . Il eft bien conftant que les liens de la Société font les pouvoirs établis pour en faire éxécuter les conditions.

Le bonheur de toute conftitution dépend abfolument d'une action égale dans ces différens pouvoirs ; c'eft cette égalité feule qui en maintient l'équilibre.

Il faut néceffairement qu'il exifte à Saint-Domingue un pouvoir éxécutif ; car le malheur des Sociétés veut que la raifon n'aille jamais en politique qu'à côté de la force. Si ce pouvoir n'eft balancé par aucun autre, il finira par tout envahir, & par fubftituer l'oppreffion aux bienfaits de la régénération à laquelle la révolution actuelle donne à tous les François le droit de prétendre. Il ne peut donc être contenu dans fes bornes que par
une

une maffe proportionnée de pouvoir légiflatif, dont il ait à re- CHAP. III.
douter la furveillance. p. 31.

5°. LES principes de l'Affemblée Nationale s'oppofent à ce
qu'elle décrète la Conftitution particulière de Saint-Domingue.
Celle de la France a pour bafe la liberté, l'égalité; celle de
Saint-Domingue repofe malheureufement fur la fervitude, & une
diftinction de claffes, d'où dépend la confervation de cette fu-
perbe Colonie. Tous les raifonnemens poffibles échoueront
contre cette vérité.

Ces différentes obfervations, bien analyfées dans l'Affemblée
générale, la raffurèrent fur la crainte qu'elle avoit de ne point fe
trouver d'accord avec les principes de l'Affemblée Nationale,
& de prêter à la calomnie le prétexte d'inculper fes intentions.

Les différens Membres de l'Affemblée générale étoient bien
éloignés de prévoir que l'heureufe révolution qui a porté la joie
& l'enthoufiafme dans les cœurs de tous les Francois, finiroit
par porter à Saint-Domingue le deuil & la défolation. Qu'importe à la France, quelque foit notre régime domeftique, pourvu
qu'il tende à augmenter les productions de la Colonie? pourvu
que nous foyons affujettis aux Loix générales de l'Empire?
pourvu que nous refpections les rapports commerciaux? pourvu
que nous regardions la fujétion de ne traiter qu'avec la France,
comme un jufte dédommagement de la protection & des fecours
qu'elle nous accorde? pourvu que nous éxécutions les Décrets
de l'Affemblée Nationale, en tout ce qui n'eft point contraire aux
localités.

Il

Il importe à la France que nous foyons heureux, que nous confommions les denrées & les marchandifes qu'elle peut nous fournir, & que nous lui envoyions en échange beaucoup de fucre, de café, d'indigo, de coton, de cacao, &c. Enfin, il lui importe que la Conftitution de Saint-Domingue foit telle, qu'elle uniffe pour jamais cette Colonie à la Métropole, & qu'elle concoure, par fes richeffes, à la profpérité de l'Etat.

D'après ces réflexions, fimples & vraies, l'Affemblée générale de Saint-Domingue pofa fes bafes conftitutionnelles dans fon Décret du 28 Mai (N°. 3.)

CHAP. IV. p. 49.

Suppreffed it certainly was, and the miferable Ogé hurried to immediate execution, as if to prevent the further communication and full difclofure of fo weighty a fecret.

THIS is a very remarkable fact, and leads to moft ferious reflections concerning the conduct of the French loyalifts in St. Domingo; I fhall therefore prefent the reader with Ogé's dying declaration at length, as copied *verbatim* from the public records, when the difclofure was made nine months afterwards to the Colonial Affembly.

TESTAMENT

TESTAMENT DE MORT D'OGÉ.

EXTRAIT des minutes du Confeil Supérieur du Cap, l'an mil fept cent quatre-vingt-onze et le neuf mars, nous Antoine-Etienne Ruotte, confeiller du roi, doyen au Confeil Supérieur du Cap, et Marie-Francois Pourchereffe de Vertieres, auffi confeiller du roi au Confeil Supérieur du Cap, commiffaires nommés par la cour, à l'effet de faire exécuter l'arrêt de ladite cour, du 5 du préfent mois, portant condamnation de mort contre le nommé Jacques Ogé, dit Jacquot, quarteron libre ; lequel, étant en la chambre criminelle, et après lecture faite dudit arrêt, en ce qui le concerne, a dit et déclaré, pour la décharge de fa confcience, ferment préalablement par lui prêté, la main levée devant nous, de dire vérité.

Que dans le commencement du mois de février dernier, fi les rivières n'avoient pas été débordées, il devoit fe faire un attroupement de gens de couleur, qui devoient entraîner avec eux les àtéliers, et devoient venir fondre fur la ville du Cap en nombre très-confidérable ; qu'ils étoient même déjà réunis au nombre de onze mille hommes ; que le débordement des rivières eft le feul obftacle qui les a empêchés de fe réunir ; cette quantité d'hommes de couleur étant compofée de ceux du Mirebalais, de l'Artibonite, du Limbe, d'Ouanaminthe, de la Grande-Rivière, et généralement de toute la Colonie. Qu'à cette êpoque, il était forti du Cap cent hommes de couleur pour fe joindre à cette troupe. Que l'accufé eft affuré que les auteurs de cette révolte font les Declains, négres libres de la Grande-Riviére, accufés

au

CHAP. IV.
p. 49.
au procès ; Dumas, n. l. ; Yvon, n. l. ; Bitozin, m. l. efpagnol ;
Pierre Godard et Jean-Baptifte, fon frère, n. l. de la Grande-
Rivière ; Legrand Mazeau et Touffaint Mazeau, n. l. ; Pierre
Mauzi, m. l. ; Ginga Lapaire, Charles Lamadieu, les Sabourins,
Jean Pierre Goudy, Jofeph Lucas, mulâtres libres ; Maurice,
n. l. ; tous accufés au procès.

Que les grands moteurs, au bas de la côte, font les nommés
Daguin, accufé au procès ; Rebel, demeurant au Mirebalais ;
Pinchinat, accufé au procès ; Labaftille, également accufé au
procès ; et que l'accufé, ici préfent, croit devoir nous déclarer
être un des plus ardens partifans de la révolte, qui a mu en
grande partie celle qui a éclaté dans les environs de Saint-Marc,
et qui cherche à en éxciter une nouvelle ; qu'il y a dans ce moment plufieurs gens de couleur, dans différens quartiers, bien
réfolus à tenir à leurs projets, malgré que ceux qui trempéroient
dans la revolte perdroient la vie ; que l accufé, ici préfent, ne
peut pas fe reffouvenir du nom de tous ; mais qu'il fe rappelle que
le fils de Laplace, q. l. ; dont lui accufé a vu la fœur dans les
prifons, a quitté le Limbé pour aller faire des récrues dans le
quartier d'Ouanaminthe ; et que ces récrues et ces foulevemens
de gens de couleur font foutenus ici par la préfence des nommés
Fleury et l'Hirondelle Viard, députés des gens de couleur auprès
de l'affemblée nationale ; que lui accufé, ici préfent, ignore fi
les députés fe tiennent chez eux ; qu'il croit que le nommé
Fleury fe tient au Mirebalais, et le nommé l'Hirondelle Viard
dans le quartier de la Grande-Rivière.

Que

CHAP IV.
p. 49.

Que lui accufé, ici préfent, déclare que l'infurrection des re-
voltés exifte dans les fouterrains qui fe trouvent entre la Crête
à Marcan et le Canton du Giromon, paroiffe de la Grande-
Rivière ; qu'en conféquence, fi lui accufé pouvoit être conduit
fur les lieux, il fe feroit fort de prendre les chefs des révoltés ;
que l'agitation dans laquelle il fe trouve, rélativement à fa pofition actuelle, ne lui permet pas de nous donner des détails plus
circonftanciés ; qu'il nous les donnera par la fuite, lorfqu'il fera
un peu plus tranquil ; qu'il lui vient en ce moment à l'efprit
que le nommé Caftaing, mulâtre libre de cette dépendance ; ne
fe trouve compris en aucune manière dans l'affaire actuelle ; mais
que lui accufé, nous affure que fi fon frère Ogé eût fuivi l im-
pulfion dudit Caftaing, il fe feroit porté à de bien plus grandes
extrémités ; qui eft tout ce qu'il nous a dit pouvoir nous déclarer
dans ce moment, dont lui avons donné acte, qu'il a figné avec
nous et le gréffier.

Signé à la minute J. OGE', RUOTTE, POURCHERESSE
DE VERTIERES, et LANDAIS, gréffier.

EXTRAIT des minutes du greffe du Confeil Supérieur du Cap,
l'an mil fept cent quatre-vingt-onze, le dix mars, trois heures
de rélévée, en la chambre criminelle, nous Antoine-Etienne
Ruotte, confeiller du roi, doyen du Confeil Supérieur du Cap,
et Marie-François-Jofeph de Vertieres, auffi confeiller du roi
audit Confeil Supérieur du Cap, commiffaires nommés par la
cour, fuivant arrêt de ce jour, rendu fur les conclufions du procureur général du roi de ladite cour, à l'effet de procéder au re-
colement de la déclaration faite par le nommé Jacques Ogé, q.l. ;

G g   lequel,

lequel, après ferment par lui fait, la main levée devant nous de dire la vérité, et après lui avoir fait lecture, par le gréffier, de la déclaration du jour d'hier, l'avons interpellé de nous déclarer fi ladite déclaration contient vérité, s'il veut n'y rien ajouter, n'y diminuer, et s'il y perfifte.

A répondu que ladite déclaration du jour d'hier contient vérité, qu'il y perfifte, et qu il y ajoute que les deux Didiers frères, dont l'un plus grand que l'autre, mulâtres ou quarterons libres, ne les ayant vu que cette fois ; Jean-Pierre Gerard, m. l. du Cap, et Caton, m. l. auffi du Cap, font employés à gagner les ateliers de la Grande-Rivière, qu'ils font enfemble de jour, et que de nuit ils font difperfés.

Ajoute encore que lors de fa confrontation avec Jacques Lucas, il a été dit par ce dernier, que lui accufé, ici préfent, l avoit menacé de le faire pendre ; à quoi, lui accufé, a répondu audit Jacques Lucas, qu'il devoit favoir pourquoi que ledit Jacques Lucas n'ayant pas infifté, lui accufé n'a pas déclaré le motif de cette menace, pour ne pas perdre ledit Jacques Lucas ; qu'il nous déclare les chofes comme elles fe font paffées ; que ledit Lucas lui ayant dit qu'il avoit foulevé les atéliers de M. Bonamy et de divers autres habitans de la Grande-Rivière, pour aller égorger l'armée chez M. Cardineau ; qu'au prémier coup de corne, il étoit fur que ces atéliers s'attrouperoient et fe joindroient à la troupe des gens de couleur ; alors lui accufé, tenant aux blancs, fut révolté de cette barbarie, et dit au nommé Jacques Lucas, que l'auteur d'un pareil projet méritoit d'être pendu ; qu'il eut à l'inftant à faire rentrer les négres qu'il avoit appofté

dans

dans différens coins avec des cornes ; que lui accufé, ici préfent, nous déclare qu'il a donné audit Lucas trois pomponelles de tafia, trois bouteilles de vin et du pain ; qu'il ignoroit l'ufage que ledit Lucas en faifoit ; que la troifième fois que ledit Lucas en vint chercher ; lui accufé, ici préfent, lui ayant demandé ce qu'il faifoit de ces boiffons et vivres ; ledit Lucas répondit que c'étoit pour les nègres qu'il avoit difperfé de côté et d'autre ; que ce qui prouve que ledit Lucas avoit le projèt de fouléver les nègres efclaves contre les blancs, et de faire égorger ces derniers par les prémiers ; c'eft la propofition qu'il fit à Vincent Ogé, frère de lui accufé, de venir fur l'habitation de lui Jacques Lucas, pour être plus a portée de fe joindre aux nègres qu'il avoit débauché ; que fi lui accufé n'a pas révélé ces faits à fa confrontation avec ledit Jacques Lucas, c'eft qu'il s'eft apperçu qu'ils n'étoient pas connus, et qu'il n'a pas voulu le perdre ; qu'il a du moinsla fatis-faction d'avoir détourné ce crime horrible et cannibale ; qu'il s'étoit réfervé de révéler en juftice, lors de fon élargiffement ; que ce même Lucas eft celui qui a voulu couper la tête a deux blancs prifonniers, et notàmment au fieur Belifle, pour lui avoir enlevé une femme ; que Pierre Roubert ôta le fabre des mains de Jacques Lucas, et appella Vincent Ogé, frère de lui accufé, ici préfent, qui fit des rémontrances audit Lucas ; que cependant ces prifonniers ont déclarés en juftice que c'étoit lui accufé qui avoit eu ce deffein ; que même à la confrontation ils le lui ont foutenu ; mais que le fait s'étant paffé de nuit, lefdits prifonniers ont pris, lui accufé, pour ledit Lucas, tandis que lui accufé n'a ceffé de les combler d'honnêtetés ; qu'à la confrontation, lui accufé a cru qu'il étoit fuffifant de dire que ce n'étoit pas lui, et d'affir-mer qu'il n'avoit jamais connu cette femme ; mais qu'aujourd'-

G g 2

hui

hui il fe croyoit obligé, pour la décharge de fa confcience, de nous rendre les faits tels qu'ils font, et d'infifter à jurer qu'il ne l'a jamais connue.

Ajoute l'accufé que le nommé Fleury et Periffe; le premier, l'un des députés des gens de couleur près de l'affemblée nationale, font arrivés en cette Colonie par un bâtiment Bordelais avec le nommé l'Hirondelle Viard; que le capitaine a mis les deux prémiers à Acquin, chez un nommé Dupont, homme de couleur, et le nommé l'Hirondelle Viard, également député des gens de couleur, au Cap. Ajoute encore l'accufé, qu'il nous avoit déclaré, le jour d'hier, que le nommé Laplace, dont le père eft ici dans les prifons, faifant des récrues à Ouanaminthe, eft du nombre de ceux qui ont marché du Limbé contre le Cap; que pour éloigner les foupçons, il eft allé au Port-Margot, où il s'eft tenu caché plufieurs jours, feignant d'avoir une fluxion; que ledit Laplace père a dit, à lui accufé, qu'il étoit fûr que fon voifin, qui eft un blanc, ne dépofera pas contre lui, malgré qu'il fache toutes fes démarches; qu'il étoit affuré que le nommé Girardeau, détenu en prifon, ne déclareroit rien, parce qu'il étoit trop fon ami pour le découvrir; qu'enfuite, s'il le dénoncoit, il feroit forcé d'en dénoncer beaucoup d'autres, tant du Limbé que des autres quartiers.

Obferve l'accufé que lorfqu'il nous a parlé des moyens employés par Jacques Lucas pour foulever les nègres efclaves, il a omis de nous dire que Pierre Maury avait envoyé une trentaine d'efclaves chez Lucas; que lui accufé, avec l'agrément d'Ogé le jeune, fon frère, les renvoya, ce qui occafionna une plainte générale, les gens de couleur difant que c'étoit du renfort; que lui

accufé

CHAP. IV.
p. 49.

accufé eut même à cette occafion une rixe avec le plus grand des Didiers, avec lequel il manqua de fe battre au piftolet, pour vouloir lui foutenir qu'étant libre et cherchant à être affimilé aux blancs, il n'étoit pas fait pour être affimilé aux nègres efclaves; que d'ailleurs foulevant les efclaves, c'étoit détruire les propriétés des blancs, et qu'en les détruifant, ils détruifoient les leurs propres; que dépuis que lui accufé étoit dans les prifons, il a vu un petit billet écrit par ledit Pierre Maury à Jean-François Teffier, par lequel il lui marque qu'il continue à ramaffer, et que le nègre nommé Coquin, à la dame veuve Caftaing aînée, armé d'une paire de piftolet garni en argent et d'une manchette que ledit Maury lui a donné, veille à tout ce qui fe paffe, et rend compte tous les foirs audit Maury; qui eft tout ce que l'accufé, ici prefent, nous déclare, en nous coujurant d'être perfuadés que, s'il lui étoit poffible d'obtenir miféricorde, il s'expoferoit volontièrs à tous les dangers pour faire arrêter les chefs de ces révoltés; et que dans toutes les circonftances, il prouvera fon zèle et fon refpect pour les blancs.

LECTURE à lui faite de fa déclaration, dans laquelle il perfifte pour contenir vérité, lui en donnons acte, qu'il a figné avec nous et le gréffier.

Signé à la minute J. OGE', RUOTTE, POUCHERESSES DE VERTIERES, et LANDAIS, gréffier.
Pour expedition collationée, figné LANDAIS, gréffier.

A COPY of the preceding document, the exiftence of which I had often heard of, but very much doubted, was tranfmitted
to

to me from St. Domingo in the month of July 1795, inclofed in a letter from a gentleman of that ifland, whofe attachment to the Britifh cannot be fufpected, and whofe means of information were equal to any: This Letter is too remarkable to be omitted, and I hope, as I conceal his name, that the writer will pardon its publication: It here follows.

Je vous envoye ci joint, le teftament de Jaques Ogé executé au Cap le 9 Mars 1791. Voici mes reflexions fur les dates et les faits:

1°. Jaques Ogé depofe le projet connu dépuis long tems par les Briffotins dont il étoit un des Agents. Il nomme les chefs des Mulâtres, qui dans toutes les parties de la Colonie devoient éxécuter un plan digne des Suppôts de l'enfer.

2°. Il depofe que l'abondance des pluies et les cruës des rivières avoient empèché l'éxécution du projet au mois de fèvrier.

3°. Il déclare que fi on veut lui accorder miféricorde, il s'expofera aux dangers de faire arrêter les chefs.

Ogé eft éxécuté, avec vingt de fes complices, le 9 Mars 1791. Son teftament eft gardé fecret jufqu'a la fin de 1791 (après l'incendie générale de la partie du Nord) qu'un arrèté de l'Affemblée Coloniale oblige impèrieufement le Gréffier du Confeil du Cap à en délivrer des copies. Que conclure? Hélas, que les coupables font auffi nombreux qu' atroces et cruels!

3

1ᵉʳˢ. Coupables:

1ᵐ. Coupables: Les hommes de couleur nommés par la dé- CHAP. IV.
pofition d'Ogé. p. 49.

2. (et au moins autant s'ils ne font plus) Le Confeil du Cap,
qui a ofé faire éxécuter Ogé, et qui a gardé le fecret fur fes de-
pofitions fi interreffantes.

3. Le Général Blanchelande et tous les chefs militaires qui
n'ont pas fait arrêter fur le champ toutes les perfonnes de Couleur
nommes par Ogé et ne les ont confrontés avec leur accufateur.
Mais non: on a precipité l'éxécution du malheureux Ogé; on
a gardé un fecret dont la publicité fauvoit la Colonie. On a
laiffé libres tous les chefs des révoltés; on les a laiffés pour
fuivre leurs projets deftructifs.

Si les Chefs militaires, le confeil, les magiftrats civils, avoient
fait arrêter au mois de Mars 1791, les mulâtres Pinchinat,
Caftaing, Viard, et tous les autres, ils n'auroient pas pu con-
fomer leur crime le 25 Août fuivant. Les Régimens de Nor-
mandie et d'Artois qui venoient d'arriver de France, etoient
affés forts pour arrêter tous les gens de couleur coupables, et
s'ils ne l'avoient pas été, et que ce fut le motif, qui eut empèché Blanchelande d'agir, pourquoi Blanchelande envoya tíl,
au mois de Mai 1791, des troupes de lignes que lui envoyoit de
la Martinique, M. de Behague?

La férie de tous ces faits prouve évidement la coalition des
contre révolutionaires avec les Mulâtres, dont ils ont été la dupe,
et la victime après l'arrivée des Commiffaires Polverel et Santhonax.

CHAP.

CHAP. V. p. 56.

Mauduit started back, &c.—while not a single hand was lifted up in his defence.

In this laft particular I was mifinformed, and rejoice that I have an opportunity of correcting my miftake. The following detail of that bloody tranfaction has been tranfmitted to me from St. Domingo fince the firft fheets were printed: " Les grenadiers du regiment de Mauduit, et d'autres voix parties de la foule, demandent que le Colonel faffe reparation à la garde nationale. On éxige qu'il faffe des excufes. pour l'infulte qu'il lui a fait. Il prononce les excufes qu'on lui demande; fes grénadiers ne font points fatisfaits, ils veulent qu'il les faffe à genoux. Une rumeur terrible fe fait entendre: ce fut alors que plufieurs citoyens, *même de ceux que Mauduit avoit le plus vexé,* fendent la foule, et cherchent à le fouftraire au mouvement qui fe préparoit. On a vu dans ce moment le bràve *Beaufoleil,* àprès avoir été atteint d'un coup de feu á l'affaire du 29 au 30 Juillet, en défendant le comité *(fee page* 34) recèvoir un coup de sàbre en protégeant les jours de Mauduit. On peut rendre juftice auffi à deux officiers de Mauduit: *Galefeau* et *Germain* n'ayant pas abandonné leur Colonel jufqu'au dernier moment; mais l'indignation des foldats étoit à fon comble, et il n'etoit plus temps.

MAUDUIT preffé par fes grénadiers, de s'agénouiller pour demander pardon à la garde nationale, et refufant conftamment

de

CHAP. V.
p. 56.

de s'y foumettre, reçut un coup de sàbre à la figure, qui le terraffa; un autre grénadier lui coupa à l'inftant la tête, *qui fut portée au bout d'une bayonnette.* Alors le reffentiment des foldats et des matelots livrés à eux memes, n'eut plus de bornes: ils fe tranfporterent chez Mauduit, où ils trainèrent fon corps, tout y fut brifé, rompu, meubles &c. on décarela même la maifon, &c. &c.

CHAP. VI. p. 77.

CHAP. VI.
p. 77.

It was compùted that, within two months after the revolt began, upwards of 2,000 white perfons had been maffacred, &c.

IN the month of October 1791 the Colonial Affembly of St. Domingo fent two Commiffioners (Mefs. *Raboteau* and *Lemoine)* to negociate a loan of money in the Ifland of Jamaica, on the fecurity of their internal taxes and port duties. As an Act of Affembly was neceffary to give effect to the meafure, it was propofed in the houfe, by the author of this work, to advance on this occafion £.100,000 of the publick money, but the motion was over-ruled by a majority. The houfe however ordered the Receiver General to advance the French Commiffioners £.10,000 Sterling on the fecurity of bills drawn by the Colonial Government on the treafury of France; but this offer was declined by the Colonial Affembly. In the courfe of this bufinefs the French Commiffioners were examined at the bar, and from the examination of one of thofe gentlemen I have felected fome

H h   of

of the particulars given in the text.   It is a curious and important document; and conceiving that fome of my readers will not be difpleafed to have an opportunity of perufing the whole, I have fubjoined it, as follows:

" On the 16th of October laft (1791) when I left Cape François, 182 fugar plantations, and 950 coffee, cotton, and indigo fettlements had been plundered and deftroyed, and the buildings thereof burnt down; one hundred thoufand flaves, as far as can be computed, were in rebellion, and the men of Colour in a ftate of infurrection in every part of the Colony except round the Cape.   All the whites that fell into their hands were indifcriminately murdered, and about 1,200 families reduced to fuch a dreadful ftate of mifery, that they were forced to receive their clothing and fufiftance either from public or private charity.

" The lofs in this year's crop was eftimated at 66,000,000 * St. Domingo livres, which are nearly equal to £. 2,650,000 of the currency of Jamaica.   The value of the capital could not then be afcertained, but it muft amount to an immenfe fum, confidering the lofs of ftock, flaves, and buildings.

" Since I left the town of the Cape, the rebellion has extended itfelf to the eaftern parts of the plain, and 246 coffee fettletiements and a few fugar plantations have been deftroyed; this will add about £. 300,000 † Jamaica currency to the lofs of this year's crop.

* Nearly £. 1,900,000 fterling.   † £. 210,000 fterling.

2   " The

" The laſt accounts I have received from St. Domingo inform me, that detachments of regulars and militia have ſucceeded in ſurpriſing and diſperſing ſeveral negro encampments, in conſequence of which a few gangs of ſlaves have returned to their maſters eſtates; but theſe advantages have occaſioned extreme fatigue to our troops, though they have not been able to reduce even the ſixth part of the rebels.

" The quarters of Doudon and Grande Riviere are occupied by ſuch a number of rebels, that without a larger body of troops than we are poſſeſſed of, we cannot attempt to attack them with any hope of ſucceſs.

" We are reduced to remain ſhut up as it were within the town of the Cape, and it is with great difficulty that we can man the line of poſts which are neceſſary to prevent the rebels from attacking the weſtern and ſouthern parts of the iſland. Notwithſtanding the activity of our troops, a body of the rebels found means to paſs thoſe poſts, in order to ſpread their ravages in the mountains of L'artibonite, called *Les Cahos*; the inhabitants whereof have united their forces to repulſe and ſtop them, but after killing a few, the reſt eſcaped into the woods, and there is reaſon to apprehend that the rebellion may ſoon extend itſelf to that part of the iſland, which would in a few days become a prey to a general conflagration.

" At this juncture we received a copy of the decree of the national aſſembly of the 24th of September laſt, whereby our rights are acknowledged; but we fear too late.   We have only

H h 2   a copy

a copy of the decree, it has not been received officially, no troops are yet arrived to enforce the execution of it; and that decree may, in our critical circumſtances, add to our calamities, inaſmuch as the free people of colour, knowing the enormity of their crimes, declare that they will ſooner periſh than ſubmit to this laſt decree; they are again forming a camp in the pariſh of La Croix des Bouquets, near Port au Prince, and every hour I dread to hear of their having commenced hoſtilities againſt the white inhabitants; if ſo, our ruin is inevitable.

" If this ſhould unfortunately be the caſe, your Iſland, Gentlemen, would of courſe be expoſed to ſimilar deſtruction, as the ſucceſs of our ſlaves would induce your own to rebel againſt you.

" Negroes have not ſufficient reſolution to encounter the whites in the field of battle; but no men bear with greater fortitude hunger, pain, and fatigue, when once their imagination is heated, and their reſolution ſettled; we have amongſt us men, who, pretending to be philanthropiſts, have preached freedom even to our ſlaves; theſe men are connected with men of weight and fortune in Old France, by whom they are greatly encouraged, and who are alſo connected with the philanthropiſts in Great Britain, *from whoſe conduct, indeed, the firſt example was taken*; and I moſt ſincerely pray, that this iſland may not be expoſed to the ſame evils as have reſulted amongſt us from ſuch an enormous miſinterpretation and miſapplication of philanthropical principles.

" The

CHAP. VI.

P. 77.

" The means left us for our defence are but few and feeble, and it is indeed surprising that we have been able to resist our enemies for so long a time; we owe much to the power of opinion, and to the superiority the negroes have been accustomed to yield to the whites. The forces we have to defend every part of the colony, consists of about 1000 men of the regiments of Artois and Normandy; 700 of the regiment of the Cape, including the sick, who are in great number; 1200 stipendiary troops, paid by ourselves; and 6000 or 7000 militia, which have been without the least discipline or order ever since our fatal political divisions. Our maritime force consists in one ship of 74 guns, two frigates, and two sloops of war.

" It is with such feeble means that we are to face the free people of colour, and the slaves in rebellion. We have applied for relief to our neighbours and allies, the Spaniards; but it has been refused by the Spanish government, with inhumanity and insult; private men among them, and some of the commanding officers on the lines between us and them, *appear to have seconded the rebels, by supplying them with ammunition, and by delivering into their hands some of the wretched inhabitants, who had fled to them for refuge.*

" Our publick treasury is not only free of debt, but there is even money due to it, yet it is absolutely empty; it being impossible at present to collect the taxes, or otherwise to provide for the vast expence occasioned by the war, and the necessity of giving relief to unfortunate families in want.

" The

" The ſtate of our monthly expences is nearly as follows :

3000 regular troops, at 3 livres a-day, is 9000
    livres a-day, equal *per* month to   -   - 270,000
4000 men, women, and children at public allow-
    ance, at 2 livres a-day, is *per* month   -   - 240,000
Expences of officers, clothing, arms, ammuni-
    tion, &c.   -   -   -   -   - 410,000
                               ——————

                  Total Livres - 920,000
                               ——————

of St. Domingo currency, or about £.34,166 * Jamaica currency *per* month, without including ſeveral other extraordinary
expences, ſuch as that of adminiſtration, rewards, maritime expeditions, &c.

" Were we deprived of the neceſſary funds to pay our troops,
and to ſupply them with proviſions, they ſoon would join the
mulattoes, and we ſhould be ruined without any reſource.   The
forces which are expected from Europe would arrive too late ;
and they could then only revenge, and not defend us.

                            " RABOTEAU."

CHAP. VII. p. 85.

*The ſociety of Amis des Noirs reſorted without ſcruple to thoſe mea-
ſures which their fellow labourers in London ſtill heſitated to adopt.*

JE répéterai éternellement que c'eſt à vous, zélateurs de
philantropie! qu' appartient l'honneur de ces bouleverſements:

              * £.24,500 ſterling.

                                     c'eſt

c'eſt à vous ſeuls que l'on doit le dépériſſement des reſſources nationales. Si vous n'aviez pas ſappé juſqu'aux fondemens la plus hrilliante colonie de l'univers, &c. &c.

CHAP. VII. p. 85.

Reflexions ſur la Colonie de St. Domingue, tom. 2. p. 66.

CHAP. X. p. 142.

CHAP. X. p. 142.

They declared by proclamation all manner of ſlavery aboliſhed, &c.—This proceeding was ratified in February, followed by the National Convention in a Decree, of which follows a Copy.

DECRET de la Convention Nationale, du 16 Jour de Plu-viôſe; an ſecond de la Republique Françaiſe, une et indivi-ſible.

5 Feb. 1794.

LA Convention Nationale déclare que l'eſclavage des Négres dans toutes les Colonies eſt aboli; en conſéquence elle decrète que tous le hommes, ſans diſtinction de couleur, domiciliés dans les Colonies, ſont citoyens Français, et jouiront de tous les droits aſſurés par la conſtitution.

ELLE renvoie au comité de ſalut public, pour lui faire in-ceſſament un rapport ſur les meſures à prendre pour aſſurer l'éxécution du préſent décret.

Viſé par les inſpecteurs. *Signé*

Auger,

Cordier,

S. E. Monnel.

Collationné

Collationné à l'original, par nous préfident et fécrètaires de la Convention Nationale, à Paris le **22** Germinal, an fecond de la République Françaife une et indivifible. *Signé*, Amar, *Préfident*. A. M. Baudot. Monnot. Ch. Pottier, et Peyffard, *Sécrétaires*.

As moft of the French iflands fell into poffeffion of the Englifh foon after that this extraordinary decree was promulgated, the only place where it was attempted to be enforced, was in the fouthern province of St. Domingo, and the mode of enforcing it, as I have heard, was as fingular as the decree itfelf. The negroes of the feveral plantations were called together, and informed *that they were all a free people*, and at liberty to quit the fervice of their mafters whenever they thought proper. —They were told however, at the fame time, that as the Republick wanted foldiers, and the ftate allowed no man to be idle, fuch of them as left their mafters, would be compelled to enlift in one or other of the black regiments then forming. At firft many of the negroes accepted the alternative, and enlifted accordingly; but the reports they foon gave of the rigid difcipline and hard fare to which they were fubject, operated in a furprifing manner on the reft, in keeping them more than ufually quiet and induftrious; and they requefted that no change might be made in their condition.

CHAP. X. p. 143.

Of the revolted negroes in the Northern province, many had perished of disease and famine, &c.

FROM the vast number of negroes that had fallen in battle, and the still greater number that perished from the causes above mentioned, it was computed in the year 1793 that this class of people at that period had sustained a diminution of more than one hundred thousand. (*Reflexions sur la Colonie, &c.* tom. 2. p. 217.) Since that time the mortality has been still more rapid, and, including the loss of whites, by sickness and emigration, I do not believe that St. Domingo at this juncture (June 1796) contains more than two fifths of the whole number of inhabitants (white and black) which it possessed in the beginning of 1791.——According to this calculation upwards of 300,000 human beings have miserably perished in this devoted country within the last six years!

CHAP. X. p. 147.

The propositions, or terms of capitulation, had been previously adjusted between the people of Jeremie, by their Agent, Mr. Charmilly, amd General Williamson, &c.

As I conceive that these articles were drawn up in England, and adjusted with the King's ministers previous to Mr. Char-

milly's

CHAP. X. milly's return from thence, I fhall prefent them to the reader.
P. 147. The paffages which I have printed in *italick* are remarkable.

TERMS OF CAPITULATION *propofed by the Inhabitants of La Grande Anfe (including the Quarter at Jeremie) reprefented by Monf. de Charmilly, poffeffed of full powers by a Commiffion from the Council of Public Safety of the aforefaid Place, dated the 18th of Auguft 1793, and prefented to his Excellency Major General Williamfon, his Majefty's Lieutenant Governor of Jamaica, for his Acceptance.*

Article I.

That the proprietors of St. Domingo, deprived of all recourfe to their lawful Sovereign to deliver them from the tyranny under which they now groan, implore the protection of his Britannick Majefty, and take the oath of fidelity and allegiance to him; and fupplicate him to take their colony under his protection, and to treat them as good and faithful fubjects till a general peace; at which period they fhall be finally fubjected to the terms then agreed upon between his Britannick Majefty, *the Government of France*, and the Allied Powers, with refpect to the Sovereignty of St. Domingo.—Anfwer. Granted.

Art. II. That till order and tranquillity are reftored at St. Domingo, the Governor appointed by his Britannick Majefty fhall have full power to regulate and direct whatever meafures of Safety and Police he fhall judge proper.—Anf. Granted.

Art. III. That no one fhall be molefted on account of any anterior difturbances, except thofe who are legally accufed, in
fome

fome Court of Juftice, of having committed murder, or of
having deftroyed property by fire, or of having inftigated others
to commit thofe crimes.—Anf. Granted.

Art. IV. That the Mulattoes fhall have all the privileges
enjoyed by that clafs of inhabitants in the Britifh iflands.—
Anf. Granted.

Art. V. That if, at the conclufion of the war, the colony remains under the Sovereignty of his Britannick Majefty, and order
is eftablifhed therein; in fuch cafe, the laws refpecting property *and all civil rights, which were in force in the faid colony
before the Revolution in France, fhall be preferved:* neverthelefs,
until a Colonial Affembly can be formed, his Britannick Majefty
fhall have the right of determining provifionally upon any meafures which the general good and the tranquillity of the colony
may require; but that no Affembly fhall be called till order is
eftablifhed in every part of the colony; and, till that period, his
Britannick Majefty's Governor fhall be affifted in all the details
of Adminiftration and Police by a Committee of Six Perfons,
which he fhall have the power of choofing from among the proprietors of the three Provinces of which the colony confifts.—
Anf. Granted.

Art. VI. That, in confequence of the devaftations which have
taken place in the colony by infurrections, fire, and pillage, the
Governor appointed by his Majefty, on taking poffeffion of the
colony, to fatisfy the demand cf the Inhabitants in this refpect,
*fhall be authorized to grant, for the payment of debts, a fufpenfion of
ten years, which fhall be computed from the date of the furrender; and*

I i 2 *the*

the fufpenfion of all intereft upon the fame fhall begin from the period of the 1ft of Auguft 1791, and terminate at the expiration of the ten years above mentioned granted for the payment of debts; but all fums due to minors by their guardians, or to abfent planters by thofe who have the management of their property, or from one planter to another, for the transfer of property, are not to be included in the above fufpenfion.—Anf. Granted.

Art. VII. That the duties of importation and exportation upon all European commodities fhall be the fame as in the Englifh colonies.—Anf. Granted. In confequence, the tariff fhall be made public and affixed, that every one may be acquainted therewith.

Art. VIII. That the manufacturers of white fugars fhall preferve the right of exporting their clayed fugars, fubject to fuch regulations as it may be neceffary to make with refpect to them.—Anf. Granted. In confequence, the duties upon white fugars fhall be the fame as were taken in the colony of St. Domingo in 1789.

Art. IX. That the Catholic Religion fhall be preferved and maintained, but that no other mode of Evangelic worfhip fhall be excluded.—Anf. Granted. On condition that fuch priefts as have taken the Oath prefcribed by the perfons exercifing the powers of Government in France fhall be fent away, and replaced by others.

Art. X. The local taxes deftined to acquit the expences of garrifons, and of the Adminiftration of the colony fhall be affeffed in the fame manner as in 1789, except the alleviations

3

and

and remittances which fhall be granted to the inhabitants whofe property has fuffered by fire, till their poffeffions are repaired. An account fhall be kept by the colony of all the fums advanced on the part of Great Britain for fupplying the deficiency of the faid taxes; which deficiency, as well as all the public expences of the Colony (except thofe of his Majefty's naval forces, deftined for its protection) fhall always be defrayed by the faid colony.—Anf. Granted.

Art. XI. His Britannic Majefty's Governor of St. Domingo fhall apply to the Spanifh Government, to obtain reftitution of the negroes and cattle fold upon the Spanifh territory by the revolted flaves.—Anf. Granted.

Art. XII. The importation, in American bottoms, of provifions, cattle, grain, and wood of every kind from the United States of America, fhall be allowed at St. Domingo.—Anf. Granted. On condition that the American fhips, which fhall be employed in this trade, fhall have only one deck; and this importation fhall be allowed only as long as it fhall appear neceffary for the re-eftablifhment or fubfiftence of the Colony, or until meafures have been taken for putting it in this refpect upon the fame footing as other Englifh Colonies; and an exact account fhall be kept of the faid veffels, with the defcription of their cargoes, and fhall be tranfmitted every three months to the Right Honourable the Lords Commiffioners of his Majefty's Treafury, as well as to one of the principal Secretaries of State; and on no account whatever fhall any of the faid veffels be allowed to take in return any production of the Colony, except molaffes and rum.

Art. XIII.

Art. XIII. *No part of the aforesaid conditions shall be considered as a restriction to the power of the Parliament of Great Britain, to regulate and determine the Political Government of the Colony.*— Ans. Granted.

C H A P. XI. p. 169.

The same fate awaited Lieutenant Colonel Markham, &c.

I CANNOT deny myself the melancholy satisfaction of preserving in this work the following honourable tribute to the memory of this amiable officer, which was given out in general orders after his death, by the Commander in Chief.

Head Quarters, 28 *March* 1795.

Brigadier General Horneck begs the officers, non-commissioned officers, and privates of the detachment, which, on the 26th Inst. proceeded under the command of Lieutenant Colonel Markham, on a party of observation, to receive his very sincere thanks for their gallant behaviour, at the attack of the enemy's advanced post; taking their colours and cannon, and destroying their stores.

At the same time he cannot sufficiently express his feelings on the late afflicting loss, that has been sustained in Lieutenant Colonel Markham; who, equally excellent and meritorious as an officer and a man, lived universally respected and beloved, and
died

died leaving a bright example of military, social, and private CHAP. XI.
p. 169.
virtue.

The Brigadier General likewise requests Captains Martin and
Wilkinson, of the Royal Navy, to receive his acknowledgments
and thanks, for the important assistance they have afforded;
not only on this occasion alone, but on every other, wherein his
Majesty's service has required their co-operation. He also
begs Captain Martin to do him the favour, to impart the like
acknowledgments to the officers of the Royal Navy, and to the
respective ships companies under his command, for the zeal and
good conduct they have shewn whenever employed.

For EU product safety concerns, contact us at Calle de José Abascal, 56–1°,
28003 Madrid, Spain or eugpsr@cambridge.org.

www.ingramcontent.com/pod-product-compliance
Ingram Content Group UK Ltd.
Pitfield, Milton Keynes, MK11 3LW, UK
UKHW030900150625
459647UK00021B/2716